Recreation and Leisure Service

a humanistic perspective

James F. Murphy

San Jose State University

WM. C. BROWN COMPANY PUBLISHERS *Dubuque, Iowa*

PARKS AND RECREATION

Consulting Editor

David Gray
California State University, Long Beach

PHYSICAL EDUCATION

Consulting Editor

Aileene Lockhart
Texas Woman's University

HEALTH

Consulting Editor

Robert Kaplan
The Ohio State University

to my mother and father

for your

love and support

my object in living is to unite

my avocation with my vocation

as my eyes make one in sight

Robert Frost

contents

PREFACE xi

ONE **INTRODUCTION TO FUNDAMENTAL CONCEPTS** 1

Recreation—a humanistic expression. Concepts of leisure, work, and time. The nature of recreation experience. Summary—Developing a meaningful work—leisure rhythm of life.

TWO **HISTORICAL DEVELOPMENTS** 19

The emergence of leisure. Leisure as the basis of culture. Leisure as a style of life. Perspectives on play behavior. Summary.

THREE **AMERICAN SOCIETY IN TRANSITION: The Institution** 39
of Leisure Service

The American recreation movement. Early forces influencing the provision of recreation. Recreation and the new American culture. Emerging leisure ethic. Summary.

FOUR **COMMUNITY RECREATION: A Dynamic Process** 55

Community involvement in recreation and leisure service. Organizing leisure service delivery: the role of the community worker. Traditional versus contemporary role of community recreation. Leisure and human development. Measuring leisure service delivery. New strategy for community recreation. Organizational renewal. Encouraging neighborhood recreation. Identifying leader competencies. Taxonomy of recreation outcomes. Organizational strategy. Summary.

FIVE **SOCIOPSYCHOLOGICAL CONSIDERATIONS: Ecological** 81
Perspectives

Leisure and society. Collective search for identity. Leisure and the individual. Leisure and anomie. Dynamics of recreation and leisure service. Life-style counseling. Psychological implications for an individual with terminal illness. Philosophical commitment. Summary.

SIX   **LEISURE AND LIFE-STYLES: Subcultural Expressions**   101

Definition of life-style. Life-style types. The rhythm of life and leisure. Alternative life-styles: youth subculture, counter-culture, blue-collar workers, minority expressions.

SEVEN   **CONTEMPORARY ISSUES AND VALUE CONFLICTS**   123

Crisis in value formulation. Race relations: leisure and civil unrest. New dimensions in sport. The ravaged environment. Urban planning: toward societal and self renewal. Life-styles and urban space. A sense of place. Urban renewal. Self-renewal. Leisure and self-actualization. Leisure and mental health. The dynamics of aging. Summary.

EIGHT   **LEISURE AS A PATH TO LEARNING**   153

Optimal learning through leisure. The school's responsibility for leisure education. Leisure and learning. A personal experience. Leisure studies: a humanistic discipline. Integrating university and community. Preparing community catalysts. A new age of learning and living. Four levels of learning. Two-track leisure studies curriculum. Summary.

NINE   **LEISURE AND WORK: A Forward Look**   173

Poverty of abundance. Historical meanings of work. Three- and four-day workweeks: timewealth. Toward a leisure ethic: new worker options. Summary.

TEN   **THE FUTURE OF LEISURE**   187

Social change and leisure. Impact of leisure on culture. The "problem" of leisure. Leisure and the quality of life. Utopian forecast of society—Cyberculture. The value of leisure—An ecological perspective. Summary—The future of leisure.

EPILOGUE—REDEFINING LEISURE: An Action Plan for   199

the Recreation and Park Movement

SELECTED BIBLIOGRAPHY   229

INDEX   235

preface

The dramatic changes in American society over the past several years have led to major shifts and changes in the structure of various institutions and organizations, including recreation and leisure service. Swift technological advancement, sweeping social reform, alternative educational approaches to learning, and other social innovations have altered the nature of community life in America and helped shape the basis for the delivery of recreation and leisure service.

This text represents a pioneering attempt to present the history, basic concepts, issues, concerns, and scope of recreation and leisure service as a *process*—a dynamic representation of the sociopsychological and developmental way in which the nature of leisure opportunity is conceived and becomes a viable community function. This book is primarily geared to introductory courses in colleges and universities dealing with the history, foundations, community development, and sociopsychological implications of recreation and leisure in American society. It is recognized by the author that several such introductory texts already exist. However, this text is not intended to duplicate these volumes, but rather, is an attempt to present a new *humanistic* perspective of recreation and leisure.

This view reflects a central concern for the dignity and worth of man and the development of human potentialities. A humanistic perspective, which is a growing trend in the social and behavioral sciences, sees man as having a measure of autonomy, choice, and self-determination. Through the study of recreation and leisure, a humanistic approach is oriented toward exploring possibilities and alternatives to improve a constantly evolving society and facilitate human development.

The book is divided into ten chapters, and includes an introduction to basic concepts of time, work, play, recreation, and leisure; the sociohistorical development of recreation and leisure; the evolution of leisure service as an institution and its impact on American culture; community recreation as a dynamic, developmental process; sociopsychological considerations and implications of leisure; various subcultural leisure lifestyles; contemporary issues and value conflicts affecting leisure service; leisure education; the relationship of work and leisure; and future considerations of leisure. The epilogue contains a paper prepared by Seymour Greben and David Gray on the future of the recreation movement.

The author has attempted to assemble the most pertinent and representative literature which either directly or indirectly has relevance to the field of recreation and leisure service. The writings of professional colleagues, particularly David E. Gray, Richard Kraus, Max Kaplan, William Niepoth, Michael J. Ellis, and H. Douglas Sessoms, and works of individuals from allied disciplines, notably Abraham Maslow, Kenneth Roberts, Stanley Parker, Victor Ferkiss, George Leonard, Walter Kerr, Theodore Roszak, and Bennet Berger, have all had a marked impact on the conceptualization and content of this text. It is the desire of the author to amplify their ideas in relation to recreation and leisure, with the hope that the availability of leisure opportunity and fostering of recreation expression may be better achieved and understood as a significant form of the individual personality system.

The author wishes to extend a special note of gratitude to David Gray who provided the impetus for this text and served as a spirited and extremely helpful source of encouragement and assistance throughout the project. Dr. Gray's inquisitive, probing mind resulted in a serendipitous writing adventure which proved to be a joyous, psychologically pleasing experience for the author. It is the author's expressed desire that a similar experience will occur for the readers of this book. Additionally, the author wishes to thank Miss Barbara Fairhurst who typed the manuscript and offered many helpful suggestions which improved the quality of the text. Her assistance was invaluable and greatly appreciated.

Recreation and Leisure Service

chapter ONE
introduction to fundamental concepts

what to look for in this chapter...

Recreation as a Humanistic Expression

Stages of Professional Recreation Development

Interpretation of the Concepts of Time, Work, and Leisure

The Nature of the Recreation Experience

Developing a Meaningful Work-Leisure Rhythm of Life

RECREATION—A HUMANISTIC EXPRESSION

As mentioned in the introduction to the text, humanism reflects a central concern for the dignity and worth of man and the development of human potentialities. It asserts that the fundamental consideration for human beings is that the individual should have a measure of autonomy, choice, and self-determination. Humanistic psychology has become recognized as a "third force" transcending the two main schools of psychology, behaviorism and psychoanalysis. It seeks to study the "health personality" and to recognize the essence and capacity of all human beings to be unique individuals. But individuals living in a highly technological society, often have to give up some measure of independence for shared decision making, and many are submerged by the overwhelming thrust of a highly depersonalized contractual system of governmental process. The humanistic movement is seen as largely a *moral* revolution, in that it challenges those religious, ideological, and moralistic philosophies that deny the most genuine qualities of human existence, and seeks to restore those aspects of life which have been suppressed or lost in postindustrial society.

Typically, social science depicts man in society in relation to a set of institutions which are designed to serve, control, and facilitate human needs. Any conflicts, changes, or alternative expressions are usually seen as deviations, not as inherent social processes. A humanistic approach to viewing life does not seek to modify science, rather it places the highest commitment on a concern for man. It seeks to embrace man's positive capacities, his expressions of joy, freedom, and self-fulfillment. The new morality of humanism views the good life as a realization of human potential.

Recreation and leisure agencies which incorporate a humanistic approach to service seek to promote the capacity and ability of groups and individuals to make self-determined and responsible choices—in light of their needs to grow, to explore new possibilities, and to realize their full potential. A humanistic perspective involves facilitation of growth potentials as well as a concern for eliminating barriers which hinder self-development. Recreation and leisure service which does not address itself to the positivistic nature of human behavior will miss the essence of humanism. Humanism is concerned with facilitating man to become what he is capable of being. It asks, "What are the possibilities of man? And, from these possibilities, what is *optimum man*, and what conditions will most probably lead to his attainment and maintenance of such a state?"

It is suggested by Carl Rogers that man is directional in his nature and that he seeks to move toward the development of all his capacities in ways which serve to maintain or enhance the organism.[1] To facilitate this directional tendency, recreation and leisure service personnel should be aware of some conditions which, according to Rogers, exist in any growth-releasing or growth-promoting relationship. Recreation catalysts must be genuine. They must have congruence between their experiencing, awareness, and communication. It is suggested that such individuals would thus be unified or integrated in the relationship and *real*. Secondly, an empathic understanding is required. Recreation personnel must increasingly be able to "stand in their participant's or client's place" and communicate something of this sensitive understanding to them. Finally, leisure service personnel need to have unconditionally positive regards for their clientele. They must relate person-to-person. The participants are respected for what they are, and accepted for that, with all their potentialities. Such unconditional relationships, which have often been fostered in therapeutic settings, are seen as fundamental to *all* areas of recreation and leisure service. It is the most growth-promoting type of relationship, in which each individual is prized for what he is and may become.

The prospect of leisure as a science may well be embraced within the tenets of humanism as applied to play research. A humanistic ethic views each person as being responsible for his own actions. While there are other contingencies, including the environment, sociocultural factors, etc., that influence behavior, the meanings that guide conduct are not imparted by institutions and agencies, but are created by individuals through their choices and their definitions of life situations.[2]

A humanistic ethic insists on the right and the necessity of each person to be the engineer of his own life. Recent studies by Howard, Bishop, and Witt (refer to chapter 2 for a discussion of their research) have provided the recreation movement with its first real scientific thread of understanding why human organisms play. Their studies provide the recreation and leisure service field with data which indicate the positive, intrinsic growth-related nature of play that contributes to man's human development.

It is important for recreation and leisure agencies to recognize that the delivery of service which incorporates a humanistic perspective is founded on the premise of aiding human fulfillment and eliminating imposing external barriers which impede growth potential. Efforts should be made

1. Carl R. Rogers, "A Humanistic Conception of Man," *Humanistic Society*, ed. John F. Glass and John R. Staude (Pacific Palisades: Goodyear Publishing Co., Inc., 1972), pp. 21-22.
2. John R. Staude, "The Theoretical Foundations of Humanistic Sociology," *Humanistic Society*, ed. John F. Glass and John R. Staude (Pacific Palisades: Goodyear Publishing Co., Inc., 1972), p. 263.

to organize leisure service delivery in a way which fosters individuality and autonomy (as depicted on the chart, "Changing Values and Approaches in Recreation and Leisure Service," in chapter 5). Often, recreation programs which employ standardized service approaches to serve all the public (without really providing meaning to anyone) tend to accentuate the degree of banality of the consumer-oriented, Madison Avenue type of "packaged" approach to meeting people's needs. Such approaches often create false impressions of what really are the essential human wants and desires. A humanistic leisure service approach accents the positive qualities of life experience, and seeks to rediscover joy and love, creativity and growth, shared experience and fraternity, uniqueness and diversity, achievement and excellence.

According to Kurtz "A significant life which fuses pleasure and creative self-realization is possible . . . and men can again discover ways of enriching experience, actualizing potentialities, and achieving happiness."[3] *Recreation and leisure service agencies are seen as catalysts of human growth and stewards of individual rights of self-expression.* Such agencies recognize that there is a wide diversity of human values, and efforts should be made to allow for divergent life-styles and modes of expression to avoid the imposition of uniform standards upon all individuals. Agencies must be sensitive to the plurality of human needs and to the diverse means that may be required for their satisfaction.

The development of the recreation movement in America has evolved over the last century from the initial gestures of private citizens concerned about wholesome play opportunities for children, and of socially conscious individuals who believed that the cumulative effects of the Industrial Revolution were potentially disruptive to the human condition, particularly in urban communities. The challenge confronting the recreation movement today involves the ability of its leaders to identify, and then implement, a diversified, flexible, and comprehensive leisure service opportunity system which will embrace the needs of people living on the frontiers of a postindustrial society.

Weiner states, "For the municipal recreation professional, this means his *focus* must now be on the individual and his family—to what extent does leisure and recreation contribute to their physical and psychic growth and to the quality of their lives.[4]

The focus of the recreation movement in the future appears to be centered on an understanding of all aspects of the environment and the

3. Paul Kurtz, "The Moral Revolution," *The Humanist* March/April 1971, p. 4.
4. Myron E. Weiner, *Systems Approach to Municipal Recreation* (Storrs, Conn.: Institute of Public Service, University of Connecticut, 1970), p. 9.

movement's ability to merge with it to create a milieu serving a central goal of human development. The integration of human experience is viewed as an important conceptual approach that is necessary to enable the individual to realize his potentiality within an environment which allows him to flourish according to his interests and capabilities, meet individual needs, and find his own life solution.[5]

CONCEPTS OF LEISURE, WORK, AND TIME

Concepts of Leisure

To properly approach the coordination and servicing of individual leisure opportunities it is important to understand the theoretical basis and the terms used and applied to the recreation movement. The most all-inclusive term used to describe the attitude and time reference in which recreation occurs is leisure. Refer to Figure 1.1, a diagram of the relationships of three essential elements—time, work, and leisure—that are seen as the primary determinants affecting the basic rhythm of community life.

The term *leisure* is derived from the Latin *licere* or "to be permitted to abstain from occupation or service," with direct reference to the aristocratic elite who were absolved from daily work requirements and free to engage in intellectual, cultural, civic, and artistic endeavors. Additionally, the Greek influence of leisure may be traced to the word *schole,* which was closely related to leisure and education and is the derivation of the English word *school. Schole* referred to a place where one was permitted to engage in scholarly pursuits. The implication of leisure in this sense refers to a disregard for material concern and is strongly linked to individual freedom and self-determination and an immunity from occupational requirements.

Leisure according to the *classical* or *traditional* interpretation places emphasis on "cultivation of self"—a perspective developed by Aristotle in which the individual pursued intellectual, cultural, civic, and artistic activities. The view of leisure is characterized as a state of being, a condition of the soul, having no relation to linear, clock-time. Its origin dates to ancient Greece and Rome. This highly elitist dimension of leisure placed emphasis upon contemplative pursuits and was strongly intellectual and moral in character. De Grazia and Pieper view this concept of leisure as being most representative of the nature of the intent of classical philosophers, scientists, theologians, politicians, artists, and educators who en-

5. Refer to Stanley R. Parker, *The Future of Work and Leisure* (New York: Praeger Publishers, Inc., 1971), p. 139, for a discussion on the role of recreation and leisure service professionals as enablers and encouragers of human development and self-determination through the provision of leisure opportunities.

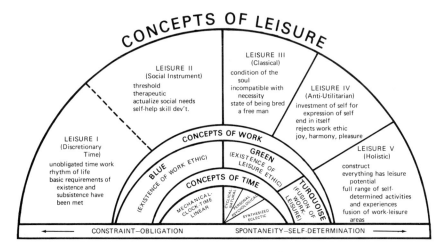

Figure 1.1   Toward a Dynamic Conceptualization of Leisure.

Adapted from diagram in "Toward A Dynamic Conceptualization of Leisure," by James F. Murphy, *Concepts of Leisure: Philosophical Implications* (Englewood Cliffs, New Jersey: Prentice-Hall, Inc., 1974).

gaged in aesthetic, religious, philosophical, and political pursuits.[6] Pieper views leisure as an attitude of mind and a condition of the soul—the highest value of culture. To Pieper, leisure is the foundation of any culture and is rooted in divine worship. Pieper's interpretation serves as a useful link to the spiritual conceptualization of leisure, which religious sects within the youth subculture have identified as an integral part of their communal living experience—the foundations of life beyond the utilitarian world.

A contrasting view of leisure, the *discretionary time* concept, conceives of leisure as that portion of time which remains when time for work and the basic requirements for existence have been satisfied. This dominant conceptualization of leisure, an outgrowth of the Industrial Revolution, divides time into three categories—time for existence and meeting biological requirements; time for subsistence, involving work; and leisure, time left over after the basic necessities of living and work requirements have been satisfied.

The discretionary time concept of leisure recognizes work as the dominant rhythm of community life which, therefore, revolves around

6. Sebastian de Grazia, *Of Time, Work and Leisure* (Garden City, New York: Anchor Books, Doubleday and Company, Inc., 1964); Joseph Pieper, *Leisure: The Basis of Culture* (New York: Pantheon Books, Inc., 1952).

industrial clock-time. Leisure is seen as unobligated time, and justifiable only as it relates to release from basic obligatory and work time requirements. There is an obvious relationship between clock-time and leisure where the concept of discretionary time is central. According to Gray:

> "Time, unlike purchasing power, cannot be expanded or accumulated. It is permanently and irretrievably fixed at 168 hours per week per person. Time can be reallocated among uses, but even here the limits are narrow. Time then can become more and more scarce compared to goods. Thus the "price" of time can rise faster than the price of goods.
>
> One of the outcomes of the dynamic relationship between time and goods may be that we will seek things to buy with rising income, that take little time to enjoy and maintain. As time becomes more scarce and goods more plentiful, there is a tendency to invest in the activities which involve the purchase and consumption of goods in place of activities which involve the commitment of time. These activities like eating out, racing cars, or water skiing, which are high consumption activities with relatively low time requirements take precedence over low consumption, high time commitment activities like contemplation, writing, or sculpture."[7]

For most Americans, the discretionary time concept of leisure is most representative of the industrial worker. The primary goal of the blue-collar laborer is the daily work routine; leisure is viewed as a respite from work—time for rest, relaxation, and recuperation.

Another concept of leisure is the *social instrument* view, in which leisure is seen as a means of meeting needs of the poor through human service agencies, such as VISTA and Headstart, and serving as a *threshold* for the ill, disabled, and deprived through which they might be helped to actualize social needs and develop self-help skills. This therapeutic concept has been most recently articulated by Frye and Peters, and Kraus, and broadened by Kaplan into a formal conceptual scheme.[8] Kraus also recognized that recreation and leisure service has traditionally been designed to meet the needs and interests of middle-class Americans, which represents a somewhat idealistic and narrow view of American society. Kraus states:

7. David Gray, "This Alien Thing Called Leisure," in *Reflections on the Recreation and Park Movement*, ed. David Gray and Don Pelegrino (Dubuque, Iowa: Wm. C. Brown Company Publishers, 1973), p. 11.
8. Virginia Frye and Martha Peters, *Therapeutic Recreation: Its Theory, Philosophy, and Practice* (Harrisburg, Pennsylvania: Stackpole Books, 1972), p. 41; Richard Kraus, *Public Recreation and the Negro* (New York: Center for Urban Education, 1968), p. 7, and *Therapeutic Recreation Service: Principles and Practice* (Philadelphia, W. B. Saunders Company, 1973), pp. 2-3; Max Kaplan, "Aging and Leisure" (Speech delivered at American Psychological Association, Washington, D.C., September 4, 1971).

Today it must be recognized that the United States has become pre-dominantly an urban society and that it is marked by major differences in terms of social class, racial affiliation, economic status, and attitudes of morality. Particularly in the cities, the pressure upon the tax dollar is tremendous. Within this context, the notion of recreation as an experience which, by definition, is not designed to meet important social needs or achieve "extrinsic" outcomes can no longer be applicable. Every area of service that is provided by government and voluntary agencies today *must* be purposeful and *must* achieve significant outcomes.[9]

An *antiutilitarian* approach to conceptualizing leisure has been identified by Gray, articulated by Walter Kerr in *The Decline of Pleasure*, and discussed in a number of popular essays on the counter culture.[10] This view suggests that leisure is a state of mind that is a worthy end in itself. This concept rejects the "position that every investment of human energy must produce a useful result. It rejects the work ethic as the only source of value and permits the investment of self in pursuits that promise no more than the expression of self. This concept accepts joy and seeks pleasure."[11]

According to the antiutilitarian concept of leisure, the Protestant work ethic, or the philosophy of utilitarianism, focused more on tangible, productive outcomes and hindered more rhythmical, expressive forms of joy, spontaneity, and engagement in activities that have no useful end. Like Kerr, John Farina sees leisure as a personal response which consists of activities not directly related to utilitarianism except insofar as they may promote self-realization.[12] "His concept reflects a more personal, psychological time reference, in which the essence of leisure is seen as self-expression through activity, whether it be intellectual, spiritual, or physical, in which the individual strives toward his full potential as a human being.[13]

Finally, there is a fifth concept of leisure, a *holistic* perspective, which is an integrating view that seeks to fuse

9. Richard Kraus, *Recreation and Leisure in Modern Society* (New York: Appleton-Century-Crofts, 1971), pp. xii-xiii.

10. Refer to Gray, *Recreation and Park Movement*, pp. 7-13, for a discussion of the antiutilitarian concept of leisure; Walter Kerr, *The Decline of Pleasure* (New York: Simon and Schuster, Inc., 1962); refer to Charles Reich, *The Greening of America* (New York: Bantam Books Inc., 1971); Philip Slater, *The Pursuit of Loneliness* (Boston: Beacon Press, 1970), particularly pp. 81-118; Abraham Maslow, *Toward a Psychology of Being*, 2nd edition (New York: Van Nostrand Reinhold Company, 1968); and Theodore Roszak, *The Making of a Counter Culture* (Garden City, New York: Anchor Books, Doubleday and Company, Inc., 1969).

11. Gray, *Recreation and Park Movement*, p. 9.

12. John Farina, "Toward A Philosophy of Leisure," *Convergence* 2:(1969)14-17.

13. James F. Murphy, *Concepts of Leisure: Philosophical Implications* (Englewood Cliffs, New Jersey: Prentice-Hall, Inc., 1974).

. . . work and nonwork spheres and establish the relationship and relevance of leisure in terms of other human behavior. Leisure is not seen simply as activity but rather includes time and attitudes toward time and nonwork activities . . . Leisure in the holistic orientation is seen as a complex of multiple relationships involving certain choices which indicate both societal and individual aspirations as well as life styles.[14]

The holistic concept of leisure is seen as a synthesizing theoretical perspective in which elements of leisure are to be found in work, play, education, religion, and other social spheres. This view of leisure incorporates all possible interpretations of leisure into one definition. The evolution of this new concept of leisure is characterized by a convergence of elements; a neoprimitive fusion of work and nonwork. "Elements of leisure, . . . pleasant expectation or self-growth—become ideals in the work situation; meantime, elements of work—such as fulfillment of oneself, discipline and craft—find their way into leisure."[15] Bacon suggests that leisure is a multidimensional concept, composed of many elements, which interact to generate particular styles of life.[16] The predicted fusion of institutions and social relationships possible in a postindustrial society serves as an indicator of the interaction between work and leisure relationships, once enmeshed in preindustrial societies. The main consequence of fusion is to improve work as well as leisure, so that each may be fulfilling to the individual.

Concepts of Work

Work is perceived as the dominant rhythm of society, and leisure (according to the discretionary time concept) is valued as reward for people gainfully employed in American culture. The central focus of society has traditionally revolved around a steady pattern of productive work. All other aspects of social life, including family relationships, existence requirements, enjoyment in community and civic activity, political, educational, and religious participation, gain their significance and place in society in relation to work requirements of the culture.

The traditional work rhythm of life, oriented around a scarce economy, necessarily required people to work long hours and to be frugal with their time and money to survive. As American society is shifting from an

---

14. Joe Hendricks and Rabel J. Burdge, "The Nature of Leisure Research: A Reflection and Comment," *Journal of Leisure Research* 4 (1972): 216.
15. Max Kaplan, "Implications for Gerontology from a General Theory of Leisure" (Paper presented at the Third International Course, "Leisure and the Third Age," Dubrovnik, Yugoslavia, May 15-19, 1972).
16. A. W. Bacon, "Leisure and Research: A Critical Review of the Main Concepts Employed in Contemporary Research," *Society and Leisure* 4 (1972): 83-92.

economy of scarcity to one of abundance, the resulting increases in non-work time, longer vacations, earlier retirement, increased longevity, less physically demanding work, and rising incomes are causing an adjustment in the individual's central life interest which will focus upon the leisure domain.

Johnston has developed three concepts of work for interpreting work's meaning in the life pattern of the individual.[17] The first perspective, the *green* concept, anticipates an automated society in which a small elite of cybernetic engineers would be responsible for the production and distribution of goods, and the remainder of the population would be limited to consumption. The emergence of a leisure ethic is viewed in this configuration as taking over the intrinsic and personally satisfying aspects of life which work now provides, primarily through the monetary rewards it brings. This concept is supported by the continually diminishing workday, week, and year, the increase in length of paid vacations, and the reduced proportions of one's life spent in the labor force.

The second and most dominant model of work, the *blue* concept, envisions the "realization and maintenance of a full employment economy, together with the progressive removal of remaining barriers to the employment of those groups whose desire for employment has been frustrated by a variety of handicaps or by discrimination.[18] This concept assumes the continuance of the work ethic with a steady flow of appropriately trained persons willing to work, as an expansion in the number and variety of professional, technical, and service occupations geared to the generation of automated machinery has continued to occur.

The third approach, the *turquoise* concept, suggests a gradual unification of work and leisure into a holistic pattern as was characteristic in most preindustrial societies. The humanization of the work setting reflects society's increasing recognition of the worker's desire for greater opportunities for growth and fulfillment within the work setting. The major transformation in this concept of work is a movement of worker interest from economic to sociopsychological concerns. "This shift links the economic sector more closely to noneconomic forces, such as changes in lifestyles, so that nonmaterial cultural values tend to become the primary determinants of what we produce and consume."[19]

The turquoise setting, a synthesized cybernated environment, is characterized and accompanied by sustained demand for work in four major areas:

17. Denis F. Johnston, "The Future of Work: Three Possible Alternatives," *Monthly Labor Review* 95(1972):3-11.
18. Ibid., p. 5.
19. Ibid., p. 6.

1. A core of highly trained technicians and engineers needed to maintain and improve the machinery of production and distribution, supplemented by a growing corps of ombudsmen to provide the feedback information needed to direct this machinery in accordance with public wishes and agreed-upon social values;
2. A growing number of workers in the fields of public and personal services;
3. A growing number of craftsmen and artisans whose handiwork continues to be valued because of its individualistic, nonmachine characteristics and stylistic qualities; and
4. A major expansion of employment in what Toffler has aptly termed the experience industries—a blending of recreational and educational opportunities packaged to appeal to the interests of an increasingly affluent and educated population enjoying greater amounts of leisure time.[20]

Cybernation refers to the systematic application of both automation and computers in a technological society. The means of processing work and information is synchronized and controlled through a communications network which may improve on human capacities for performing work and related functions, and may even increase man's ability to understand the complex interrelationships and information demands of a technological social order.

The turquoise scenario for the future appears to represent a view that work will not be greatly reduced. The nature of work may change, but a life without work does not appear to be a tenable proposition for the next twenty-five years. Not only is there some speculation as to whether or not work will be replaced by something else, there are projections which suggest there will be an uneven distribution of free time in which a technological elite will have less opportunity for leisure while working classes, retired persons, and displaced workers will have extended free time at their disposal. Unemployed and working class groups appear to have adverse psychological reactions to excess free time, while retired people are often unable to make the necessary adjustment away from the work ethic.

"The limited evidence . . . derived from a study of steelworkers with extended vacation periods indicates that there might be some increase in travel, but no substantial increase in educational pursuits, community activities, or hobbies."[21]

While production and manufacturing jobs may be scarce in the future, such types of work may be replaced by more socially useful, service-

---

20. Ibid., p. 6.
21. Irene Taviss and William Gerber, "Technological Change in Industry," *Freedom and Tyranny,* ed. Jack D. Douglas (New York: Alfred A. Knopf, Inc., 1970), p. 253.

oriented jobs. The turquoise arrangement of society, recognizes a humanizing of both work and leisure spheres of life.

Concepts of Time

According to Figure 1.1, there are four kinds of time: *cyclical* or *natural* time; *mechanical* or *clock* time; *personal* or *psychological* time; and a synthesis of the previous three types, *eclectic* time.

Cyclical time refers to the nomadic hunting life of primitive man. Time was conditioned by the rising and setting of the sun, ebb and flow of the tide, and seasonal rhythms of the universe. These circular conceptions of time were constant and recurring. Time was never lost or wasted. The image of time was based on the repetition of social and natural activities.

The mechanization of time occurred when it became necessary for nomads and food-gatherers to barter and trade goods and wares at specified times. Since the industrial revolution, leisure is viewed as being *linear.* Anderson states: "The time by which most of us regulate our lives is called *mechanical,* because it reflects the interdependence of man and the rhythm of his machines."[22]

This time perspective is regulated by the clock, and it is possible to speak of "wasting time" or letting time "escape." There is an urgency that it be shaped well since time can pass and not be recovered. While it seems possible to arrange for more optimum work and play schedules by varying the years, months, and days, the acceptance of artificial time may have diluted man's inner biological rhythm of movement and oriented it to the mechanical beat of the clock.

Psychological time relates to one's inner sense of space and movement, independent of natural time, the beat of the clock and calendars. The complexity of highly industrialized societies has tended to submerge individuality. The continuing passage of time has fragmented man. The individual must learn to perceive time and space as an opportunity to add experience and knowledge, through a broadening and deepening consciousness.

An eclectic approach to viewing time recognizes a relationship between the various dimensions, the biological, mechanical, and natural rhythms of life. It does not maximize one time value over any other, but fuses them in such a way as to encourage individual understanding of one's own movements through time and space, combined with a series of temporal alternatives for work and leisure from which to select.

22. Nels Anderson, *Dimensions of Work* (New York: David McKay Co., Inc., 1964), p. 106.

THE NATURE OF RECREATION EXPERIENCE

Definitions of recreation have typically been derived from the discretionary time concept of leisure and designated as occurring within a clock time reference. This somewhat restricted perspective has limited its potential application as a more personal, psychological experience which supersedes mechanical time, social approval, and extrinsic reward. Gray has suggested that recreation is not an activity, but that it is the *result* of an activity.[23] Generally the psychological responses, considered to be independent of activity, have been largely ignored as planning bases for the provision of recreation programs. Ordinarily, programs are planned with certain activities as the sole point of reference. The use of activity categories as the bases for determining a well-rounded program, reflecting the needs and interests of the community being served, has little or no meaning if one were to consider that a given activity may provide recreation for one individual and not for another.

Most park and recreation agencies have focused their attention on the provision of leisure activities designed to fulfill expressed community needs and interests. This approach has tended to limit the goals of the agencies and restrict their services to the delivery of activity opportunities with little or no regard for the influence such activities have on the participants. Gray offers a definition which reflects accelerated interest in humanistic psychology and a contemporary assessment of the human condition. He states:

> Recreation is an emotional condition within an individual human being that flows from a feeling of well-being and self-satisfaction. It is characterized by feelings of mastery, achievement, exhilaration, acceptance, success, personal worth, and pleasure. It reinforces a positive self-image. Recreation is a response to aesthetic experience, achievement of personal goals, or positive feedback from others. It is independent of activity, leisure, or social acceptance.[24]

Gray's definition of recreation views it as an internal, individual, pleasurable response of the organism. The challenge of recreation and leisure service agencies should include a developmental concern for facilitating the delivery of opportunities necessary for man to optimize his arousal level.[25] Accordingly, play is seen as a class of behaviors that is concerned with increasing the level of arousal (stimulation) of the human organism.

---

23. David Gray, "Exploring Inner Space," *Parks and Recreation* 7(1972):18-19,46.
24. Ibid., p. 19.
25. Refer to M. J. Ellis, "Play and Its Theories Reexamined," *Parks and Recreation* 6(1971):51-55, 89-91, and *Why People Play* (Englewood Cliffs, New Jersey: Prentice-Hall, Inc., 1973) for a discussion of the concept of play as arousal-seeking.

This is an optimistic perspective for recreation and leisure service personnel. Successful operations will be ensured to the degree that "they deliver opportunities for their patrons to engage in behavior that optimizes their arousal during nonworking hours."[26] Principles for operation may be derived from this exploration, and credibility for service will be heightened since professional delivery of recreation opportunities will be based on a recognition of why their patrons play.

The principles for play that serve as the foundation for the arousal-seeking approach are:

1. children play for the stimulation they receive (adult patterns apply to their activities at both work and play);
2. that the stimulation must contain elements of uncertainty (they are to some extent novel, complex, or dissonant); and
3. that the interactions producing the stimulation must rise in complexity with the accumulation of knowledge about or experience with the object (the extent to which the uncertainty concerning the object is reduced).[27]

The concept of leisure service functioning to produce optimal arousal is a dynamic one, in which the basic ingredients of recreation are exploratory, investigative, manipulative, and epistemic (cognitive) behaviors. According to Ellis, such behaviors are active engagements with the environment that escalate in complexity. The goal of all leisure service agencies, no matter the setting, is to conceivably produce an environment that encourages direct and spontaneous human use. Human response to facilities, leadership, and program is not conducive to mass, stereotyped leisure opportunities provided by recreation agencies, based on a generalized or typical portrait of a community. According to Gray:

> The imperative is that persons planning programs and parks must know intimately the culture, wishes, social patterns, and life-style of the people who are to use them; the park or program must fit those conditions. There is no such thing as a universal man and there is no such thing as a universal park and there is no such thing as universal recreation. There is an individual emotional response, by an individual person in an individual park.[28]

By viewing recreation as an individual response which may reflect social, physical, and emotional behavior, the *primary objective of leisure*

26. M. J. Ellis, *Why People Play* (Englewood Cliffs, New Jersey: Prentice-Hall, Inc., 1973), p. 143.
27. Ibid., p. 135.
28. Gray, *Park and Recreation Movement*, p. 46.

agencies is to provide opportunities for people to optimize and satisfy internal need-drives, opportunities which cater to the total human personality. Recreation in this text is seen as a human experience and is best understood from an ecological perspective representing the interrelationships of the agency, the participant, the physical environment, and the social environment. Since recreation behavior is goal-directed, the perceptions of the individual are fundamental to determining the bases for the response. Recreation experience therefore represents a wide and complex variety of individual differences which have potentiality for influencing recreation behavior. Recreation must be viewed as an important element within the total spectrum of community services. While recreation's role in some cases may appear to have only a secondary position for some groups within the community, it is often seen as playing a primary role in meeting the needs of the ill, disabled, and aged.

SUMMARY—DEVELOPING A MEANINGFUL WORK-LEISURE RHYTHM OF LIFE

By integrating the various time, work, and leisure spheres, one is able to construct several alternative life patterns. The prerequisites for the various leisure life-styles are conditioned by one's time and work orientation and vice versa. The significance of leisure in a postindustrial era gains relevance when the individual makes of it what is pertinent and meaningful to his personal life rhythm.

The various dimensions of time, work, and leisure presented in this chapter are all possible future societal patterns—each with alternative options. However, as depicted in Figure 1.1, each time, work, and leisure configuration is best conceived when understood in relation to its respective elements. The recognition of leisure's changing and broadening perspective parallels the country's expanding awareness in other spheres of life. Traditionally, most definitions of leisure use work as the reference point. As suggested by the discretionary time concept, leisure activities are associated implicitly or directly, with work or productive activities. Leisure is recognized by some as antiutilitarian and encompasses all nonwork time; while others state that it is only that time which is free of all commitments. As America moves into a postindustrial stage, leisure is increasingly recognized as that time available to be used at the individual's discretion—a *self-deterministic condition*.

Psychic fulfillment has traditionally been derived from one's accomplishments at work. As suggested by the turquoise concept of work and holistic leisure configuration, people will increasingly seek a more socially and psychologically satisfying work experience and equally satisfying nonwork fulfillment. There has been an erosion of the meaning of work, and increasingly people are turning to other forms of expression to realize pleasure, achievement, mastery, and fulfillment. The challenge of post-industrial society will seemingly be to provide its members the moral reinforcement to express their leisure attitude and behavior—whether it occurs during free time or work—and the opportunity to be identified by their leisure life-styles and cultural bases rather than solely by occupational roles. At the same time an environment characterized by a fusion of major social institutions recognizes the importance of improving the conditions of work.

historical developments

what to look for in this chapter...

Depiction of the Interrelationships and Transformation of Community Life, Work Life, and Leisure through Time

Historical Emergence and Development of Leisure
    Greek and Roman Culture
    Feudal Societies and the Renaissance
    The Industrial Revolution

Leisure as the Basis of Culture — Contemporary Developments
    A Discussion of Why People Play

Leisure as a Style of Life — A Way of Understanding Individual Leisure Patterns

Photograph by Harold M. Lambert

The flow of historical events is often presented in a disjointed, fragmented manner. The developments in one culture or civilization are not seen in relation to another. The emergence of recreation and leisure has had a profound impact on the life-styles, rituals, rest, and working conditions of various cultures. The particular social system associated with each culture has had varying degrees of impact on the meaning and distribution of leisure. The respective social system's values, beliefs, and rituals have exercised an influence on the acceptance of leisure as a worthwhile and beneficial experience.

The existence of the attributes of community life, work life, and leisure is best understood when viewed according to their dynamic relationships. *The prevalence of leisure in a culture may modify, reinforce, or contradict existing values, roles, and patterns of relationships in community and work life, but conversely, certain values, roles, and patterns of relationships in community and work life may influence the choice and use of leisure.*

A simplified model of ideal historical social orders and leisure is presented to provide a basis for communicating the developments, contrasts, and relationships of the transformation of leisure through time and is represented in Figure 2.1. Figure 2.1, "Social Orders and Leisure," is an adaptation of a model developed by Kaplan.[1] The Figure 2.2 shows the interrelationships and transformation of community life, work life, and leisure through time.

The first social order illustrated in Figure 2.1, the primitive or folk (phase A) order recognizes an integration of all aspects of social life in which leisure is spontaneous, spiritual, and personal in nature and interwoven into the main fabric of life. Leisure serves utilitarian as well as nonutilitarian functions. Because of the fusion of institutions, leisure may serve as an integral part of a religious ceremony but may also be revealed in various drawings, paintings, sculpture, and other art forms. Time is cyclical and society revolves around the seasons.

The next historical leisure configuration, the feudal order or phase B, initiates a stage of development in which leisure is seen as an opportunity available primarily to aristocracy, although leisure is more-or-less integrated into the rituals, celebrations, weddings, and day-to-day routines of the masses. The total way of community life of the rich is beyond the masses, with fairly rigid social and economic lines drawn between the rich and poor. Relatively stable preindustrialized societies are characterized as organic, communal, homogeneous, religious, and rural social or-

1. Max Kaplan, "Leisure and Design" (Paper presented to the American Iron and Steel Institute, Chicago, Illinois, March 23, 1972).

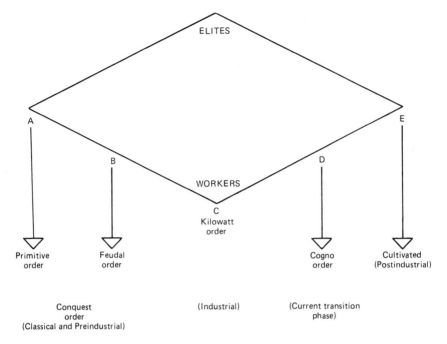

Figure 2.1. Social Orders and Leisure.

Adapted from Max Kaplan, "Leisure and Design" (Paper read at the American Iron and Steel Institute, Chicago, Illinois, March 23, 1972).

ders. It is during this phase that workers and the elite ruling class became sharply divided (as shown by their separation on the diagram) with class and power lines well-delineated. Time is geared to special occasions and rituals.

The existence of industrial society (phase C) brings about a major demarcation between the elite and the poor. Urban communities serve as the centers of social life and regulate the flow of work, community life, and leisure according to the fixed patterns of machines and demands of industry. The complexity of community life fosters a multitude of organizations. Contractual arrangements foster personal freedom and diversity in which technological change accelerates the pace of living. Time is mechanized and geared to the industrial work rhythm of life. Leisure emerges as an unobligated block of time available to the masses. Socially acceptable leisure behavior predominates.

The transition phase (phase D) of an advanced technological social order similar to American society in the 1920s, is a stage in-between indus-

TABLE 2.1

TRANSFORMATION OF CULTURE: TOWARD A SOCIETY OF LEISURE

	FOLK SOCIETY	FEUDAL SOCIETY	INDUSTRIAL SOCIETY	POST-INDUSTRIAL SOCIETY
Community Life	Small, isolated, non-literate, homogeneous communities with a strong sense of group solidarity. No distinction of class. Social structure is rigid. Mobility is slow and infrequent.	Relatively large peasant population and small elite. More stratified and more heterogeneous. Small core of literate persons, priestly class. Some government apparatus.	Large community size and relatively dense population. Heterogeneity of people and cultures. Anonymity, transitory and impersonal relationships. Social mobility. Fluid class system, mass literacy. Predominance of secondary contracts.	Shared community decision making based on pluralistic, cooperative relationships.
Work Life	Energies wholly oriented toward the quest of food. Little or no specialization of labor. No food surplus. People produce their own artifacts.	More occupationally differentiated than folk communities. Trade, commerce, and craft specializations are well developed.	Occupational specialization, division of labor. Economy of scarcity dominated by manual labor, assembly-line work.	Economy of abundance. Economic independence. Still large work force—dominated by science and technology and computerized work.
Leisure	Behavior is traditional, spontaneous, spiritual, personal. Sacred prevails over the secular. Leisure is part of living, condition interwoven into the main fabric of life. Characterized by oneness with nature and an integral part of on-going processes and institutional functions.	Leisure is class bound. Leisure available to upper classes—a symbol of hierarchy and a value of the creative elite minority. It is integrated into the rituals, celebrations, weddings and day-to-day routines of the masses.	Mass leisure. Leisure is a specific block of time—earned from work. Socially acceptable leisure behavior predominates. Changing accessibility by the masses to opportunities for leisure and to power.	Individualized and liberated leisure (freed by technology)—based on inherent right and specified by particular developmental needs of the individual. Many personal options, diverse styles of life. A fusion of work-leisure relationships.

Source: Adapted from figure in "Transformation of Culture: Toward a Society of Leisure," by James F. Murphy, **Concepts of Leisure: Philosophical Implications** (Englewood Cliffs, New Jersey: Prentice-Hall, Inc., 1974).

trial and postindustrial cultures. The advent of automation, high-speed transportation, electric technology, and rising literacy contributes to a stage of reappraisal and inward quest for moral, aesthetic, and sociopolitical directions. A movement toward synthesis and integration of community and work life with leisure emerges, and a reordering of social life is pursued along humanistic channels.

The appearance of postindustrial or cultivated social order[2] (phase E) is seen as a general return to the fusions of work and nonwork which characterized the primitive period. Individualized and self-determined leisure emerges, based on inherent right and motivated by particular developmental needs of the individual.

A cybernated era, characteristic of the postindustrial period, provides for an integrative-cultivated fusion of work and nonwork spheres of life, and allows for the establishment of a relationship and relevance of leisure in terms of other human behavior.[3] This social order relies less on the precision of the clock, and the concept of time may revert back to the primitive notion of time which is oriented to natural, cyclical rhythms.

THE EMERGENCE OF LEISURE

The recognition of leisure as a separate, identifiable part of life emerged in classical Greece and Rome. In preclassic times there was a constant intermingling of cultures, and religious festivals and ceremonies were fused with other aspects of the life routine. Leisure, as such, did not exist. Agriculture was the main form of economic sustenance. Leisure was intertwined with religious observances and feasts following hunting forays and other ceremonial occasions. Kraus states:

> Primitive man does not make the clear distinction between work and leisure that we tend to make in modern society. Industrial man sets aside periods of time each day for work and other periods for rest and relaxation. Primitive man has no such precise separation; instead, he tends to work only when it is required and available. He may engage in an extended period of steady labor and then pause for a lengthy period to enjoy the fruit of his toil. Work itself is often infused with rites and customs that lend it variety and pleasure.[4]

The hunting society is usually made up of nomads and differs from the agricultural society which has a more stable economy and community

2. Max Kaplan, "Leisure: Theory and Policy," *Society and Leisure* 4(1972):138.
3. Joe Hendricks and Rabel Burdge, "The Nature of Leisure Research—A Reflection and Comment," *Journal of Leisure Research* 4(1972):216.
4. Richard Kraus, *Recreation and Leisure in Modern Society* (New York: Appleton-Century-Crofts, 1971), pp. 129-130.

pattern. The simple, fused life pattern of both preclassical periods (also characteristic of some primitive tribes today), constructed a society in which ritual and work were integrated into the life sequence to celebrate the success of a planting or harvest, a hunting expedition, or completion of a hut or dwelling. Art was infused into the process of daily living; and while architecture, painting, and sculpture may be less decorative or stylistic by contemporary standards, the experience was probably as aesthetically pleasing and rewarding.

The play behavior of preclassical civilization was an essential element of the life process and was often an important part of education, religious ritual, healing, communication, entertainment, and recreation of the tribe or nomadic community. As human societies became more complex and functions became more clearly specialized, play became a more distinct component of culture. Individuals who composed such preclassical societies commonly shared the same experiences and expectations, providing the bases for a more homogeneous population held together by similar sentiments and points of view.

Greek and Roman Cultures

The rise of cities in ancient Greece led to the emergence of self-governing communities—city-states with political independence. Some believed in leisure as the foundation of civilization, but one had to be bred to it. The scholar-philosopher Aristotle generated a concept of leisure which conceived of it as being free from the necessity of work. The Greeks invented the gymnasium and Olympic games and nurtured philosophical, political, intellectual, artistic, and religious pursuits. However, these aesthetic, primarily contemplative activities were available only to the rich, while the slaves and foreigners toiled in the fields and ships. The classical ideal was an aristocratic amenity. Music, art, drama, sports, and poetry were seen as mutually beneficial play activities. Physical prowess and intellectual imagination were recognized as necessary ingredients for a well-balanced citizen. A strong relationship was encouraged which would unify mind and body into an integrated personality.

The contemporary discretionary time concept of leisure would have little relevance to ancient Athenians who made a sharp distinction between rest and relaxation, entertainment and leisure. The first principle of all action was leisure, while amusements were merely seen as recuperative diversions. Leisure was recognized as giving pleasure, happiness, and enjoyment to one's life, in which members of the aristocracy were wholly divorced from obligation and "free" to pursue intellectual cultivation. The Greek equivalent of rest, relaxation, and "discretionary" recreation is

noted by Miller and Robinson: "The Athenians combined religious worship and athletic and cultural events in a large number of annual festivals
occupying perhaps seventy days of the year."[5]

Ancient Greece can be divided into roughly two stages of leisure development. The rise of Greek city-states involved a more utilitarian approach to play which was characterized by physical fitness, courage,
endurance, and rest and relaxation. This period is contrasted by the Per-
iclean "Golden Age" which stimulated a culture of humanistic concern,
creative, intellectual, moral, physical, and aesthetic living, and civic participation.

The Roman empire was somewhat different from the aesthetic expressive Greek civilization. Rome exploited culture with grandiose architecture and lush gardens for the pleasure of a few. Rome was more
practical, and although sports, for example, were valued as a worthwhile
pursuit, they were seen primarily for their utilitarian benefits. Rome
lacked sensitivity and inventiveness, which were traits of Athens, and was
less interested in varied forms of cultural, aesthetic, and civic activities.

Rome exploited leisure, although some members of the ruling classes
valued a liberal education and a cultured life. But the prevalent forms of
leisure activities were oriented to sensuous, gaudy forms of entertainment
highlighted by chariot races, gladiator contests, circuses, fights between
beasts, and Roman gymnasia and baths. The indigent poor were mainly
entertained by the baths and games. Kraus notes how the rulers of Rome
had to have a large number of holidays for popular entertainment to
maintain their political popularity:

> As early as the reign of the Emperor Claudius, in the first century
> A.D., there were 159 public holidays during the year; of these 93 were
> devoted to games at public expense. These included many new festi-
> vals in honor of national heroes, foreign victories, and other occasions.
> by A.D. 354 there were 200 public holidays, including 175 days of
> games. Even on working days, the labor which began at daybreak
> ended shortly after noon during much of the year.[6]

The folk communities of classical Greece and Rome are generally
characterized as being elitist societies where the upper classes built an
elaborate leisure culture in which a philosophy emerged to justify and
rationalize the aristocratic concept of leisure values. However, Rome did
extend entertainment to the working masses by providing opportunities

5. Norman P. Miller and Duane M. Robinson, *The Leisure Age: Its Challenge to Recreation* (Belmont, California: Wadsworth Publishing Co., Inc., 1963), p. 390.
6. Kraus, *Recreation and Leisure,* p. 140.

for relaxation and recreation to the semi-idle workers, craftsmen, and indigent urban dwellers. While there was some cultivation of the arts in the Roman empire by prominent citizens, notably Cicero, Seneca, Virgil, and others, the decline of scholarship, philosophy, literature and other "cultured" activities begun in Greece continued.

Feudal Societies

The preindustrial societies of the Middle Ages and Renaissance were more stratified, heterogeneous, and occupationally differentiated than folk communities. The existence of trade, commerce, and craft specializations did not totally lie dormant during medieval feudalism. Traders and merchants were only nominally influenced by priestly or feudal rule. Cities did decline in importance, and there was a long period of cultural and economic stagnation.

Leisure was primarily available to the feudal nobility and secondarily to urban workers. Serfs, who were bound by the rhythms of the seasons, did have some limited opportunity for leisure as it was normally integrated into their rituals, celebrations, and day-to-day routines.

Leisure was class bound, and the traditional activities of the upper class included hunting, riding, and combating. The castle was the center of social life for these groups with indoor activities including feasting, singing, drinking, chess, backgammon, listening to jesters, etc. After the rise of Christianity, other social classes were heavily influenced by the church, which replaced many of the Greek and Roman festival days with saints' days, and public holidays were reduced to approximately one-half of the total enjoyed in clasical times. During the Middle Ages play was seen as useless and evil, as intellectual and political leaders combined to suppress sports, games, and other forms of entertainment.[7]

Medieval communities were centers for cultural developments and religious worship. The crafts of the carpenters, sculptors, stoneworkers, and architects were exemplified in the building and design of cathedrals. Dancing, drama, and festivals ordinarily reflected religious influences, although secular cultural expressions, like street pantomime, became more prevalent in the late stages of the medieval period. The country life of the serfs was more characteristic of folk society entertainment in which seasonal celebrations incorporated simple games, dances, and songs. Peasant folk expressions eventually influenced the music and dance of the church, opera, and ballet of the upper classes and conveyed the simple, vital, and beautiful life of the serfs.

7. Refer to Martin H. Neumeyer and Esther S. Neumeyer, *Leisure and Recreation: A Study of Leisure and Recreation in Their Sociological Aspects,* 3rd ed. (New York: The Ronald Press Co., 1958), p. 55.

The Renaissance began roughly in the fifteenth century and marked an awakening of cultural activity, including science, philosophy, literature, and the arts. The reemergence of cities as active and thriving centers for intellectual, economic, and political activity was accompanied by increased opportunity for more active pursuit of cultural enlightenment, made possible largely by the invention of the printing press.

While life was still hard for urban workers and peasants, with few moments for rest and relaxation from toil, the Renaissance marked a transformation from the ruralism of the Middle Ages to an urbanity brought on by increasing trade and expanding intellectual horizons. A philosophy of humanism, which was incorporated in the field of the arts—painting, sculpture, dance, drama and music—was representative of the right of man to exercise his physical senses and emotions, and it accelerated a fresh and vigorous appreciation and fusion of cultural concerns into the cities of Europe.

While the Renaissance is seen as a period of rich stimulation of the arts, literature, and sciences, it was a hectic, tense period in which the conflicting life-styles of men who followed classical traditions, engaged in contemplation, and studied nature, love, beauty, and the liberal arts were contrasted with more active men who saw the need to breed horses, hunt, dance, and explore the universe. This conflict centered on the essence of the dignity of man which was torn between action and contemplation, with each laying claim to being the highest purpose of mankind.

The Industrial Revolution

The period following 1750 saw the rapid rise of the use of industrial machinery which replaced human labor, through the introduction of steam, water, oil, and electric power, and which brought an increase in the size of cities. Industrial expansion meant replacement of individual craftsmen by large-scale machine operations and occupational specialization as a result of the division of labor into small, component parts. The Protestant ethic which emerged during the Reformation under Calvin became even stronger as a consequence of the Industrial Revolution. Protestantism glorified work and demeaned leisure. Work was seen as a path to religious salvation as a high value was placed on an active rather than a contemplative life; thus, the Protestant ethic fostered economic rationality in which unremitting labor was seen as a moral virtue and duty. Work was established as the cornerstone of society and a basis for man's self-justification. Kraus notes:

> As industrialization became more widespread, there was a renewed emphasis on the importance of 'honest toil' and a strong antagonism

expressed against play. The church fell in with the attitude of the merchant-manufacturing class that idleness led to drinking and vice and that consequently long hours of labor should be maintained for the sake of the wage-earner's moral welfare.[8]

The peasant revolts against the Catholic church during the Reformation were symbolic of the mass resistance growing out of the peasant's miserable condition and the frustration of being repressed by ruthless feudal rulers. The reformed social order gave powerful motivation to work, as it too placed a high moral value on the material consequences of one's work. It fostered a code of ethics that ranked work highly. "It was a set of beliefs consonant with the technological innovations of industrial capitalism."[9]

Under Puritanism folk festivals and drama were discouraged and even banned; musical instruments and art pieces were removed from the Church. The highly stratified class structure which divided the society into two great classes began to give way with the emergence of a middle class, whose materialistic aspirations were in conflict with spiritual values. Work was viewed as more than a necessity; it became a source of social and moral values. While Puritanism suppressed forms of leisure, some new and varied forms of play and recreation emerged with the rise of a new middle class.

The first half of the nineteenth century was witness to a number of religious repressions in America. Consequently, there was a gradual expansion of many popular forms of recreation and amusement which increasingly found a role of importance in the way of life. Dulles states:

> The first half of the nineteenth century witnessed the growth of the theatre as entertainment reaching out to all classes of people. It saw the beginnings of variety shows, minstrel shows, and the circus; the establishment of amusement parks, public-dance halls, concert-saloons, and beer-gardens; a revival of horse racing, and the rise of spectator sports. By the Civil War, the nation was in the midst of those far-reaching changes in the recreational scene which were a natural corollary of the broader social changes through which it was passing.[10]

The Civil War served as a stimulus to recreation involvement, as soldiers, fighting in different sections of the country, learned new forms of games and sports. While cities, particularly larger ones, began to re-

8. Kraus, *Recreation and Leisure*, p. 171.
9. Noel P. Gist and Sylvia F. Fava, *Urban Society*, 5th ed. (New York: Thomas Y. Crowell Co., 1964), p. 32.
10. Foster Rhea Dulles, *A History of Recreation: America Learns to Play*, 2nd ed. (New York: Appleton-Century-Crofts, 1965), pp. 98-99.

construct their communities and as machinery was introduced to the production processes, new forms of commercial recreation—the circus, burlesque, vaudeville, melodramas, shooting galleries, dance halls, bowling alleys, billiard parlors, and saloons—emerged. Additionally, amusement parks developed on the fringe of cities, where parachute jumps, open-air theatres, bicycle races, band concerts, roller-coasters, and fun houses were popular. Various sports, including horse racing, professional baseball, prize fighting, and a number of college sports drew large crowds and became increasingly popular. Kraus summarizes the inevitable consequence of this Industrial Revolution:

> Americans now lived in greater numbers in large cities, where the traditional social activities of the past and the opportunity for casual, wholesome play were no longer available. They had increasing amounts of free time and, more and more, were able to afford to pay for recreation. It was increasingly apparent that there was a need for organized recreation services that would provide wholesome and enriching leisure experiences for all classes.[11]

The growth of cities during the Industrial Revolution resulted in a shift from primarily agricultural, rural societies of Europe and America to urban nations. The Industrial Age brought factories, factory workers, long hours, cluttered and heavily populated cities, and the possibility of leisure for the masses as a result of the specialization and mechanization of work. Industrialization in America led to a democratization of leisure and the promise that more people could enjoy the benefits of free time and share in the values derived from leisure.

The development of leisure during the seventeenth through the nineteenth century led to a greater participation of the lower middle classes and other groups in music and dance as a means of expressing the joy and playfulness of the common people during their leisure. While there was some disagreement as to the place of leisure in industrial society, the emergence of machine power, urbanization, complex social organizations, science, and relative abundance for the common man led to the recognition of leisure as a specified, unobligated block of time—free from the necessities of work. Miller and Robinson comment:

> . . . we can see that the industrial revolution and capitalism on the one hand created new problems of city crowding, poverty, and the wear and tear of industrial labor. On the other hand, a tremendously greater wealth could be produced and, potentially, shared by all, and a much greater leisure could be provided by the productivity of the

11. Kraus, *Recreation and Leisure,* p. 179.

machine. The contradictions between the promise of comfort and leisure and the stark reality of discomfort, poverty, and dreary labor
became clearer to the poorer classes. They realized that a better world
could be brought into being and that it is man's right and duty to work
for such a better world and to share in its pleasures. Much of the turmoil and instability of these centuries was the result of efforts by the
masses to seize a larger share of all those things that meant a good
life.[12]

LEISURE AS THE BASIS OF CULTURE

The glorification of work through industrialism led to the separation
of work and leisure. This resulted in an emphasis on economically productive functions as the most significant aspects of life, with the eventual
relegation of leisure to the status of spare time. At the turn of the twentieth
century work commanded the moral attention of a society still predomi-
nately based on a scarce economy. The resultant growth in the economy,
increased educational opportunity, medical advancements, automated industry, earlier work retirement, and shorter workweek have all contributed to an erosion of the view of leisure as discretionary time, time that is
earned from increased efficiency and productivity. These conditions have
caused a corollary dissipation in the tradition of work being at the moral
and religious core of life.

The highly specialized, assembly-line nature of modern industrial work
has left the individual with little opportunity to use individual judgment
or initiative. The autonomous craftsman, individually responsible for the
total creation and performance of a product has virtually disappeared from
the American industrial scene. Work still continues to provide most people
with an important source of identity and opportunity for self-fulfillment;
these values accrue particularly in industries and agencies where the
individual is allowed an opportunity to create his own work schedules, or
be a part of a team which rotates tasks, divides up the work, and sets its
own work pace. The content and the environment of work are conditions
which seem to be at the core of the problems of alienation, dissatisfaction,
and absenteeism in industry and the misuses of leisure and boredom
which arise generally in nonwork hours.

The social patterns associated with the technological changes that
began in the eighteenth and nineteenth centuries were incorporated into
the values of American society. They remained dominant until the end of
the second World War. Industry effectively integrated many of the concepts of the Protestant ethic into work and even conditioned the worker

12. Miller and Robinson, *The Leisure Age,* p. 80.

in his off-work hours. There is a belief held by some people that the industrial and technological thrust in America has had a detrimental influence on the appreciation and fostering of leisure. But as our society enters a postindustrial era, in which the economy has primarily moved away from production-oriented to consumer-oriented characteristics (a society based on technology and the flow of information and new knowledge and not manufacturing), leisure has become a distinct part of the social structure. A society is said to become *leisure-based* when the self-consciousness of man is oriented primarily upon the interests and activities which are associated with leisure. In such a society leisure will exercise a generalized influence throughout all aspects of people's lives. Since leisure is self-motivated and self-directed, it is in nonwork hours that individuals express their real personalities. In large measure, the individual's self-concept is based upon, and reinforced by, the values, activities, and the life-style he pursues during his leisure.

While work is still an essential component of man's social orientation, it has increasingly commanded less reverence. For example, when an individual is at work, he may feel relatively detached from the role that he is playing and not identify his own personality with the qualities which his job demands that he display. Therefore, we may expect that as other institutions accommodate their own values and structures to conform to the emerging leisure-based orientations, leisure may increasingly become the source of man's sense of self-identity and the basis of all social life.

The emergence of recreation and leisure services as a separate, distinguishable institution in America to provide opportunities for leisure expression for the public is a major social development in the twentieth century. That the public is willing to support a group of professional planners, organizers, and community catalysts for the primary function of encouraging and fostering leisure pursuits, has aided the process whereby leisure service agencies have evolved into an identifiable and reputable institution.

Recreation and leisure agencies emerged at the outset of the twentieth century to meet the various social, recreational, and community needs of an urbanizing industrial nation. Today the complexity of social issues and problems has increased, and the nature of leisure service has expanded in response to the needs of a highly diverse, multiracial population.

LEISURE AS A STYLE OF LIFE: THE WIDENING CIRCLE

Leisure experience, in a behavioral context, represents *all* of the potential nonwork opportunities available to an individual. As such, leisure behavior must be recognized as an expression of an individual's total self in which all of man's intellectual, physical, and emotional capacities are potentially engaged. Niepoth[13] suggests that the perceptions of the individual engaging in leisure experience are the bases for his response. Behavior is goal-directed. The experience is a direct result of goal-seeking. Success or failure influences continuation, modification, or termination of recreation participation. The level of aspiration of an individual conditions perceptions of success or failure.

Recreation behavior is a behavioral sequence. From the standpoint of the individual, it is an experience. Motives for recreation participation vary from individual to individual, and from occasion to occasion. Therefore, those engaged in the delivery of recreation and leisure service and providing program opportunities must recognize the varied and complex interrelated individual differences which have potentiality for influencing recreation behavior. The recreation and leisure service agency must make a commitment to provide opportunities for people, individually and collectively, to engage in recreation behavior. "Leisure services, then, are those activities, which, through the creation and/or manipulation of human and physical environments, provide opportunities for the expression of a wide variety of recreation behaviors."[14]

Recreation as seen from a behavioral context is an experience that results from one's engagement in activities to meet certain personal needs. Recreation engagements are viewed as self-rewarding experiences and must be perceived as a process. Recreation consists of more than participation in an activity, as its value must be measured as a process of responses. Several disadvantages are involved in viewing recreation from an activity perspective (e.g., a program which is categorized according to whether it encompasses sports, arts and crafts, drama, special events, or some other type(s) of activity). One disadvantage is that such a perspective doesn't explain why an individual is participating in an activity. Another is that it doesn't explain what satisfactions or rewards are received from activity. Additionally it doesn't help recreation programmers understand how the quality of the experience can be enhanced. Essentially those designing and programming recreation experiences from an activity viewpoint tend to focus on supply and give little attention to demand—to the personality, expressive needs, and life-style of the participants.

13. E. William Niepoth, "Users and Non-Users of Recreation and Park Services," *Reflections on the Recreation and Park Movement,* ed. David Gray and Donald A. Pelegrino (Dubuque, Iowa: Wm. C. Brown Company Publishers, 1973), pp. 135-136.
14. James F. Murphy, John G. Williams, E. William Niepoth, and Paul D. Brown, *Leisure Service Delivery System: A Modern Perspective* (Philadelphia: Lea & Febiger, 1973), p. 78.

By perceiving recreation as an experience, planners will understand that a person's responses are reflective of an attempt to realize need satisfaction or obtain a goal. *Individuals are motivated to recreate by internalized needs which are set in motion by a multitude of forces or drives in an attempt to respond and achieve internal consistency.* The recreation experience is culminated with the attainment of the goal. Recreation catalysts must be perceptive to recommend complementary and supplemental opportunities to enhance the realization of a participant goal and should similarly attempt to reduce points of conflict which are encountered in the pursuit of a goal.

The recreation state in this context is perceived as a state of mind, an attitude set, and the experience exists to the extent to which the needs or desires to be fulfilled are gratified. The recreation experience is a highly personal response. It can, however, be influenced by others and the intervening factors that are a part of the physical environment. The satisfaction level of attainment of the recreation experience will vary from person to person, with some people "peaking" during the anticipation phase, others at the point of goal attainment, and still others at some later time during recollection of the event.

The effective recreation and leisure service delivery system is based on (1) initial assumptions about participant behavior (motivations and influencing individual characteristics, such as age, sex, income level, etc.), and on (2) the individualization and modification of service at the point of actual contact with the participant. This process should be viewed within an *ecological* framework, in which the participants, the agency-structured environment, and the conditioning aspects of both the social and physical environment are seen as complimentary elements of a whole system. The individual, for example, is influenced by the agency, and in turn, he influences it.

PERSPECTIVES ON PLAY BEHAVIOR

Individuals perceive experiences on the basis of their compatibility with existing evaluations of their own personalities. Those experiences which are inconsistent with this self-evaluation are rejected or discarded; those experiences which are consistent are accepted by the person. The personality system reflects a degree of unity across a number of expressive behaviors.

Studies by Bishop, Howard, and Witt have shown that there are stable dimensions of leisure activities that can be used to describe individual patterns of leisure behavior.[15] It is suggested by their research that people tend to prefer similar leisure experiences because there is a need by man to maintain an internal consistency. According to Murray, the concept of need represents the significant determinant of behavior within the person.[16] One's needs are modified and set in motion through his interaction with the environment. One is aroused (stimulated) when a need is in a state of tension and is satisfied through reduction (play) of the tension. By applying Murray's needs concept to leisure activity preferences, it is possible to see why people select certain activities to experience satisfaction (reduce tension) and fulfill their needs.

Howard states that leisure activity preferences satisfy the needs of individuals better than others, and that the individual's own unique personality determines what is appropriate for him.[17] An individual chooses specific leisure activities on the basis of their ability to satisfy certain needs. One may deduce that a person will select those activities whose inherent values are consistent with his personality style.

Howard's findings indicate that individuals who prefer *outdoor-nature* activities are more persevering, forceful, adventurous, self-reliant, and intellectually curious. Those individuals who prefer *sports* activities are more aggressive, incautious, spontaneous, and pleasure-seeking. Individuals inclined to *aesthetic-sophisticate* or culturally-oriented activities tend to be more attention-seeking, domineering, and affiliative. These results lend support to the notion that different leisure activities attract individuals with different needs.

The use of personality indicators as measured by Howard account for a little over one-half (53 percent) of the determination of leisure choices and elevates our understanding of why people choose one activity over another. An important finding of this study is that people with similar personalities tend to make the same type of leisure activity choices. Previous demographic factors of age, income, sex, and occupation used to explain leisure behavior have accounted for only 30 percent. By combining psychological aspects with biological, social, and occupational determinants into a life-style perspective, we may soon understand more clearly the reasons, patterns, and outcomes of leisure behavior.

15. Doyle Bishop, "Stability of the Factor Structure of Leisure Behavior: Analysis of Four Communities," *Journal of Leisure Research* 2(1970):160-170; Dennis R. Howard, "Multivariate Relationships Between Leisure Activities and Personality" (Unpublished Doctoral Dissertation, Oregon State University, Corvallis, Oregon, June, 1973); Peter A. Witt, "Factor Structure of Leisure Behavior for High School Age Youth in Three Communities," *Journal of Leisure Research* 3(1971):213-219.

16. Henry Murray, *Explorations in Personality* (New York: Oxford University Press, 1938).

17. Howard, *Leisure Activities and Personality*, pp. 85-90.

Howard's study lends credence to the Bureau of Outdoor Recreation's efforts to more accurately meet the outdoor recreation needs of the American people. At a series of forums held by the Bureau of Outdoor Recreation to develop a nationwide Outdoor Recreation Plan, it was indicated that more comprehensive studies should be undertaken to measure the physical, psychological, and/or emotional satisfaction derived from each outdoor recreation activity; that these measurements should be derived through use of a social-psychological approach rather than the traditional socio-economic approach. "Measurements derived from such an approach would determine this desire for specific types of recreation experience, rather than for particular activities or facilities, since several types of activity may satisfy the same need."[18]

Increasingly, greater consideration is being given the total life-style of the participant. With the proliferation of a diversity of subcultures in American society, the term *life-style* has become an important social indicator for determining leisure interests and is based upon such factors as cultural heritage, family life, education, income, and/or occupation. A person's life-style is a unique pattern of individual behavior. Knowing how an individual with an identified life-style behaves in one area of his life gives important insights into what he might do in other segments.[19] In spite of the unique life-style developed by individuals, there is enough commonality among people of similar life-styles to permit generalizations about some groups. However, life-style generalizations drawn across the whole of American society have little validity.

The concept of life-style provides more of a comprehensive view of leisure participants, since various groups in American culture are characterized at the same time by both great uniformity and great diversity.

The style of life context is seen as a qualitative view of people's lives in that it is an integrating and unifying approach to behavior study and analysis. It allows for the formulation and development of a reliable guideline for man's behavior as a whole, as a unified expression of various forms of life. For a more complete discussion of leisure and life-style see chapter 6.

A question arises as to whether there is such a typical leisure life-style pattern in American society. Most often American life-style is expressed by middle-American, middle-majority consumption patterns. However, American society embraces several class and ethnic groups,

18. *America Voices Its Recreation Concerns* (Washington, D.C.: U.S. Government Printing Office, 1973) p. 12.
19. Refer to Saul D. Feldman and Gerald W. Thielbar, ed., *Life Styles: Diversity in American Society* (Boston: Little, Brown and Co., 1972), pp. 1-3, for a discussion on the meaning of life-style.

including blacks, Chicanos, blue-collar people, Jews, and Indians. In response to this question recreation and leisure service has tended to broaden its base of leisure service delivery by incorporating a *pluralistic* approach which preserves separate ethnic and racial life-styles.

A pluralistic approach seeks to incorporate all ethnic and racial minorities within the system. It implies that a group may seek toleration for its cultural and life-style differences—the idea being that variant cultures can flourish in harmony in the same society—a pattern acceptable to the dominant culture. The possibility that all groups may reflect their own cultural, ethnic, and racial life-styles while supporting an overall democratic political philosophy appears to have strengthened the meaning and vitality of American society.

SUMMARY

Historically leisure has evolved in relation to community life and work life and is best understood when viewed according to their dynamic relationship. The figures were presented to show the transformation and interrelationships of community life, work life, and leisure through time. Briefly, during primitive eras leisure was intertwined with religious observances and feasts following hunting forays and other ceremonial occasions. Leisure emerged as a separate, identifiable part of life during the time of classical Greece and Rome. The Greeks, as represented by Aristotle, saw leisure as being free from the necessity of being occupied to engage in intellectual contemplation. Rome exploited culture with grandiose architecture, as leisure activities were oriented to sensuous, gaudy forms of entertainment. In preindustrial societies of the Middle Ages leisure was primarily available to the feudal nobility, as serfs were bound by the rhythms of the season. Their leisure expression was integrated into their ritual, celebrations, and day-to-day routines. During the Renaissance, there was a reawakening of cultural activity and infusion of a philosophy of humanism.

During the Industrial Revolution work was viewed as more than a necessity; it became a source of social and moral values as Puritanism suppressed forms of leisure. The glorification of work through industrialism led to the separation of work and leisure at the height of the Industrial Revolution. Since the turn of the twentieth century leisure service has emerged as a separate distinguishable institution in America. Leisure behavior may be viewed as an expression of an individual's total self in which all of a person's intellectual, physical, and emotional capacities are potentially engaged. Life-style is seen as an important indicator for determining leisure interests and is based on such factors as cultural heritage, family life, education, income, and/or occupation.

chapter THREE
american society in transition:
the institution of leisure service

---

what to look for in this chapter...

Origin and Development of the Recreation Movement in America

Early Forces Influencing the Provision of Recreation

Recreation and the New American Culture

Emerging Leisure Ethic

American society is no longer oriented primarily around a scarce economy in which materialistic striving was a central focus. Increases in nonwork time, longer vacations, rising incomes, earlier retirement, less physically demanding toil, and increased longevity have sparked a shift in American institutional focus and central life interest to more intrinsic, self-fulfilling areas, including leisure.

The Recreation Movement grew out of the humanitarian concerns of dedicated private citizens who saw the need to help urban dwellers overcome the problems of overcrowding, poverty, lack of recreation opportunity and who led social reform to improve the blighted conditions of city life. According to Gray, "The earliest practitioners had a human welfare motivation in which the social ends of human development, curbing juvenile delinquency, informal education, cultural enrichment, health improvement, and other objectives were central."[1]

The Recreation Movement's early success and impact upon local government was a result of the actions of socially conscious individuals who believed organized recreation should be a basic and legitimate function of each community. The role of social change was dramatic at the height of the Industrial Revolution. The attention of play leaders and social reformers in the early days of the Recreation Movement was directed to satisfying the lower level needs of people, including physiological (food, rest, exercise, shelter, protection from the elements), safety needs (protection against danger, threat, deprivation), and social needs (need for belonging, for association, for acceptance by one's fellows). Likewise, the persistence of world wars, the Depression, and national recovery kept the leisure service field oriented to meeting basic human needs.

A rekindling of the humanitarian spirit which marked the early years of the Park and Recreation Movement was again prevalent at the beginning of 1960s, the period of the New Frontier which produced a significant shift in the direction of social commitment. A revitalized concern for the problems of the "deprived" or "disadvantaged," excluded from the benefits of an age of affluence, brought the movement back to issues of social concern. This coincided with the era of "flower children," "hippies," "growth centers," and "humanistic psychology" which was symbolic of a focus on higher order human needs, including ego needs (self-esteem, need for self-confidence, independence, achievement, competence, status, and recognition) and self-actualization (needs for realizing one's own potentialities, for continued self-development, for being creative).

1. David Gray, "The Case for Compensatory Recreation," *Parks and Recreation* 4 (1969):23.

Various human service institutions, including leisure service organizations, began to develop a common strand of development and participation which was an extension of sociotechnological change in the 1960s. The need for fulfillment and satisfaction of basic needs became a twofold goal of institutions who were challenged to meet both the need of the poor and downtrodden as well as the more affluent.

The discrepancy and hypocrisy of nationally shared standards of achievement, equality, and material success and the actual conditions of social life affecting the poor, disadvantaged, and youth have become more apparent in recent years. They have served as a sufficient social problem to cause leisure service agencies and organizations to search for new values, goals and programs in an attempt to bring the field into a closer, more harmonious relationship with the disaffected and disadvantaged. Refer to Table 3.1 for a contrast between the differences of the traditional belief patterns symbolized by the Protestant ethic and the changing pattern of beliefs representative of a Humanistic ethic as they relate to social institutions. The rate of social change is so rapid and disruptive to the daily routine of most people, particularly "outsiders" who do not fit within the established social order that institutions have become important sources of and links to stability in a highly transient society. Leisure service agencies may be recognized as filtering agents, in which the rapidity of technological developments and the human consequenecs of change may be interpreted and synthesized for people looking for guidance in a highly unstable world. Leisure service agencies may serve as agents of social control, particularly in urban communities where impersonality, a sense of impotence, alienation, and the need for primary group contact are pervasive expressions and elements of city life-styles.

THE AMERICAN RECREATION MOVEMENT

The Recreation Movement was spawned in the latter part of the nineteenth century because of the recognition by such socially concerned leaders as Jacob Riis, Jane Addams, Joseph Lee, Luther Gulick, and others, that there was an imperative need to provide constructive leisure opportunities for children and youth in urban slums. In fact, many of the pioneers of the movement conceived recreation as a means of counteracting some of the affects of poverty, such as bad housing and juvenile delinquency.

The beginning of the movement is credited to the Boston Sand Garden, established in 1885, where public-spirited citizens converted a pile of sand into a much needed play area in a working-class district. Similarly

TABLE 3.1.

CHANGING SOCIAL VALUES AS RELATED TO INSTITUTIONAL
GOALS FOR THE SOCIETY

	Protestant Ethic	Humanistic Ethic
Political Institutions	Are to protect the rights of the individual and to encourage the free enterprise system on which our society has grown and prospered. Minimum intervention in the lives of the people.	Are to protect the right of all people, especially the poor, the sick, the downtrodden. Increased intervention in the lives of the people to guarantee civil rights of all.
Economic Institutions	Must grow and prosper, for material progress leads to social progress. Hard work and long hours lead to material success.	Must provide economic security for those at the bottom of the ladder. Economic success no longer an important goal for the individual.
Leisure Institutions	Are to be used only so that one is then able to do a better job at work.	Self-expression, "doing your own thing" are legitimate, important, necessary activities in their own right.
Family Institutions	Nuclear as well as extended family groups are important in the life pattern and the value and belief structure of the individual members. Close psychological and geographical proximity of members.	Family is less important in the life pattern and the value and belief structure of individual members. Peer group is more important. Generation gap.
Religious Institutions	Are highly respected. They define morality for the individual. Moral men are economically successful men.	Religious experience is an individual rather than an institutional affair. Individual acts of kindness, gentleness, love toward one's fellow men constitute morality. Economically successful men are not necessarily moral men.
Educational Institutions	Are important avenues to material advancement. Not as important as hard work, though, and too much education is certainly suspect.	Are respected for their own sake, i.e., for the gaining of knowledge rather than the achieving economic success. Importance of "relevant" social studies.

Source: Mary Lystad, **As They See It** (Cambridge, Massachusetts, Schenkman Publishing Co., Inc., 1973), p. 4.

other areas were developed by socially conscious individuals in run-down communities. Butler states:

> . . . the conscience of civic leaders and social workers such as Jacob Riis in New York City and Jane Addams in Chicago was stirred into

action by the slum conditions and their effect upon the children and youth living in blighted neighborhoods. Joseph Lee was shocked to see boys arrested for playing in the Boston streets, and George E. Johnson was moved at the pathos of the attempts of little children to play in the narrow crowded alleys of Pittsburg.[2]

The early efforts of the Recreation Movement in America were oriented to the needs of underprivileged white youth. The initial attempts to meet the leisure needs of children and youth did not include a consideration for black children, still confined largely to the southern states in rural areas.

EARLY FORCES INFLUENCING THE PROVISION OF RECREATION

The formation of the Playground Association of America in 1906 culminated some three decades of concern in what many people consider as the most significant development of the Recreation Movement. The organization of the association served to unite the various scattered attempts of communities to provide recreation leadership, equipment, and facilities for people and to serve as a means for interrelating individual efforts and concerns.

A plan for such interrelation was formulated when a few dedicated and visionary individuals, competent observers, who defined the situation as constituting a social problem requiring readjustment, met in Washington, D.C. in 1906 to plan what was to become the first true attempt at organization of the American recreation movement.[3]

The initial impetus of the Recreation Movement came from social and civic workers who provided funds for the establishment of the first playgrounds and began building up public opinion favorable to governmental support and direction of public recreation facilities. At the time the Playground Association of America was started in 1906, there were some 41 cities that were maintaining municipally supported and operated playground programs. By 1915, 83 communities reported public recreation departments, and the number had increased to 465 by 1920.

It became clear, as the importance of recreation as a necessary part of normal life was increasingly recognized, that government should assume responsibility for the provisions of recreation. High governmental

2. George D. Butler, "A Fair Share," *Recreation and Leisure Service for the Disadvantaged*, ed. John A. Nesbitt, Paul D. Brown, and James F. Murphy (Philadelphia: Lea & Febiger, 1970), p. v.
3. Reynold Carlson, Theodore Deppe, and Janet MacLean, *Recreation in American Life*, 2nd ed. (Belmont, California: Wadsworth Publishing Co., Inc., 1972), p. 45.

officials, prominent organizations, citizens, and economists voiced the opinion that public parks and recreation centers were, like schools, essential to the health, safety, and welfare of the community. State legislatures passed enabling laws empowering municipalities and counties to conduct recreation activities. Decisions by state and federal courts declared recreation to be an essential governmental function.

The development of public, tax-supported recreation service was primarily a northern urban phenomenon. a response to overcrowding, inadequate housing, and generally deleterious social conditions arising from the Industrial Revolution. The welfare-motivated leaders of the play movement in America were not primarily concerned about the needs of blacks and other nonwhite minority groups. The early propagation of play in urban areas was a consideration for the needs of white immigrant slum children.

The specific interest in providing recreation opportunities for blacks was a consequence of the first World War which resulted in great numbers of blacks migrating to the northern urban communities. For the first time blacks were brought into contact and competition with whites on a large scale, involving employment, education, housing, and recreation. The expanding concern for race relations necessitated a change in the provision of public recreation service, resulting in a specialized attempt to meet the leisure needs of black citizens through the Bureau of Colored Work of the Playground Recreation Association of America (renamed in 1911), the major professional agency of the Recreation Movement. It provided consultation services aimed at assisting racially segregated community recreation programs until World War II. The prevailing "separate but equal" doctrine (a result of the *Plessy v. Ferguson* 1896 Supreme Court ruling) which dictated the nature of relations between blacks and whites, was also applicable to recreation during the first half of the twentieth century.

The National Recreation Association (renamed in 1930) maintained the Bureau of Colored Work, under the guidance of Ernest T. Attwell, from 1920 to 1942 to facilitate and expand recreation opportunities for blacks and encourage such programs as were provided. The early efforts of the Bureau of Colored Work were significant in helping to establish facilities and programs for blacks, although programs tended to continue to be inferior to those run in white neighborhoods, and in most cases they were maintained on a "separate but equal" basis.

The effects of World War I served as a watershed for the Recreation Movement. During the war 600 recreation programs were initiated in communities near military centers. The War Camp Community Service, which was mobilized by the Playground and Recreation Association of America at the request of the War Department, served to broaden the philosophy of community recreation to make available leisure opportunities to all citizens during World War I.

The broadened role of recreation during the 1920s improved its image in communities, and it was during this phase that the concept "recreation for all" developed as a consequence of wider and more representative recreation opportunities for everyone. By the outset of the 1930s the need for special training of aspiring recreation administrators was recognized, and the NRA began a one-year graduate course through the National Recreation School which lasted until 1935. The Depression resulted in an increased emphasis on community recreation. Black leaders benefited from special training courses set for thousands of blacks employed by the Works Progress Administration and the National Youth Administration. The courses, in many instances, constituted the only training in recreation the workers had ever had.

Because of the reduction in the workweek and the high unemployment, recreation received more attention during the Depression. "The resulting increased demand for recreation and decreased supply of opportunities available caused federal agencies to try to take up the slack, giving the recreation movement more impetus than it had ever had before.[4]

The Recreation Division of the Works Progress Administration provided direct leadership and guidance in the offering of recreation activities in over 23,000 local communities during the 1930s. Other federal programs, including the National Youth Administration and the Civilian Conservation Corps, provided service to communities and outdoor areas by constructing various kinds of recreation facilities, including picnic grounds, camps, parks, trails, swimming pools, and playgrounds.

With the advent of World War II in 1939 and America's involvement in 1941, the government renewed its emphasis on recreation. Several services, including the USO, American Red Cross, Army Special Services Division, the Welfare and Recreation Section of the Bureau of Naval Personnel, and the Recreation Service of the Marine Corps promoted programs on the battlefields, in hospitals, and in camps. The Federal Security Agency's Office of Community Service set up a new Recreation Division which assisted in establishing programs in over 300 communities, assisting the construction and operations of child-care centers and recreation buildings, of which several were taken over by cities as tax-supported recreation departments.

4. Ibid., pp. 49-50.

At the same time as recreation programs and facilities were expanding during World War II throughout the United States, Myrdal found a uniformly inferior provision of facilities for black in the South. He claimed that blacks had a greater need for public recreation facilities than whites:

> . . . the visitor finds Negroes everywhere aware of the great damage done Negro youth by the lack of recreational outlets and of the urgency of providing playgrounds for children. In almost every community visited during the course of this inquiry, these were among the first demands on the program of local Negro organizations.[5]

By the mid-1940s the condition of the black man had improved slightly but had not changed significantly. He certainly had increased opportunities for leisure through expanded recreation service, but his subordinated status deterred his ability to participate in community recreation programs. It was during this decade that a concern among professional recreators emerged to support the inclusion of blacks in the mainstream efforts of the municipal recreation program. The recreation center was seen as a community laboratory where persons of different races, creeds, and social stratas would be able to work, play, and interact together, developing attitudes of tolerance and understanding.[6]

The recognized importance of recreation in city-wide planning included a trend to involve representation from all groups in the postwar developing communities. The potential visualized in recreation and leisure service, as a medium for unifying and integrating various social and cultural strains in communities consistent with democratic tenets and ideals, was an outgrowth of post-World War II events. This development, which conceived of public recreation service at a catalytic agent for making available leisure opportunities for all races and creeds, reflected a new position. The belief supported the integration of all community groups in the overall recreation program, and the doctrine of "separate but equal" was abandoned as a guide to the formulation of public policy applied to most areas of community life. While there were regional differences, the general stance of public recreation service was the concern for adequate leisure opportunity for all groups.

The consideration of the "race problem" in post-World War II American society, with respect to the Recreation Movement, resulted in an important realization by the Movement that problems could not be solved by sentiment nor by superficial ideas concerning the relationship of race

5. Gunnar Myrdal, *An American Dilemma*, rev. ed. (New York: McGraw-Hill Book Co., 1964), pp. 346-347.
6. Refer to James F. Murphy, "Egalitarianism and Separatism: A History of Approaches in the Provision of Public Recreation and Leisure Service for Blacks, 1906-1972" (Ph.D. diss., Oregon State University, 1972), p. 98.

and the provision of public recreation opportunities. Meyer and Brightbill suggested that the race issue could not be ignored or allowed to run its course.[7] It was their contention that frank and honest recognition by all races of the difficulties involved was essential for a viable solution to be developed.

State-imposed racial discrimination was struck down as unconstitutional in the *Brown v. Board of Education,* Topeka, 1954 Supreme Court decision.[8] The Supreme Court ruling on segregation of public schools had a direct effect on the provision of recreation service in those communities where public leisure service was conducted cooperatively with the school system. While there was a tendency for cities to go out of the recreation business, stop further development, and slow down service, the desegregation decision brought about a general improvement in black welfare and a corollary decline in segregation in the public sectors of community life.

During the decades of the 1950s and 1960s organized recreation's profile had a marked increase on community life, advanced by an increasing concern for physical fitness, programs for the ill, aged, and disabled, an upsurge in outdoor recreation and park development, involvement in the arts, professional education, unification of the parks and recreation professional organizations, and the impact of civil unrest and youth dissent. The federal government provided greater assistance, through agencies in the Department of Health, Education and Welfare, Department of Interior, and Department of Housing and Urban Development.

Three significant developments appear to stand out as highlights during this two-decade period. First, the amalgamation of five national organizations (the American Institute of Park Executives, the American Recreation Society, the National Recreation Association, the National Conference on State Parks, and the American Association of Zoological Parks and Aquariums) in 1966, who constituted the National Recreation and Park Association, presented an opportunity for the field to yield a stronger voice for recreation and leisure concerns at the national level.

A second highlight of the period was stimulated by the report on outdoor needs and interests made in 1962 which led to the formation of the Bureau of Outdoor Recreation. The Bureau of Outdoor Recreation

7. Harold D. Meyer and Charles K. Brightbill, *Community Recreation: A Guide to Its Organization,* 1st ed. (Boston: D. C. Heath and Co., 1948), pp. 639-640.
8. It required later Supreme Court rulings to provide the full meaning of the *Brown* decision that all state-imposed racial discrimination was unconstitutional per se. Relying specifically on the 1954 *Brown* determination, the court declared segregation involved in municipal and public parks, *Muir v. Louisville,* 1954; swimming pools, *City of St. Petersburg v. Alsop,* 1957; beaches, *Mayor and City Council of Baltimore v. Dawson,* 1955; golf courses, *New Orleans Park Association v. Ditiege,* 1954; and public parks and municipal recreation facilities, *Watson v. Memphis,* 1963 to be unconstitutional.

(BOR) was an outgrowth of a series of recommendations of the Outdoor Recreation Resources Review Commission (ORRRC), established in 1958 by Congress during the Eisenhower Administration.

The Commission made more than fifty specific recommendations intended to assure that the benefits of outdoor recreation would be available to all Americans, now and in the future. The commission found that there were inadequate provisions being made for the expanding outdoor recreation needs. Additionally it found that the existing gap between demand and supply would increase if prompt and effective action were not taken. It also found that many of the programs were not oriented to the desires of the public.

The BOR was the first federal agency to be established principally for recreation purposes and the first one to carry the word *recreation* in its name. The establishment of the BOR helped to unify and promote all federal programs related to open space, the protection of natural resources, and outdoor recreation development.

The general concern for the quality of the environment precipitated by this event led to the creation of the Land and Water Conservation Fund in 1964, the Open Space Program of HUD, which assisted communities developing park and recreation sites, the Wild and Scenic Rivers System, and a National System of Recreational and Scenic Trails in 1968, the Council on Recreation and Natural Beauty in 1966, and the Environmental Quality Council established in 1969. State planning and increased municipal land acquisition programs, and a renewed public awareness, were a result of these acts and other environmentally based recreation legislation.

The third significant development of the period 1950 to 1970 was a return by the Recreation Movement to issues of social concern, stimulated by rioting and racial disorder in many of the nation's cities during the summer months of 1964, 1965, 1967, and 1968. It was not really until the decade of the 1960s that the recreation and leisure service field began to give special attention to the leisure needs of the poor—especially the nonwhite poor in urban slums. The federal government antipoverty program, funded principally by the Office of Economic Opportunity, which provided money and assistance to disadvantaged groups, gained impetus following a wave of rioting which erupted throughout the nation in 1964 and 1965. It was only after these "civil disturbances" that the needs of inner-city residents were brought forcefully to the attention of the public.

Prior to the establishment of the various OEO summer "crash programs" and community self-directed recreation programs beginning in 1964, the delivery of leisure service was still largely outside the sphere of the relatively powerless and unorganized slum dwellers. As the pace of racial unrest increased, the response of public officials to the various needs of deprived citizens, including public recreation and leisure service, expanded in most communities. Many summer programs, and special seasonal "cooling off" cultural, employment, health, education, and recreation programs were instituted to improve the condition in the slums and provide ghetto residents with improved service.

Throughout America, with the help of private enterprise and the federal government, attempts were made to supplement municipal and voluntary youth agency recreation efforts to reach out to the various economically and culturally deprived groups in slums. Kraus states:

> In city after city, recreation and park administrators began to develop expanded recreation programs in black and Spanish-speaking neighborhoods. Sports clinics and tournaments were initiated, along with busing programs, workshops in Afro-American arts, dance, and the theatre, and similar activities . . . Since recreation and park facilities in Negro neighborhoods were often minimal, vacant lots, littered with garbage, were quickly transformed into vest-pocket parks, often with community participation and supervision. Portable pools and other mobile recreation units were rapidly built or purchased and trucked into disadvantaged neighborhoods. Busing programs transported large numbers of Negro children and youth to municipal, county, or even nearby state parks.[9]

The major initial weakness of these programs was that they were often only designed for the summer needs of black slum residents. Many of them ended abruptly as soon as the "peak" danger period was passed, because they failed to recognize the more permanent need of leisure service opportunity as a year-round concern in the ghetto, as elsewhere, and as more than a last-minute enrichment program. The value of the programs was seen in recreation's revitalized role "as a means of improving the self-concept of participants, of overcoming apathy, and encouraging community involvement.[10] Leisure service came to be viewed as a *threshold* activity which drew participants to other forms of involvement for the purposes of improving community life, organizing neighborhoods for socially constructive activity, and providing an opportunity for individuals to actualize their potential for leisure expression.

As a result of these major developments recreation and leisure service increasingly came to be seen as an opportunity to improve the quality of

9. Richard Kraus, *Recreation and Leisure*, p. 389.
10. Richard Kraus, "Providing for Recreation and Aesthetic Enjoyment," *Governing the City: Challenges and Options for New York*, ed. Robert H. Connery and Demetrios Caraley (New York: Praeger Publishers, Inc., 1969), p. 99.

life, reduce social pathology, build constructive values, and generally make communities a better place to live. It became more apparent that recreation experience contributes to individual growth and fulfillment and to social development.

Another form of protest, a youth rebellion against the traditional mores, customs, and values of American society served to propel the Recreation Movement into a new era during the 1960s and the decade of the 1970s.

RECREATION AND THE NEW AMERICAN CULTURE

It has been suggested by Charles Reich that there is a quiet revolution festering in America that is originating with youth who seek to reject the present impersonal, plastic, and desensitizing, advanced technological state of affairs of American society.[11] This new sense of emerging reality, dubbed "Consciousness III" by Reich, is a repudiation of earlier patterns and values and represents liberation and the primacy of natural, humanistic, and sensory experiences. Young people have stimulated altered thinking concerning the provision of leisure opportunity, particularly public sponsored programs which have traditionally been guided by the majority viewpoint within the community.

Some of the elements of the relaxed, more permissive expressions of youth include a concern for the preservation and the restoration of the natural environment, spiritual values, and ceremonial rituals, self-fulfillment, self-determination, and a concern for fostering a sense of community.

EMERGING LEISURE ETHIC

The yearning by youth to determine their own life-style and evolve a pattern of behavior which will integrate work, leisure, and family life into a unitary configuration, is a desire in part for a return to a society in which art, ritual, ceremony, spirituality, and work endeavors are combined into a single, dynamic, and meaningful life pattern. As the young seek new kinds of sensory experience and personal relationships, many of the traditional forms of recreation opportunity no longer are as relevant as they have been in the past. Through the pursuit of leisure, education, reflection, and relevant work, it is contended by some of the youth movement that individuals will be able to *synthesize* their experiences into an integrated, meaningful life pattern.

11. Charles A. Reich, *The Greening of America* (New York: Random House, 1970).

Reich's concepts are also shared by other contemporary writers of the technological age. McLuhan, Ellul, and Ferkiss suggest that the technological system has created "false needs" in individuals which serve to sustain the system while repressing true human needs.[12] Such effects of technology are indeed manifesting changes which are present in contemporary human character.

In an age of increasing nonwork time and widespread leisure, when meaningfulness of life in society is being questioned, the foundation upon which the delivery of leisure service was developed is in need of revision to meet the needs of a new postindustrial age. Much of the search by youth is a quest for deeper meaning in self. Loss of prestige and moral sanctity of work, and even the opportunity to work, has meant that youth have sought identity through leisure expressions, through a pursuit of "kicks" (an attempt to realize oneself), through fun as a "peak experience."

SUMMARY

The emerging American culture does not appear to be a total rejection of the basic social structure of society but is a rejection of the frustrating opportunity structure in which people are bored, lack meaning in their lives, and desire to exercise more individuality and make more choices in their leisure. The humanistic movement is essentially an aesthetic and a moral one; it is a rejection of the previous condition of alienation; it is a movement toward what may be real, meaningful, and self-fulfilling. Expectations of self-fulfillment are arising precisely because a highly industrial society provides incentives for individual expression. The new leisure consciousness represents a rejection of artificial enticements while promoting natural, spontaneous behavior patterns. According to this consciousness a child's or an adult's natural curiosity for investigation and experimentation would be encouraged, a fostering of health and vital organisms would occur, and the stimulation of *all* of the person's senses would be promoted.

The Recreation Movement has passed through several stages of professional development, including a phase dominated by the concern of park professionals for pleasant, passive surroundings in which people could enjoy leisure at their own pace; a period of time which included the propagation of an egalitarian "recreation for all" principle, which stimulated an almost compulsive concern for programs and activities, and

12. Marshall McLuhan, *Understanding Media: The Extensions of Man* (New York: McGraw-Hill Book Co., 1964); Jacques Ellul, *The Technological Society* (New York: Alfred A. Knopf, Inc., 1964); Victor C. Ferkiss, *Technological Man: The Myth and the Reality* (New York: George Braziller, Inc., 1969).

the legitimatizing of local government responsibility for recreation and leisure service; a tumultuous period of social upheaval and civil unrest which brought the movement back to issues of social concern and commitment to the provision of recreation designed to meet important social needs; and most recently, a human developmental phase, which focuses on the individual and the need to build and nurture human services responsive to his needs. An *ecologically* based perspective, this evolving stage of the Recreation Movement is concerned primarily with the interrelationships among people in their physical and social environment and the way these relationships contribute to or hinder their ability to realize their human potential.

The Recreation Movement, then, grew out of humanitarian concerns, and it appears that it has now come full circle, to an era which again is focusing on the individual. Recreation opportunities are increasingly being fostered with the intent to build and nurture arousing situations which are responsive to human needs. They are not seen as trivial, but as fundamental to the developing individual.

community recreation:
a dynamic process

---

what to look for in this chapter...

Characteristic Features of Mass Society

Community Involvement in Recreation and Leisure Service

Organizing Leisure Service Delivery — Various Roles of the Community Worker
Enabler
Advocate
Organizer
Developer

Comparison of the Traditional and the Contemporary Role of Community Recreation
Facility Managers vs. Community Catalyst/ Encouragers

Leisure and Its Relationship to Human Development

Assessing the Delivery of Leisure Service

New Strategy for Community Recreation

Identifying Leader Competencies

Taxonomy of Recreation Outcomes

Organizational Renewal — Strategies for Leisure Service Delivery
Adaptive, Flexible, Problem-Solving, Temporary Systems

The social fabric of society which serves as a functional, moral, and spiritual phenomenon is the essence of the concept of community. The term *community* is often used to refer to a condition in which human beings find themselves engaged in a close-knit web of meaningful relationships with one another.

America is recognized as a mass society in which the members of community life have a wider and more diffused role to play. Some characteristic features of a mass society include: (1) a sense of *alienation,* a feeling by members of being cut off from meaningful group affiliations; (2) *moral fragmentation,* in which members pursue divergent goals and feel no sense of oneness with other people; (3) *disengagement,* a feeling by members that they have no need to participate in the collective activities of various groups; and (4) *segmentation,* a view held by members in which they regard each other as means to ends and give little or no intrinsic worth or significance to the individual.[1]

The place of the individual in mass society can be contrasted with more intimate, deeply committed moral communities by the following characteristics: (1) *identification,* members have a deep sense of being a part of a significant, meaningful group; (2) *moral unity,* members have a sense of common goals and a feeling of oneness with other community members; (3) *involvement,* community members are entrenched in various groups and have a compelling need to participate in these groups; (4) *wholeness,* each member regards the other as a whole person who is of intrinsic significance and worth. This description of community involves a sense of identity and unity with one's group and social environment and a feeling of involvement and wholeness on the part of the individual.

Toffler has suggested that we live in a transient society in which established institutions, social relationships, and traditional values are cracking under the pressure of change.[2] The foundations of society are being eroded by high speed social change, and the individual finds himself becoming alienated and anxiety-ridden. Human beings function best when they understand their actions and when they are able to determine and participate in the entire process. Community life in America, particularly in urban centers, has become disintegrating for a growing number of people. The relationship between family, education, leisure, and work has become increasingly fractionalized and disjointed. Man's relationships to things and people are increasingly temporary. There is a need for a web

1. Refer to Dennis E. Poplin, *Communities: A Survey of Theories and Methods of Research* (New York: The Macmillan Co., 1972), p. 6.
2. Alvin Toffler, *Future Shock* (New York: Random House, 1970).

of human relationships which will provide a relatively unified, stable, personal, and enduring basis for community life.

Even temporary communities are being built along the thousands of interchanges on the interstate highway system. This form of new town cannot be found on the map, it usually doesn't have a name and is unincorporated. While pioneers built towns to live in, this newest form of community is designed to pass through. These communities are transient towns which cater to a large percent of the population who utilize a credit card and seek only to fill their gas tanks, walk their pets, eat a meal, and stretch their legs before moving on.

Temporary community life, while representative of uprootedness and transience, also reflects a self-selected consequence of life-style preferences and life-style changes. While this new migratory life-style represents low degrees of community involvement, small numbers of intimate friends, its pattern also suggests a new sense of community life based on a greater degree of individual flexibility, vocational choice and selectivity, and avocational options within a highly mobile nationwide society. There is little question that neighborhood life is breaking down—people no longer develop a close social network of friends in their residential locale. People increasingly are seeking a new sense of community, which transcends kinship ties, geography, and social distance barriers. The traditional social web of relationships once embedded in the context of the family has been replaced by a wider community network based on mutual compatability and shared interests, made possible by mobile-conscious people.

Leisure service, as an institution represented in community life, may provide an opportunity for people to achieve *maximum human interaction and development,* in which each subcommunity is interwoven into the total community network of communication by the leadership of community catalysts/encouragers. Social interaction is facilitated by catalysts/encouragers who seek to foster a moral sense of community by fostering an interrelationship of efforts. Such a holistic process recognizes community life as a dynamic developmental process. It is important for leisure service personnel to recognize the sociopsychological implications of community life, as member involvement, a willingness on the part of each individual to participate in local neighborhood and city-wide affairs serves as a key to developing a meaningful sense of community.

Some sort of identity and sentiment tends to strengthen the member support to various activities and aspects of community life. A positive, qualitative relationship may be nurtured in a community where each individual feels a sense of belonging, attachment, and commitment. It is within this context that recreation and leisure service may aid the planning process and may further community goals by enabling individual members to realize personal ambitions and make a contribution to the total effort through participation and involvement.

COMMUNITY INVOLVEMENT IN RECREATION AND LEISURE SERVICE

In recent years most human service fields adopted a more affinitive community role. Workers moved away from providing strictly direct service and concentrated on developing an enabler's profile, which focused more closely upon local residents, in an attempt to help solve vexing social problems. The emergence of community action programs in the 1960s served as an important social development in America, particularly for urban slum dwellers who, feeling frustrated and overwhelmed by the complexities of a highly industrial nation, felt a need to exercise some control and leadership over their own lives.

"Maximum feasible participation" of the poor in the planning and execution of federal programs became a major theme of the Community Action Project (CAP) provided by the legislation of the Economic Opportunity Act of 1964. The patterns of paternalism were being felt with increasing dissatisfaction by welfare recipients and slum dwellers, enmeshed generally in the social, economic, education, health, and recreation concerns. While these programs failed for obvious reasons, including limited budgets, poorly trained personnel, restrictive legislation, unfulfilled promises, and mismanagement, they did offer a nontraditional approach to community problems, with a focus on the social environment which was causing the pathology and "deviant" behavior of inner-city residents. Attempts to ensure an awareness among low income and economically deprived residents of their rights and privileges and to provide an opportunity whereby their needs could be articulated to appropriate agencies for improved service were only partially successful strategies of the CAP structure.[3]

However, several of the CAP programs did increase the community profile of many human service agencies, including recreation and leisure service, and improved the ability of these agencies to be responsive to the needs of the urban poor. This perspective served to thrust recreation and leisure service into the limelight and improve its viability among the disaffected and deprived. Recreation was seen as a *social instrument* whereby citizens could realize certain goals. Personnel increasingly became recognized as *change-agents*, who could blend social action and community

3. Refer to Joseph J. Bannon, ed., *Outreach-Extending Community Service in Urban Areas* (Springfield, Illinois: Charles C Thomas Publishing Co., 1973).

development into an effective service approach. As a result of this conceptual service design, programs were evaluated with greater scrutiny than ever before to determine whether they had a direct bearing on community life and were an integral part of local concerns.

The community action concept has broader application beyond the slums. Initiated community action may actually serve as a broader framework for all service offerings, no matter the socioeconomic status of the clientele. Its characteristics include: "(1) an emphasis upon problem solving or achieving a concrete goal, (2) the voluntary participation of local citizens, groups, and institutions, and (3) a democratic orientation."[4]

The community action concept may serve as a way to encourage each community to design programs uniquely suited to its own needs, although most of the funds expended during the 1960s sponsored efforts with a national emphasis, including Head Start. The community action process appears to offer a framework which will enlist the maximum feasible participation of the poor, elderly, handicapped, and "outsiders" in planning and implementing programs of particular importance to them. Traditional service offerings usually do not take into account the culture, needs, values, and interests of neighborhood groups so far removed from decision making and visibility of highly complex and centralized operations.

ORGANIZING LEISURE SERVICE DELIVERY: THE ROLE OF THE COMMUNITY WORKER

There are several possible styles of leadership which may be utilized in stimulating a responsive leisure service delivery system. Spergel[5] identifies four basic roles for human service workers engaged in community development. They are the enabler, advocate, organizer, and developer. At times each of these concepts has been used interchangeably although they are different ideas and approaches to social service.

The *enabler* serves as a guide or adviser and assists people who are usually representatives of the dominant interests of the community to work together to solve various agency and community problems. The results of his tasks are expected to move the community to a higher level of moral or value integration.

An *advocate* is usually a social reformer who directly represents or persuades other professional groups to represent the interest of alienated,

4. Poplin, *Communities*, p. 187.
5. Irving A. Spergel, *Community Problem Solving: The Delinquency Example* (Chicago: The University of Chicago Press, 1969), pp. 58-105.

deviant, or disadvantaged groups. He serves as enthusiastic ombudsman or a mediating function on behalf of dispossessed groups in their relation to public, voluntary, or private organizations. He believes that his constituents or clientele receive the service rightly due them, and he is generally more interested in the achievement of specific needs than the facilitation of a group process of social development.

The *organizer* is concerned about change of the social system at any level so that people may more fully achieve their human potential. This approach embodies more of an antagonistic or conflict profile. He usually is less interested in the problems of specific groups than in the larger issues of poverty, racism, and educational reform. He utilizes a more militant approach in an attempt to neutralize the capacity of the opposition to generate certain programs and policies. He is not usually committed to the established tenets of any professional organization.

The *developer* ordinarily depends on the resources, motivations, values, and institutions for self-help of an indigenous population, particularly impoverished groups. He attempts to develop the viability of the community's pattern of adopting to several conditions. Usually he is more concerned with process than with content as his role is integrated with the daily life of the population. He intimately shares the problems and frustration, and joys and camaraderie of the group he is serving. His allegiance and primary identification is one with the immediate community and only nominally to professional organizations.

Within recreation and leisure service at least two community worker approaches appear to have value—the enabler and advocate roles. The enabler recognizes the problems of leisure as being centralized in particular individuals and groups within a community and aggravated by inadequate social resources and inefficient and insensitive agency operations. The advocate views the problems of leisure as primarily resulting from a breakdown or failure of particular institutional patterns. The enabler may be said to work from a *micro*community perspective while the advocate operates from a *macro*community standpoint. The enabler will initiate intervention within a segment of the community concerned about the particular actions of a phase of an agency's operation, while the advocate will seek to confront the entire organization and achieve institutional change.

Since an enabler may only be a part-time resident of the community he is working in, he may have a hard time gaining the trust of the community. However, since he is often not viewed as a threat to the existing system, he may be able to have easy access to key people of other organizations. The advocate usually undertakes an extensive and systematic investigation of every aspect of a problem, but he may not be accessible to clientele at the grass-roots level since he must confront organizations head-on and challenge established institutional patterns.

Both perspectives mentioned have appeal for recreation and leisure service. While each approach seeks to bring about improved service and ameliorate social conditions, the enabler may serve in the most relevant community process service approach, since he seeks to bring about neighborhood or community change by reaching out to individuals, groups, and agencies with the goal of human development. The advocate's involvement of people at the grass-roots level is minimal, since his efforts are primarily directed at established institutional patterns in which he will utilize only highly specialized professionals and experts effective in influencing social change.

TRADITIONAL VERSUS CONTEMPORARY ROLE OF COMMUNITY RECREATION

Traditionally, most leisure service agencies, like other local and state government services, have operated under a centralized authority which has perpetuated a "chain-link fence" philosophy for the operation of recreation facilities. Gray suggests that the most deleterious effect of the "chain-link fence" delivery approach is on the deployment of staff.[6] Such a philosophy holds that the primary concern of the staff is to operate the center or playground. It identifies the primary tasks as surveillance of grounds to assure compliance with rules, safety, proper use of facilities and control of equipment; development of a schedule for use of the facility; planning and execution of a program of activities with the staff in face-to-face leadership roles; and coordination of maintenance activities to ensure the readiness and sanitary condition of the premises. Such a philosophy rewards *facility managers* and holds that what happens in the center is what matters.

In contrast to this view, there is a role concept for professional recreation personnel which perceives them as community figures. This concept identifies as central, development of people, human interaction, improvement of the community, preservation of the virtues of urban life, and concern for the social problems of our time. The chain-link fence concept has little or no relevance to the contemporary needs of urban America.

It is expected that recreation and leisure personnel will increasingly assume a posture of *community catalyst* or *encourager* (terms used synonymously with enabler) in which areas of concern outside their immediate

6. David E. Gray, "The Tyranny of the Chain-Link Fence," *California Parks and Recreation* 10(1968):10.

realm will have significant influence on the delivery of leisure service. Leisure service will be seen in relation to the whole field of human services, in which health, education, employment, and welfare concerns will function in concert with each other. For example, leisure service offerings will be devised to impart basic skills and knowledge which will help welfare recipients to cope with consumer problems, provide basic insight and information which can subsequently lead to employment opportunities, and improve environmental conditions. In this way, leisure service personnel will adopt their skills and knowledge to fit more realistically with the new functions of recreation and parks necessary in contemporary urban life.

This approach involves a redefinition of the role of recreation and leisure service personnel. This concept involves moving the facility personnel and supervisors out into the community where they can confront and satisfy complex human needs at the grass-roots level with less rigidity and greater flexibility. This new role suggests that leisure service personnel assume an outreach perspective and become enabler/encouragers of human development and social change in which the people become increasingly able to satisfy their own needs. At the same time, encouragers of human development who manifest a concern for the social environment will possess an equal commitment to the concerns and issues of the physical environment. The environment requires support on the part of leisure service personnel who must be cognizant of open space, greenbelts, and park area planning, acquisition, and development needs for communities.

The adoption of the encourager role will require that the field of recreation and leisure service reorient its concept of community recreation to align itself more closely with those of allied human service fields, including social group work, counseling, community action, and health care. "Recreation personnel seemingly must become skilled in the *art* of community development in which emphasis in continuously placed upon the overall quality of community life instead of any particular specialization, project, or program."[7]

The alienating tendency of urban life requires that a more personal and meaningful pattern of interpersonal and intergroup relationships be fostered. The goal involves a deeper and more widespread feeling of local pride and responsibility to be stimulated in community recreation programs. People have tended to adopt attitudes of helplessness and dependency. By encouraging primary group experiences where fundamental social units may be developed, the community recreation encourager has

7. James F. Murphy, "Community Recreation: A Dynamic Process," *California Parks and Recreation* 28(1972):14.

not only provided a setting in which pleasurable leisure opportunities are available, but he has instigated the nucleus of a more close-knit, self-sustaining social group.

Essential qualities that a community recreation encourager seeks include the following:

1. To stimulate the community's ability to accomplish things for itself—solve its own problems
2. To make appropriate use of various related human services and resources
3. To recognize and take effective steps to meet community needs
4. To recognize leisure service as a holistic process

It appears reasonable to envision leisure service agencies in the future as a self-help process by which people develop an increasing skill to cope with various social problems (including the misuses of leisure) and gain a sense of pride in their community.

LEISURE AND HUMAN DEVELOPMENT

Increasingly, more Americans are devoting their attention and energies to questioning and examining man's existence as a social being. According to Gray this "new frontier is the exploration of inner space. The motive is a deeper participation in life."[8] This growing humanistic ethic which is permeating American society has broad implications for the country as a whole, and most certainly the field of recreation and leisure service. There is a growing concern for improving the outmoded processes of human interaction, redefining success and achievement in intrinsic terms, and building a viable community base founded upon a concern for human development and the quality of the environment.

Leisure expression is not seen as a separate entity, wholly divorced from other aspects of human endeavor, and a disengaged segment of one's personality. Leisure is an actively receptive condition of the whole personality. "Leisure is both the occasion and the capacity of the whole personality to open up to all stimuli from within and without. The personality is not passive or detached, but wholly engaged in this process."[9]

Viewing leisure as a holistic process enables the individual to transcend the narrow and limited conception of the dominant, but eroding, work-oriented world and perceive all elements of the social and physical

8. David E. Gray, "Exploring Inner Space," *California Parks and Recreation* 7(1972): 18.
9. Alexander Reid Martin, "Man's Leisure and His Health," *Quest*, Monograph 5 (1965):28.

environment as *complimentary* and essential to growth. The direction of all human service fields would have a common goal and direction: *growth would be toward greater consciousness of our wholeness and uniqueness.*

Gray's definition of recreation (noted in chapter 1) views it as an internal, individual, pleasurable response of the organism. While it may occur in the company of others and even be stimulated by the presence of others engaged in the same activity, the recreation experience occurs independently of activity. Gray states:

> We must recognize the potential role of recreation in the development of people. The goal of organized recreation programs is to provide people opportunities for the exercise of their powers, opportunity for recreational experience, opportunity for the development of a positive self-image. Any program that receives a participant whole and sends him back damaged in self-respect, self-esteem, or relationships with others is not a recreation program. The fact that it may be a basketball program with games played during leisure is irrelevant. Such a program is not a recreational program unless the response of the participants is positive.[10]

Maslow has indicated that a self-actualizing person transcends the dichotomizing of work and leisure. Perhaps Maslow embraced a holistic perspective. It was also his view that a real problem with the materialistic values which pervade our culture is that many people, particularly the young, are deprived of intrinsic values and frustrated by a society they see mistakenly motivated by only material needs. Leisure service agencies which focus entirely upon the lower level or "materialistic" human needs (physical and safety needs), serve to deprive highly motivated individuals who seek to satisfy deeper, more intrinsic needs.

The conditions of modern life provide only limited opportunity for individuals to become self-actualized, the ability to realize one's own potentialities. The deprivation most people experience in work and leisure, with respect to the satisfaction of lower-level needs, diverts their energies into the struggle to constantly satisfy those needs while the higher order needs of self-esteem and self-fulfillment are never realized. Much of the depression, alienation, anxiety, and turmoil which exists is suggestive of the "emotionally starved" people in our society. Self-actualized people are not constrained by the arbitrary barriers of work-leisure and do not feel anxiety-ridden, insecure, unsafe, rejected, or unwanted. The self-actualized person has a sharpened perception of reality. He is free from the fears and inhibitions which cause others to cover up and mask reality. He

10. Gray, *"Inner Space,"* p. 19.

accepts himself, others, and nature. There is a pervasiveness of spontaneity and creativity among self-actualizing people. Farina suggests that self-actualization is the goal of leisure.[11] He sees leisure as the state or condition of being free from the urgent demands of the lower level needs. He sees leisure as freedom to express oneself through activity—be it intellectual, spiritual, or physical—in order to strive for one's full potential as a human being.

If man can fulfill his basic needs, he may then be driven by his own internal necessities to try and discover what will allow him to further develop his own capabilities. Conceivably, leisure service agencies can provide a full range of opportunities which will create an environment conducive to self-development. The rigidity of response and seemingly endless specifications, rules, and regulations often required of participants, only serves to suppress and frustrate individuals from realizing their potential through recreation. As people increasingly come to identify leisure as a central life interest, the likelihood will correspondingly be advanced that discontented people will vent their frustration in negative ways and seek to draw attention to their needs through withdrawal, protest, or even violence.

MEASURING LEISURE SERVICE DELIVERY

The leisure service field has only a few measurable indicators which can successfully appraise the outcome of a recreation experience. Most of the traditional approaches to evaluation have incorporated quantifiable services which have indicated, for example, the number of people participating in programs; the variety of activities offered; and age, sex, and other biographical information of participants. While this information is helpful, it does not tell us what happened to the participant, by reaction to leadership, facility, and other stimuli, and it does not give us any clues as to what aspects of the program were beneficial or poor. Many of our evaluation tools lack precision and do not render a meaningful appraisal of the recreation experience.

According to Gold the traditional approach to urban recreation planning may be challenged for several reasons:

1. it projects only the past and present;
2. it considers the quantitative instead of the qualitative aspect of a recreation experience;
3. it does not reflect a behavioral approach to accommodating expressed or latent demand or user needs;

11. John Farina, "Toward A Philosophy of Leisure," *Convergence* 2(1969):14-17.

4. it does not relate to the stated objectives of most recreation plans;
5. it does not relate to the overall objectives, priorities, and resources of most communities or acknowledge possible trade-offs with other public or private services;
6. it does not reflect citizen participation in the planning process or a systematic survey of user preferences and satisfaction; and
7. it reflects a quantitative statement of an idealized system as envisioned by the supplier, not the user.[12]

The lack of goals has hampered the field from identifying what leisure service is attempting to do in the community. Hatry and Dunn state: "Traditional measurement practices generally focus on matters such as acreage, facilities, and personnel. While these are useful, alone they will not indicate the degrees to which recreation services are meeting the needs and desires of the public."[13]

Every community is unique, and it is important that leisure service agencies be cognizant of the significance of the attachment and mutual feeling of belonging by residents of each neighborhood. By assessing each neighborhood's composition, resources, and other social factors, individuals planning leisure opportunities could better determine the distinctive aspect and form of recreation expression that may be successfully developed and blended into the style of people's lives. Since each community is different, the values of various measures of effectiveness (e.g., delinquency and crime indices, index of overall perceived satisfaction of participants, program variety indices, etc.) that pertain to each population group should be identified.

Optimum utilization of potential recreation resources is not being achieved in most cities in America. The National League of Cities reported that many publicly owned facilities are underused because they are not available in the evening or for use on the weekends or they are not relevant to the needs of the community.[14] Several new approaches have been developed which incorporate criteria of social need (median family income, juvenile delinquency rate, changing ethnic composition, etc.) as the bases for planning leisure services in communities. This perspective centers upon the identity and definition of needs and problems before the development of services. This concept differs from many of the traditional approaches of leisure service agencies where a "packaged" program is planned, implemented, and individuals encouraged to accept it.

12. Seymour Gold, "Nonuse of Neighborhood Parks," *AIP Journal* 38(1972):370.
13. Harry Hatry and Diana Dunn, *Measuring the Effectiveness of Local Services: Recreation* (Washington, D.C.: The Urban Institute, 1971), p. 5.
14. *Recreation in the Nation's Cities: Problems and Approaches* (Washington, D.C.: Department of Urban Studies, National League of Cities, 1968), p. 2.

By realistically assessing community needs, program priorities may be determined which reflect the philosophy, goals, and objectives of the agency. The agency philosophy provides a set of values and beliefs which are reflected in its professional approach to service. The criteria defined for program priorities should reflect the agency's philosophy about values of leisure as an essential human need and about the special functions which it views as its particular mission in the community.

NEW STRATEGY FOR COMMUNITY RECREATION

The Recreation Movement has passed through several stages of professional development (as noted in chapter 1). Each phase contributed to the structure of leisure service delivery and also has yielded conflicts which have affected the relevancy of current operations in community life. The presently evolving phase is seen as a human developmental service approach. Seymour Gold notes that during the period beginning in the early 1960s (post-Outdoor Recreation Resources Review Commission report) the idea of visualizing recreation as an experience instead of an activity became accepted, and a new way of classifying areas, which integrated their use instead of separating their form and function, came into being.[15]

The Recreation Movement is moving into a new stage of development where the focus is on the individual and on creating an environment in which the individual may realize his potential. Since both work and leisure together may be seen as environments where people will seek opportunities for self-fulfillment, each setting must focus on the individual as a *totality* The latest phase of the Recreation Movement includes a recognition that the individual should be allowed to select from among alternatives.

If community recreation is to assume responsibility of creating an environment responsive to the needs, desires, and interests of its citizens, it must adopt a new strategy of organization and management. Recreation and leisure service must be recognized as a part of a complex system involving other highly interrelated public, private, and commercial agencies reacting to other systems (e.g., economic, transportation, health, etc.). The traditional organization of a municipality into separate functions cannot cope with complex, interrelated social issues. Weiner states:

> It is the municipal recreation department's responsibility to give them a sense of personal and communal worth, otherwise it is not fulfilling

15. Seymour M. Gold, *Urban Recreation Planning* (Philadelphia: Lea & Febiger, 1973), p. 192.

its function in society. The lines between recreation and other profes-
sions are disappearing; the imparting of cultural values, of skills
necessary for employment or to face old age, of abilities to cope with
modern education . . . all are legitimate recreation objectives.[16]

ORGANIZATIONAL RENEWAL

The traditional bureaucratic organization form, characterized as a
pyramidal, centralized, functionally specialized, impersonal mechanism,
lacks relevancy to contemporary realities of a technological society. This
model was appropriate to late nineteenth century and early twentieth
century conditions, but it is no longer relevant in light of several conditioning factors not apparent at the turn of the twentieth century. The rapidity and unexpectedness of social change makes it extremely difficult
for large bureaucracies, with their tight controls, impersonality, outmoded
rules and organizational rigidities, to respond adequately to the new
demands of society. The complexity and interrelatedness of a technological
society requires an *integration* between activities and persons. Also there
has been a movement of managerial values toward more humanistic
democratic practices.

Recreation and leisure service agencies must necessarily be viewed,
not as an organizational structure, but rather as a strategy, in which the
delivery system is subdivided into managerial pieces, with a technically
competent and diverse staff able to make decisions and engage in problem
solving by recognizing the relationships of various societal elements and
how they influence the leisure environment. Weiner comments on the new
role of recreation catalysts.

> If he views an organization as a strategy, not as a structure, the task
> of the recreation director would be to ascertain the public's interests
> and needs, inventory the community's capabilities (existing and poten-
> tial) to satisfy interests and needs, and augment his budget with
> additional resources in a way to be most effective in achieving com-
> munity and recreational goals.[17]

This form of "postbureaucratic" leadership recognizes that recreation
and leisure service agencies are obligated to service the *full* leisure needs
of an individual. The recreation catalyst/encourager, then, must focus on
particularizing programs for individuals to help create an environment
responsive to human developmental needs. The agency then makes the

16. Myron Weiner, "A Systems Approach to Municipal Recreation," *The Municipal
Year Book* (Chicago: International City Managers Association, 1971), p. 169.
17. Ibid., p. 169.

commitment to provide a breadth of affective, cognitive, and motor developmental choices for varied life-styles which encourage human involvement, participation, and satisfaction.

ENCOURAGING NEIGHBORHOOD RECREATION

Playground, community center, and other recreation settings need to be designed in such a way as to represent a conscious attempt to add complexity to the individual's neighborhood environment, so that opportunities are available to explore, investigate, and manipulate. A recreation environment will promote use and satisfaction to the extent that its arrangement is to some extent novel and complex. Adventure or junk playgrounds that evolved in Europe since World War II and the few that exist . in the United States, such as the one in Milpitas, California, are successful · because each child is able to explore, investigate, and manipulate the · playthings he comes into contact with. The setting is dynamic as children . are able to add their own modifications. A visit to Disneyland will serve to sensitize many a recreation director to the stimulating power of a setting designed to emphasize exploration and investigation. While it would be extremely difficult to reproduce a mini-Disneyland in each neighborhood park, most community play areas seem to be designed to produce only a small diversion in some motor activity and lack a scientific premise of the nature of play.

The idea of adventure playgrounds was developed in Denmark in 1943, when it was determined by C. Sorensen that children seemed to prefer messing around in junkyards and building sites, and developing their own brand of play with the waste objects that they found there. Lady Allen of Hurtwood comments on the purpose of adventure playgrounds.

> Adventure playgrounds are places where children of all ages can develop their own ideas of play. Most young people, at one time or another, have a deep urge to experiment with earth, fire, water, and timber, to work with real tools without fear of undue criticism or censure. In these playgrounds their love of freedom to take calculated risks is recognized and can be enjoyed under tolerant and sympathetic guidance.[18]

It was Sorensen's belief that youth ought to be free and by themselves to the greatest possible extent and that they should have only essential supervision. While the purpose of adventure playgrounds is to foster

18. Lady Allen of Hurtwood, *Planning for Play* (Cambridge, Mass.: The M.I.T. Press, 1968), p. 55.

autonomous, self-directed play, the "leader" is an extremely important ingredient. His role is to provide the environment for the children's own initiative and to serve more as a counselor than as a "leader." Hurtwood describes it thus.

> The successful leader of an adventure playground is one who has confidence in the children's positive attitude to make and create things in their own individual way, and in their ability to make good relationships with each other. He is less concerned with their physical development, or with organizing them into 'teams' for games or joint activities, or showing them 'how to play.' He does, however, act as referee when a situation is in danger of getting out of hand, or when children are unable to resolve their transient difficulties by themselves. He needs to be many steps ahead, to anticipate what materials and tools will be suitable for emerging projects, and he must be willing to discuss and support whatever activity seems to meet the needs of the moment. Above all, he will be eager to praise any endeavor that has patently brought pleasure to a group of children or, indeed, to an individual child, and not show his despair when the whole thing is abandoned and never completed.[19]

The supervisor of an adventure playground develops a committee of people from the surrounding neighborhood to assist in the administration of the site, including securing funds, developing local interest, and managing publicity. The fostering of a sense of community evolves through the committee and the participants, where progressive human development occurs through a growing sense of responsibility toward the playground itself, toward care of the younger children and others outside the playground. Each adventure playground is shaped by the children and youth themselves according to their needs, although certain equipment and material is procured by the committee.

The adventure playgrounds offer more than a permissive atmosphere which invites opportunities for self-expression; they are also noted for the intensive use that is made of the space and facilities. They are generally open from 9:00 A.M. to 10:00 P.M. throughout the week.

In addition to the junk playground in Milpitas, California, another comparable example to the European adventure playground is found in a housing project in the Lower Roxbury section of Boston. It was developed in cooperation with the Lenox-Camden Tenants Association. The experimental playground, geared to foster individual development, was designed

19. Ibid., p. 56.

a. To provide an environment that would stimulate creative and imaginative play, motor action and manual skills, cognitive development and the acquisition of knowledge, sensory stimulation and
powers of perception, and finally the social aspects of play—self-
knowledge, personality development, and social adeptness.
b. To provide a clear, identifiable locus for more general community
activities.[20]

The experimental playground attempted to provide an environment
that would be a place for free expression, where most activities that were
unwelcome elsewhere could be indulged in. The playground was designed
to facilitate creative and imaginative play. Hurtwood, in relating Robin
Moore's study findings[21] of the project, states the investigator's interpretation of play.

Creative play is an opportunity for children to manipulate their environment to achieve their own ends and to sense the fact that the world
around them can be changed and need not be taken as given.
Materials that normally appear as 'junk' in other people's eyes are very
relevant to much creative and imaginative play.
In the context of creative and imaginative play it was fascinating to
observe what might be called group imagination in operation at close
quarters. There was the important social aspect of play operating at
its highest level. Typically, a creative play sequence would start in a
leisurely way with a small group; as time went on more would join in,
children of diverse ages. Different members would make suggestions,
try something out and meet, or not meet, with the approval of the
group. One idea or action would suggest another, with different members taking the initiative and leadership.[22]

Adventure playgrounds may offer some insight into the developmental
and self-initiated parameters of play. While many such play areas are
often regarded as unsightly by adults, it is the child whose play expression
must be guided and nurtured.

When facilitating human development through recreation, leisure
service personnel have a primary responsibility to the individual. In order
to optimize a recreation experience for an individual a catalyst/encour-
ager must first recognize that there will be differing requirements for
attainment. Therefore, there must be graded levels of instruction and

20. Ibid., p. 72.
21. Robin C. Moore, Dipl. Arch. University College, London, 1962. Submitted in partial fulfillment of the requirements for the degree of Master of City and Regional
Planning at the Massachusetts Institute of Technology, November, 1966.
22. Hurtwood, *Planning for Play*, p. 76.

opportunities for expression to allow for a natural (developmental) progression towards highly complex performance. Second, professional recreation and leisure service personnel must employ architects and designers who will plan an environment in which the encounters engaged in and skills acquired can be applied by each individual to progressively more complex situations. It is extremely important that recreation personnel working in a face-to-face leadership situation recognize that play in human beings results from arousal (stimulus)-seeking. It is evoked by novel, complex, and dissonant interactions. Since it must be related to the individual, a successful recreation program will result only when the setting is related to an individual's expectations.[23]

IDENTIFYING LEADER COMPETENCIES

A recent study undertaken by a team of investigators from four recreation and leisure studies curricula in California attempted to determine perceptions about competencies of recreation leaders in order to more adequately assess the potential success of recreation major students entering the leisure service field.[24] A tentative model of leadership was developed which provides revealing and supportive data related to the research of Ellis and Gold. The model suggests that competency is a function of *processes*, carried out by an individual, which are influenced by the individual's *personal characteristics*, and by the specific environmental *situation* within which he or she is operating. This model may help educators and practitioners to more clearly understand the dynamics of leadership in recreation settings where participants seek guidance, direction, or instruction.

The model does recognize certain personal characteristics as belonging to the leader, including work enthusiasm, health, appearance, creativity, flexibility, likeableness, and work efficiency. However, it does *not* signify that the personal influence of the leader is the most relevant variable affecting leadership. Additionally, it recognizes that certain processes, including motivation, working with groups, teaching, planning, organizing, and problem solving are all factors which facilitate recreation behavior and must be applied in specific circumstances. Various situations, including giving directions to others or carrying out directions, relating

23. M. J. Ellis, *Why People Play* (Englewood Cliffs, New Jersey: Prentice-Hall, Inc., 1973), pp. 119-148.

24. "Competency Assessment Processes in Recreation Curricula," E. William Niepoth, project director (Program funded through the New Program Development and Evaluation Division, Office of the Chancellor, California State Universities and Colleges, 1973-74).

to community groups or agency staff, working in conflict situations, working on special projects or unusual demand situations, or operating as an individual or as a staff or team member affect the ability of a leader to facilitate achievement of the benefits or goals sought by participants.

It seems apparent that the maximum results to be obtained by recreation agencies will be attained to the degree leisure service personnel can assess individual leader traits which lend themselves to effective interaction with certain types of participants; the ability of the leader to be cognizant of the dynamics of the processes which are operating; and the degree to which the leader can facilitate the participants' satisfaction in a variety of situations which require the leader to be sensitive to the diversified and unusual circumstances which occur.

The leader's ability to recognize that people seek recreation expression for a variety of reasons, which may or may not coincide with agency goals or objectives (refer to Table 4.1), becomes an important consideration in the future, particularly with the proliferation and differentiation of life-styles, increasing individualization and ego conscious behavior. The ability of the leader to be aware of and understand the dynamics of the influencing factors, involving the leader, processes, and situations, will increase the satisfaction and enhancement of recreation expression.

TAXONOMY OF RECREATION OUTCOMES

In any setting, including the leisure environment, the individual participates as a totality. His cognitive (knowledge), affective (feeling), and motor (skill performance) capacities are a part of his recreation experiences and behavior.[25] It is important for recreation and leisure service personnel to have some basic understanding about the factors which motivate recreation behavior. Individual needs manifest themselves in accordance with the particular socioeconomic, cultural, ethnic background, and personality of the person.

Behavioral objectives have been set forth by Benjamin S. Bloom and his associates which classify objectives in three major domains: the cognitive, the affective, and the psychomotor.[26] There are many possible outcomes which will aid human development and foster the interaction of

25. James F. Murphy, John G. Williams, E. William Niepoth, and Paul D. Brown, *Leisure Service Delivery System: A Modern Perspective* (Philadelphia: Lea & Febiger, 1973), p. 82.
26. Benjamin S. Bloom, ed., *A Taxonomy of Educational Objectives: The Classification of Educational Goals, Handbook I: Cognitive Domain* (New York: David McKay Co., Inc., 1956), and David R. Krathwohl, Benjamin S. Bloom and Bertram Masia, *A Taxonomy of Educational Objectives, Handbook II: The Affective Domain* (New York: David McKay Co., Inc., 1966).

the individual with certain factors in his environment to produce a satisfying behavioral response.

Potential recreation outcomes include: *physical* (relief of tension, relaxation, exercise, skill development, rehabilitation, fitness, and coordination); *psychological* (anticipation, reflection, challenge, accomplishment, excitement, achievement, aesthetic appreciation, self-expression, self-image, introspection, pleasure, enjoyment, security, contemplation, self-confidence, and self-actualization); *social* (involvement, interpersonal relationships, friendship, trust, companionship, sportsmanship, belongingness, interaction, communication, awareness, cooperation, group unity, community spirit, status, socialization, compatibility, concern for others, appreciation, and human relations); and *educational* (mastery, new skills, intensified skills, discovery, insight, exploration, learning, mind expansion, and expansion of perspective). These are but a few of the possibilities for individual expression in a recreation experience. They illustrate the possibilities for self-fulfillment and potential integration of human needs which may be realized through recreation expression.

To be effective, recreation and leisure personnel must recognize the interaction of the individual with his environment and facilitate this ecological perspective when designing recreation places. For a program (opportunity complex) to be successful it must seemingly provide an environment for each individual to realize certain wants, desires, and fantasies at various developmental need levels. In this way leisure service personnel don't act as leaders in the traditional sense; they serve to promote self-realization and satisfaction. The recreation setting must foster opportunities for interaction, excitement, novelty, challenge, diversity, adventure, involvement, and identity. It has been suggested by Gold that the lack of these opportunities (potential recreation outcomes) in our neighborhood playground and park facilities may be the reason for their nonuse. Additionally he notes:

> The goal and value differences between the supplier and user are demonstrated in a number of ways which may contribute to nonuse. Much American leisure behavior is now marked by spontaneity, choice, and diversity. Although the recreation movement commonly gives lip service to the idea of spontaneity in leisure, it emphasizes organization, program leadership and scheduling of activities.[27]

Gold has depicted how the goals and objectives of typical community reference groups often are incongruous. This often means that areas and facilities designed for community recreation do not reflect user needs and

27. Gold, "Nonuse of Parks," p. 197.

goals. It is suggested by Table 4.1 that existing neighborhood structures and various types of recreation opportunities may be obsolete and irrelevant. He suggests a new innovative approach to recreation planning which even goes beyond social need planning approaches mentioned earlier in the chapter.

> Outdoor recreation planning at the neighborhood level is an *incremental* process for the determination of opportunities based on the expressed *goals* and *objectives* of *residents*. The allocation of public resources for outdoor recreation is a direct reflection of *resident values*. These values are expressed in the opportunities, space standards, and priorities selected from *alternatives* by a *representative* body of the residents or their advocate.[28]

This innovative approach is based on a short-range, goal-oriented, value-directed, representative, advocate planning effort which is adapt-

TABLE 4.1

GOALS AND OBJECTIVES OF SELECTED REFERENCE GROUPS

Reference Group	Expressed Goals or Objectives
Community decision makers	Pride and status Cohesion and social betterment Reduction in juvenile delinquency Increase in economic development Increase in public health and safety Beautification or aesthetic betterment Increase in culture and education Community improvement
Suppliers of public recreation	Happiness or enjoyment Personal growth Physical and mental health Personal safety and welfare Integrative sociability Citizenship and democratic values
Users of public recreation	Group interaction and sociability Relief from roles or surroundings Status, identity, recognition Competition and self-evaluation Variety, excitement, challenge

Source: Seymour M. Gold, **Urban Recreation Planning** (Philadelphia: Lea & Febiger, 1973), p. 108.

28. Ibid., p. 208.

able, effective, and relevant to the particular neighborhood involved. This approach involves the following process—Population to be served → Demand → Resident Goals → Alternative Resident Standards → Programs → Allocation → Review → Revision. The traditional approaches—Population to be served + A Supplier Standard → Allocation or A Population to be served → Demand + A Supplier Standard → Allocation—focus on supplier goals and standards. The new approach suggested by Gold recognizes user goals and standards with an emphasis on alternatives, citizen participation, and revision. Gold states:

> The innovative approach requires a data base or at least a survey of existing conditions prior to goal formation by residents or the groups which represent them. It also requires a much more sensitive analysis of social and environmental problems, latent and expressed leisure preferences, existing and potential public and private leisure facilities, circulation patterns, weather and climate, community psychology, social disorders, public safety and the human and fiscal resources available to help implement any possible alternative.[29]

It is suggested by Gold's planning approach that recreation and leisure service agencies do not reflect the nature of the recreation experience, citizen participation, user goals, and standards, and lack responsiveness to a dynamic and changing society. His approach merits consideration and should be interwoven into organizations desiring to reach out to their clientele and serve neighborhoods in a meaningful way.

ORGANIZATIONAL STRATEGY

While the traditional concept of organized recreation may be at odds with the leisure patterns of many Americans, so too, has the structure of its organizations been out of phase with the realities of contemporary life. According to Bennis, the new strategy for organization in the future will be characterized by the following:

> They will be adaptive, rapidly changing *temporary systems*, organized around problems-to-be-solved by groups of strangers with diverse professional skills. The groups will be arranged on organic rather than mechanical models; they will evolve in response to problems rather than to programmed expectations. People will be evaluated, not in a rigid vertical hierarchy according to rank and status, but flexibly, according to competence. Organizational charts will consist of project groups rather than stratified functional groups, as is now the case. Adaptive, problem-solving, temporary systems of diverse specialists,

29. Ibid., p. 213.

linked together by coordinating executives in an organic flux—this is the organizational form that will gradually replace bureaucracy.[30]

It is felt that in times of turbulence, disorder, and uncertainty, the bureaucracy is unable to respond flexibly and appropriately to new information. The new organizational values based on humanistic democratic ideals, replace the depersonalized, mechanistic value system of bureaucracy. The traditional organizational model is largely unable to respond to change and typically is characterized by a paralysis, a guarded, frozen rigidity that denies the presence or avoids the confrontations which arise in a highly change-oriented environment. The new organizational strategy implies the creation of a *flexible, adaptive* form, which fosters interdependence, high intrinsic rewards, standards of openness, trust, utilization of individual talents, and clear and agreed-upon goals. This means that "postbureaucratic" organizations must allow for more individual autonomy and a lot of participation by both the providers and users of service in key decision making.

This new organizational type appears to be more suited to the realities of a technological age. Buell's research indicates that people's problems and needs are multiple and interrelated, and defy those neat categories of service reserved to them by agencies.[31] To meet their clients' needs, *recreation and leisure service agencies must have access to many types of specialized services and be able to integrate them to serve the complete person and help him adjust to the complexities of his environment.* This involves a recognition of "community-centeredness," a need to maximize the speed and quality of the agency's particular type of human service or rehabilitation.

SUMMARY

New measurement practices of effectiveness must be initiated to more adequately evaluate the effects of leisure service delivery upon human development, to supplement (and even erase) the traditional emphasis which has utilized descriptive indices (more representative of the supplier goals and standards) resources of the agencies, and lump-sum participant attendance figures. Because agencies tend to overlook *outputs* (effects), they do not adequately reveal how well leisure services are meeting the needs and desires of the public. There is need for the adoption

30. Warren Bennis, "Post Bureaucratic Leadership," in *The Future Society*, ed. Donald Michael (New Brunswick, New Jersey: Transaction, Inc., 1970), p. 34.
31. Bradley Buell and Associates, *Community Planning for Human Services* (New York: Columbia University Press, 1952).

of advocacy planning based on user goals and needs in order to more accurately provide recreation opportunities which reflect the rapidly changing conditions of neighborhood life. Additionally, the new innovative strategy must encompass developmental goals to provide recreation opportunities which cover the breadth of affective, cognitive, and motor developmental choices for varied life-styles which encourage human involvement, participation, and satisfaction.

There are several possible styles of leadership for recreation and leisure service personnel, but it appears that the enabler (encourager/ catalyst) and advocate roles are best suited for community workers. In particular the enabler seeks to bring about neighborhood or community change by reaching out to individuals, groups, and agencies with the goal of human development. The adoption of the encourager/catalyst role will require that the field of recreation and leisure reorient its concept of community recreation to align itself more closely with those of allied human service fields.

chapter FIVE

sociopsychological considerations:
ecological
perspectives

---

what to look for in this chapter...

Leisure and Society

Collective Search for Identity

Leisure and the Individual

Leisure and Anomie

Dynamics of Recreation and Leisure Service

Life-Style Counseling

Psychological Implications for an Individual with Terminal Illness

Philosophical Commitment

LEISURE AND SOCIETY

The growing awareness by citizens of the emergence of leisure as a significant aspect of life has had a marked impact on culture. It is seen as a humanistic development, a renaissance of joy, craftsmanship, group feeling, ritual, and intellectual pursuit. The erosion of the Protestant work ethic as a moral force in society, characterized by assembly line labor, is being replaced by a concern for meaningful activity and craftsmanship among commitment-oriented youth and adults who are seeking a sense of self.

The spread of leisure to all segments of the population is a characteristic feature of an advanced industrial society. "Mass" leisure is said to be a feature which is no longer the sole domain of the upper class. However, leisure is seen as a personal response and cannot be viewed as a mass expression of the total population. With today's increased emphasis upon humanistic concerns, the leisure domain becomes an opportunity for people to engage in a qualitatively wide range of personally satisfying experiences. The goal of self-fulfillment through creative expression, burdened with the requirements of a consumption-oriented economy and its plethora of leisure gadgets, mobility, and other things which one gets now and pays for later, can be contaminated unless an individual can develop his inner resources. Michael states: "Actually, the careful cultivation of self through hobbies, avocations, and any other activities involves the careful cultivation of technique and insight much more than it involves the steady acquisition of things."[1]

If our society continues to move toward amassing larger segments of free time, particularly for those individuals who have had limited amounts of leisure in the past, a serious situation may arise as people become resentful and alienated by the prospect of having neither the resources nor the training to partake in the full array of creative leisure activities potentially available. If technology continues to advance at a rapid rate, in a way which introduces new work requiring high-level skills and, at the same time, eliminates less sophisticated jobs and further reduces the work force of the less technically trained, inevitably large numbers of people will be viewed as economically useless people. They will no longer be valuable for the processes of production and distribution. The task of these people and of society will be to invent new forms of social acceptance and worth which will preserve their self-respect.

---

1. Donald N. Michael, "Free Time—The New Imperative in our Society," *Automation, Education, and Human Values,* ed. William W. Brickman and Stanley Lehrer (New York: Thomas Y. Crowell Company, 1966), p. 301.

COLLECTIVE SEARCH FOR IDENTITY

One of the main problems of our highly industrialized and urbanized society is a collective groping for identity and meaning. There is a pervasive feeling of emptiness, a lack of inner strength and stability. This collective search for identity is symptomatic of the fact that some social systems deprive people of psychological "payoffs."[2] An abundant society brings freedom to pursue new interests, luxury, frivolity, mobility, emancipation from obligatory, and status requirements. However, many people, particularly youth, minority groups, and the ill, disabled, and elderly disengaged from the mainstream of society, feel a sense of alienation which is often expressed in the form of meaningless activity. "It is paradoxical that our society, as it gains in abundance, should be losing knowledge of itself in the spiritual sense."[3]

According to Klapp leisure is seen as a maze of identity-seeking activities under the aegis of "fun." Leisure serves as an arena where the individual has an opportunity to discover himself anew, and leisure service agencies conceivably serve as catalysts which provide a sense of elevating environments for self-discovery, pleasure, and meaning. *The play environment, composed of equipment, leadership, and facilities should foster increasingly complex arousing stimuli for the participant.*[4]

Our society is in a transitional state which is extremely confusing to most Americans. The central values of work and individual competition, which underscored man's attempts to further his own economic self-interest and contribute to his material progress, have lost their hold on a growing number of people. This emphasis on individual striving is no longer recognized as a positive value which automatically brings good to the community. There is unrest, loneliness, pervasive psychological disorders, and anxiety, which is perpetuated in a highly mobile, materialistic, individually oriented society. The emotional forms of gratification, opportunities for collective celebration and sharing are all but lost in a rootless society.

A sense of self needs to be recaptured in our society and the dignity of the human being needs to be elevated.[5] Our society has become so

2. Orrin E. Klapp, *Collective Search for Identity* (New York: Holt, Rinehart and Winston, Inc., 1969), pp. 3-70.
3. Ibid., p. 4.
4. Anthony F. Gramza, Jerrold Corush, and Michael J. Ellis, "Children's Play on Trestles Differing in Complexity: A Study of Play Equipment Design," *Journal of Leisure Research* 4(1972):303-311.
5. Rollo May, *Man's Search for Himself* (New York: New American Library, Inc., 1967), pp. 49-56.

highly technological that the essence of man has been minimized by the towering thrust of machines. Modern man has been dehumanized. In the process man has lost the ability to communicate deeply personal meanings. The massive gatherings at rock festivals in the 1960s served as expressions of emotionally starved youth seeking love, attention, and emotional release in the company of others. While these events appear rather bizarre to most adults, they provided "other-directed" youth an opportunity to experience communion with others—an emotional search for identity and self worth.

There is a need on the part of leisure service agencies to provide opportunities for people to realize their own potentialities, for continued self-development, for being creative. The deprivation most people experience with respect to meeting higher level needs disallows man's consciousness of himself and contributes to the sense of emptiness in modern life. The ability to interrelate with others fosters a sense of self and growth in interpersonal relationships. Recreation programs which build cooperation among people and encourage respect for and a sensitivity to others, will help to develop a sense of community. Without an affirmation of mutual sentiment and commitment to common values and concerns, individuals who live together feel no sense of responsibility to each other. The realization of a human being's potential may be advanced if leisure service agencies will recognize their vital role in encouraging human development.

LEISURE AND THE INDIVIDUAL

The individual participant exists within a total environment, which includes an infinite number of potentially influencing factors (such as age, sex, income level, race, education, life-style, etc.). The participant and the agency-structured environment represent an *ecological* unit. The individual is involved in the experience as a totality—expressive of his intellectual, emotional, and physical capacities.

Niepoth states that the recreation behavior is goal-directed.[6] The experience is a direct result of goal-seeking. The success or failure of the experience influences continuation, modification, or termination of participation. The motives for participation vary from individual to individual. Therefore, a wide and complexly-interrelated variety of individual differences have potentiality for influencing recreation behavior.

6. E. William Niepoth, "Users and Non-Users of Recreation and Park Services," *Reflections on the Recreation and Park Movement*, ed. David E. Gray and Donald Pelegrino (Dubuque, Iowa: Wm. C. Brown Company Publishers, 1973), pp. 132-136.

The primary objective of any recreation and leisure service agency, whether it be public, private, or commercial, is to provide opportunities for people, individually and collectively, to enjoy leisure behavior. In broad dimensions, the leisure service agency's delivery system is based on a commitment to provide opportunities which encourage and facilitate arousal seeking behaviors as defined in chapter 1. The *effective* leisure service agency understands the factors which condition participant behavior and is able to individualize and modify its service to fulfill individual needs and expectations.

Alternative life-style patterns have caused problems for the "Establishment," particularly those manifested by youth. Our society increasingly must provide opportunities for a varied amount of expression. Slater suggests there are three principle human desires that are deeply frustrated by American culture:

1. The desire for *community*—the wish to live in trust and fraternal cooperation with one's fellows in a total and visible collective entity.
2. The desire for *engagement*—the wish to come directly to grips with social and interpersonal problems and to confront on equal terms an environment which is not composed of ego extensions.
3. The desire for *dependence*—the wish to share responsibility for the control of one's impulses and the direction of one's life.[7]

Each of these deprived human desires may be experienced through recreation. However, because recreation agencies have focused for so many years upon the provision of activities, more personally meaningful and satisfying needs were not typically identified. The recreation experience is a personally enriching opportunity which is influenced by the leisure service agency and the social and physical environment. Agencies which recognize the interrelatedness of people and the social and physical aspects of the environment contribute to the likelihood that the recreation experience will be a positive, meaningful, and joyful event.

LEISURE AND ANOMIE

The idea that pleasure for its own sake has value has been deliberately denied within the tenets of the work ethic. The rise of the drug subculture in America grew out of estrangement or anomie for a large number of youth who could not identify with engagement in useful activities which were to be beneficial to them and the country's future. Because the domi-

7. Philip Slater, *The Pursuit of Loneliness* (Boston: Beacon Press, 1970), p. 5.

nant culture seemed deadening and of little individual value, the use of drugs among many middle-class youth increased enormously in the 1960s. However, contrary to popular belief, the use of marijuana and LSD were not taken because of some acute need.[8]

The user pursued these drug activities because the primary attraction is fun, although for some, drug use may reflect more subtle, unconscious psychological needs. Contrary to adult users of alcohol, nicotine, and caffeine, youth drug users are hardly influenced by the compelling need to "drop acid" for any useful purpose—they see it as something to be done for kicks. What adults fail to see is that drug use is enjoyable to many youth (not withstanding its potentially harmful results). Why do drugs become the primary source of fun? According to Pope the issues of boredom, alienation, and loneliness are pervasive influencing factors among youthful drug users who cannot relate to their parents' culture which seems irrelevant to their goals.[9] The lack of excitement in their parents' lives and the promise of only transitory amusement with the use of cars, movies, television, sports, and other "acceptable" activities, deprives potential users of real involvement. Since *for these youths* school is irrelevant, and most other social institutions are similarly meaningless and rigid, the process by which the basic values of the American culture are rejected and the drug subculture emerges must be understood as a gradual sequence of events. Most drug users began as alienated youths who found no opportunities for commitment, no source for meaning.

DYNAMICS OF RECREATION AND LEISURE SERVICE

Leisure service agencies structure opportunities for individuals within an ecological web of interrelated components which includes the social environment, physical environment, the agency, and the participant. The delivery of leisure service occurs within this mutual support system. Each element of the delivery system is fundamental to a positive and enriching leisure experience for individuals. It is important therefore, for leisure service managers to understand that the social, physical, agency, and human relationships of each component of the delivery system within any community must be viewed as an ecological unit.

The quest for meaning and self-identity appears to be a significant aspect of leisure behavior, particularly as expressed by youth, minorities, and deprived groups. Since leisure activity may be viewed *both* as a plea-

8. Harrison Pope, Jr., *Voices From the Drug Culture* (Boston: Beacon Press, 1971), p. 15.
9. Ibid., pp. 15-30.

surable experience by itself and as a means of satisfying other social ends, the delivery system must be based on a commitment to provide opportunities which will fulfill a wide range of recreation interests (behaviors and desires). *It is necessary for agencies to be cognizant of the whole network of human activity that is prevalent in each community.*

LIFE-STYLE COUNSELING

Recreation and leisure agencies have recognized a responsibility to assist persons in realizing their aspirations, to overcome traumatic and difficult situations, and to realize human potential not previously attainable by the participant/client. While recreation, avocational, or life-style counseling has been largely applied in the therapeutic setting, it also has gained in popularity in public, private, and youth-serving organizations serving the able-bodied individual. Essentially, humanistic life-style counseling (an approach which focuses on the totality of an individual seeking guidance) attempts to establish rapport with the individual seeking such service; to have the individual express his/her interests, problems, and present life-style; to evaluate options and alternatives in light of the individual's "state of mind"; and finally, to have the individual make self-directed decisions to realize a desired goal. Such a participant (or client) centered approach[10] is contrasted with a behavioral approach which is oriented around institutional goals and objectives set and made by a counselor, leader, or team based on what is known about the individual. This procedure emphasizes agency-structured objectives and does not help the individual make decisions about his own life situation.

The humanistic approach attempts to assess the individual's existing life-style situation, relating to his (or her) skills, attitudes, cultural/ethnic beliefs, needs, and present work or avocational context, following a process of counselor-participant interaction designed to have the individual surface his internal and external worlds. The design of the life-style counseling model referred to here (illustrated in Figure 5.1) revolves around the central concern of encouraging a self-help process whereby the individual receiving guidance may come to assume some measure of autonomy and control over his own life.

Community recreation leaders, private consultants, or recreation therapists all have a common objective—aiding individuals to make self-directed choices which will result in a personal, self-fulfilling experience. Such a condition will be realized *only* if the client or participant is able to

10. Refer to Jerry Dickason, "Approaches and Techniques of Recreation Counseling," *Therapeutic Recreation Journal* 6(1972):74-78, 95-96.

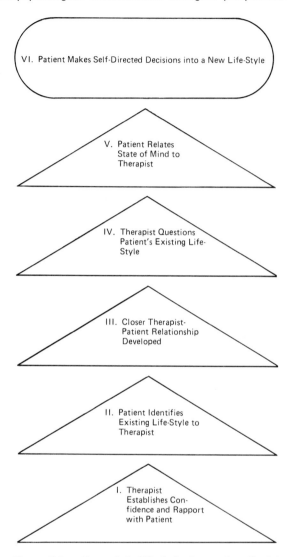

Figure 5.1. Humanistic Life-Style Counseling Model

Humanistic Life-Style Counseling Model developed by Karen Bragg Fulton, Coordinator, Therapeutic Recreation Program, Cancer Unit, Fresno Community Hospital, Fresno, California © 1973

develop trust in the counselor or community recreation leader. Meaningful life-style counseling experiences will be the natural outgrowth of the individual's ability to assess and realize his own potential in light of his awareness and recognition of community resources, prevailing social problems, individual pathos, and psychic state of being. The participant-centered, humanistic model is contrasted with several of the more popular commercial testing and referral services which are largely geared to "fill" people's free time through a series of aptitude tests.

The city of Milwaukee has been able to successfully combine the use of an avocational aptitude test with a skilled counselor to guide experiences for individuals seeking to actualize their recreation needs. Wilson comments:

> The components of the model are an interest finder test administered to assist persons in determining avocational aptitudes that can be satisfied locally; a classification system and inventory of avocational activities; and a skilled counselor who has both the ability to handle the two computerized components and the understandings, appreciations, and skills to work with people seeking assistance. The model is unique in that it enables a major public recreation/adult education agency to act as a fixed point of referral for city-wide avocational information. It serves three distinct populations—those in the mainstream of city life, those temporarily sheltered in the mainstream, and those about to return from institutions to the mainstream.[11]

The Humanistic Life-Style Counseling Model developed by Fulton is differentiated from the Milwaukee approach in that it focuses almost entirely on the individual's life-style circumstance which has been altered by an accident, disease, or illness. It involves a carefully guided program which attempts to have the individual surface his frustrations and needs, following a period of trust building between the counselor or community leader.

While there are six steps involved in the Humanistic Life-Style Counseling Model, it should be noted that there is no definite fine line between each step and that each step is not arbitrarily fixed. To better clarify the model, six phases of the process have been described so that it may be more easily perceived.[12] However, it is possible that any of the steps in the model may mesh or occur out of sequence, at any given time during the period of therapist/patient interaction.

Step 1. For the therapist (counselor) to "establish confidence and rapport" with the patient (client), several contacts may be necessary.

11. George T. Wilson, "Innovative Approaches in Community Recreation," *Leisure Today* 1973, p. 42.
12. The author wishes to express special gratitude to Ms. Karen Fulton who conceived the Humanistic Life-Style Counseling Model, provided the information, and wrote the description of the model and etiology of an individual with a terminal illness to clarify the application of the model in this situation.

Establishing rapport will, of course, involve securing a common ground of communication in accordance with the patient's capabilities. For example, communicating with the person who has been deaf since birth will necessitate the use of sign language by the therapist so that they may understand each other. The initial contact may not be a successful one in terms of free-flowing interaction between therapist and patient. It is often necessary for the therapist to be involved in several meetings with the patient in order for him to be able to express anxious feelings about his current situation. Therefore, it may take several contacts, ranging over a period of weeks or even months, for the patient to develop a sense of confidence in the therapist.

Step 2. Once the individual is able to relate to the therapist, he is able to more readily identify his "existing life-style." This entails surfacing the patient's individual accomplishments (education, hobbies, work), identifying the patient's personal environment (family, peer group), and taking into consideration his cultural background, for example.

The patient's disclosure of information regarding his personal, family, work, and educational background, enables the therapist to better identify where the patient "is at" with respect to his cultural, educational, and sociopsychological life-style pattern. At this point, too, it is of importance that the patient have an understanding as to the purpose of this interaction with the therapist. The patient should possibly be afforded a definition of the therapist's role and what part the therapist assumes in his overall care.

Step 3. Both patient and therapist now recognize and understand the existing circumstances between them, which leads to the further development of the relationship. Through the creation of this casual atmosphere, the patient can comfortably evolve a sense of trust in the therapist. This phase of the interaction is especially significant in enabling the patient to be more at ease with his illness or disability. It may be the only opportunity for this patient to do so. A similar situation occurs in an everyday friendship, whereby the extent of time involved will vary according to the individual pace of investing in and drawing from the therapist. This intense interaction, paralleled with the close relationship, aids in bringing about an assessment of the existing life-style pattern.

Step 4. To better envision and assess possible adjustments necessary in the patient's life-style, it becomes essential for the therapist to "question" it by helping the patient consider his own feelings and thoughts regarding the ramifications of the current life-style. For example, the patient may ask himself, "How do I feel now?" and "Why do I feel this way?" Both therapist and patient work together on these questions so that the individual will realize his actual limitations. This is the time many inner frustrations can be worked out, and a better acceptance of the reality of the patient's situation occurs. For many, encounters like this are an initial form of self-assessment.

Step 5. Life-style counseling occurs once the individual is able to self-express these newly assessed feelings regarding his current status. The patient is then able to relate his "state-of-mind" to the therapist by communicating his inner feelings, thoughts, and attitudes. As the patient is able to disclose these personal perspectives concerning this existing life-style, he develops a sense of awareness for what his individual needs are.

Taking into consideration the patient's situation at this time, the therapist may offer or suggest various outlets available to the patient. There is also the possibility that this opportunity for the patient to express himself openly and to be able to assess the existing life-style (for possibly the first time) is sufficient in meeting the specified needs adequately. It is also interesting to note that the patient may pursue this socialization period of interaction between therapist and patient throughout this process as his primary focus of need.

Step 6. It is through self-awareness acquired during the preceding five phases that the patient is now able to make self-directed choices and decisions as to what he shall pursue in accordance with the new life-style perspective which evolves through the counseling process. He can make necessary adjustments in seeking out an adapted life-style, which now indicates the individual's ability to control his life accordingly. This is of value because it allows the patient to gain a degree of control and self-awareness concerning his life.

PSYCHOLOGICAL IMPLICATIONS FOR AN INDIVIDUAL WITH TERMINAL ILLNESS

The life-style counseling process described previously was developed in work with individuals having a terminal illness. The following describes the etiology of terminally ill patients.

Tremendous fear with respect to progressive body mutilation, the long illness, and eventual death plagues the individual with terminal illness. Such illnesses, for example, cancer and leukemia, instill deep and realistic anxieties of the "unknown" surrounding the diseases. Questions arise about the cause of the illness, possible cures for it, and how long the person may live. The onset of weakness, of course, deprives an individual of functioning in a job setting, which can create financial difficulties. The length of the illness also affords an individual an increased amount of leisure that he may or may not be able to cope with. Inadequate finances also may be the result of a lengthy illness and the need for extensive hospitalization and medical care. The length of the illness, then, requires a person to readjust his life-style accordingly.

As it implies, terminal illness confronts a person with inevitable death. Human beings do not readily accept an end to their existence, regardless of the reason; this causes tremendous inner turmoil. An individual is faced with many phases of acceptance to the eventual death and must identify in some manner with what life experience is left for him.

Through humanistic life-style counseling an individual with a terminal illness makes a choice as to how he shall express himself for the rest of his life. A person is able to get in touch with what life exists and then strives for a qualitative life at his own discretion. Necessary adjustments can be made accordingly, on a self-directed basis as opposed to institutionally prescribed programs. Life-style counseling allows an individual to demonstrate his independent accomplishments and degree of control over his life, regardless of the terminal illness. Typically, a terminally ill patient is not able to exercise any degree of control over his own life. This approach attempts to foster an inner motivation for participating in community activities.

The humanistic approach to life-style counseling focuses on the individual. The individual is able to actualize the opportunities that exist and is able to cope more readily with life-style alternatives and perceive meaning in recreation experience because he develops the ability to discern what is best for him. Additionally, a life-style approach to counseling (encompassing all of an individual's cultural, avocational, vocational, educational, and personal background) considers and challenges an individual's full potential. The life-style counseling process will not only enable an individual to become motivated and competent, but it will also enhance the individual's self-image and status and may widen his range of social interaction.

PHILOSOPHICAL COMMITMENT

Leisure service agencies exercise an important influence upon the leisure environment. The philosophical commitment of the agency has an important impact on the nature of the leisure opportunity complex. Agencies are organized along three service continuums. First, agencies may be characterized by either a direct service or enabling service perspective; second, by providing either a cafeteria approach or a prescription approach; and third, they are organized to service instrumental or expressive activity goals.

The *direct service* approach involves the agency's commitment to provide leadership facilities and equipment for recreation participants. The agency delivers the opportunities they offer so that people can participate in them immediately and directly. Most recreation and leisure service agencies operate along this perspective. The *enabling service* approach recognizes the agency's commitment to serve as a catalyst and help people to implement their desires and interests. This perspective has recently gained more enthusiastic support among leisure service agencies, particularly as it relates to providing self-help opportunities for the ill, disabled, deprived, and aged.

The *cafeteria service* approach involves the agency's commitment to provide a wide range of opportunities which are intended to appeal to different ages, interests, and levels of skill. Ordinarily most agencies will have a variety of opportunities, including arts and crafts, music, drama, dance, sports, special events, nature programs, low organized games, and several other activities and programs, available for the public to choose. They attempt to meet the many diverse and special interests within the community by the provision of a kaleidoscope of leisure opportunities. In contrast with this all-encompassing approach, the *prescriptive service* approach is characterized by the conscious agency objective to develop certain defined benefits and values which result from taking part in the opportunities provided by the organization. Agencies utilizing this approach view leisure service as a social instrument, whereby individuals may actualize social and personal needs.

Agencies geared to provide *instrumental* goals are oriented in a way in which opportunities pursued have functional consequences for some segment of the community, the community as a whole, or the larger society. These activities are a means to an end and the participants generally derive gratification from the accomplishment of the goal and not the immediate situation. At the other extreme, agencies that foster *expressive* opportunities provide an environment in which social participation is largely self-contained, an end in itself. The consequences of engaging in expressive activities are restricted solely to the participants themselves. In pursuing expressive ends, gratification for the participants is immediate, rather than deferred as in the case of instrumental activities. On the whole, instrumental participation is more formally structured while expressive participation may be either formal or informal.

A combination of both of the instrumental and expressive approaches, the *interactionist* service approach, is emerging as a delivery model which embraces the holistic concept of leisure. Such an approach suggests that recreation and leisure service agencies should facilitate individual potentialities according to their particular capacity, and encouraged people to find their own life solution (whether it be at work or leisure). It presents a fused life perspective in which recreation may occur when one feels it exists. Recreation along this end of the leisure service delivery continuum is seen as a spontaneous, autonomous form of expression. Such a self-deterministic approach recognizes a concern for the total human being and sees recreation as a means or as an end in itself.

The chart depicted in Table 5.1 indicates the values which affect approaches in recreation and leisure service. The first perspective, the instrumental approach, which embraces the direct service model of recreation leadership, involves the typical delivery approach. It is more pragmatic than the other models and focuses on facilitating people's desire for equipment, space, and leadership to be provided by recreation agencies. It is most representative of traditional playground, community center, and youth agency programs designed to meet the immediate recreation needs of an individual or social grouping.

The expressive approach is predicated on the individual's need to enjoy himself and engage in purposeless, joyful, self-expressive recreation. Such opportunities have an intrinsic value and serve no useful end. Such programs are typically representative of youth activities and specialty cults which seek only the sanction to recreate at any time, anyplace, when the mood "hits."

The interactionist leisure service dimension allows for the individual to define his existence in the very act of creating and experiencing, without coercion by the social structure or the preconceptions of those planning and directing recreation programs who expect only certain kinds of self-fulfilling behavior to occur.[13]

Stainbrook comments on the reasoning behind allowing persons to create their own experience as he emerges. "One should come into an association of possible, potential experiencing and be free to arrange the experiencing as it develops without the coercion of organizational structuring and restriction."[14] If middle-class people desire self-actualization and self-development, then recreation agencies should support and facilitate opportunities which give rise to self-realization. At the same time, if members of the lower class want excitement and public assistance, then recreation agencies must be responsive to these needs. Such an interactionist position views different value systems of people in different social

13. Refer to Edward Stainbrook, "Man Happening in a Leisure Society," *Leisure and the Quality of Life*, ed. Edwin Staley and Norman Miller (Washington, D.C.: American Association for Health, Physical Education, and Recreation, 1972), pp. 169-180.
14. Ibid., 178.

TABLE 5.1

CHANGING VALUES AND APPROACHES IN RECREATION AND LEISURE SERVICE

Present Leisure Service Delivery Model (instrumental approach)	Shifting (Alternative) Leisure Service Delivery Model (expressive approach)	A Possible Future Leisure Service Delivery Model (interactionist approach)
Extrinsic-environmental stimulation	Intrinsic motivation	Self-determination
Measurement assessed in terms of attendance	Individualization of activities	Agency facilitated individual potentialities, allowing each individual to find his own life solution—in work and leisure
Standardized recreation programs	Diversification of programs	
Facility orientation	Serving people "where they are"	
Discretionary time	Psychological-personal time	Fused time reference
Recreation is expression of earned, unobligated time; a relief from dissatisfaction	Recreation is an expression of self; positive, reaffirmation of internal needs, inner satisfaction	Recreation occurs when one feels it exists
		Fused life experience
Leader directed and organized activities and programs	Self-initiated activities and programs	Fostering of spontaneity, autonomy Synergistic recreation
		Concern for total human being—human development

DIRECT SERVICE LEADERSHIP ←————————————————→ ENABLER-COMMUNITY CATALYST

spheres and seeks to provide *all* people with opportunities which will meet their needs, whether it be participation in a volleyball class, stamp club, well-baby clinic, or provision for self-expression and the freedom to create one's own leisure image. Some of these programs require careful, long-range planning (direct service programs), while others necessitate minimum interference (enabling service), if the situation can be expected to provide an optimum leisure experience.

Agencies which provide opportunities for individuals to fulfill instrumental needs perceive recreation as an expression of man's biological and physiological nature. Recreation is seen as an opportunity to avoid pain and boredom and reduce tension and fatigue. However, agencies which are geared to serving expressive needs perceive recreation as an internal, psychological response of the organism to satisfy individual needs for self-realization and self-actualization.[15]

The instrumental delivery approach to recreation is concerned with the prevention of dissatisfaction, and includes a recognition of the importance of clean air, shorter working days, physical security, and longer weekends in order to prevent various physical and mental disorders. The expressive or intrinsic approach to recreation behavior is concerned about developmental growth motives, similar to Maslow's need theory previously discussed in chapters 1 and 4, and Herzberg's two-factor motivation to work theory, in which satisfaction in work (achievement, recognition, work itself, responsibility, and opportunity for advancement) is related to the nature of work itself and the rewards that flow directly from the performance of that work.[16] The satisfiers are the motivators.

In recreation Levy states that the satisfiers include achievement, recognition, a degree of risk taking, responsibility, and possibilities for growth. These factors provide satisfaction for psychological growth and the need by individuals to maintain internal consistency. This concept suggests that motivation to engage in recreation results from satisfying an individual's needs for the satisfiers (expressive, intrinsic needs) and not from elimination of the dissatisfiers (instrumental, extrinsic needs).

The enabler-community catalyst approach, which encompasses the interactionist leisure service model, attempts to engender recreation independence among citizens. Dunn states: "This condition is characterized by sufficient knowledge, skills, and resources to permit an individual or group to engage in experiences of their own choice during free or discretionary

---

15. Joseph Levy, "Recreation at the Crossroads," *JOHPER* 42(1971):51-52.
16. Frederick Herzberg, Bernard Mausner, and Barbara Synderman, *Motivation to Work*, 2nd ed. (New York: John Wiley & Sons, Inc.), 1959.

time without external direction or intervention."[17] Such a perspective assumes a low profile and catalytic dimension. An interesting aspect of the enabling role is that such an enabling process avoids creating fiscally and philosophically untenable superstructures which often are destined for irrelevance and obsolescence. Some examples described by Dunn of how the enabling role operates are:

1. The San Antonio Parks and Recreation Department has sponsored an annual ecology program in which one of the activities involved thousands of children and youth. A civic association and a beer distributor collected over 50,000 aluminum cans to aid city beautification. The program involved young people directly in improving the environment of their city.

2. The Anaheim, California, Parks and Recreation Department and the Anaheim Art Association have cosponsored an Art Festival since 1964 to meet their common objective of introducing the general public to art within their community. Since 1973 the Parks and Recreation Department has withdrawn from active involvement, because the artists, who exhibit, demonstrate, compete, and sell their art, have become adept at festival management. The art group has now assumed the enabler role (itself) and have begun encouraging a variety of new community leisure opportunities. The Parks and Recreation Department serves mainly in a liaison capacity to the art festival and is now free to respond to new community interests and nurture other leisure opportunities.

3. The Dayton, Ohio, Annual Buckeye Dance Convention, a gathering of enthusiastic square, round, and folk dancers, has evolved into a successful community program as a result of the catalytic support of the Dayton Division of Recreation which has fostered interest, and provided organization, instruction, and publicity for the event. The division's active role has diminished as the dance council now boasts a membership of twenty clubs. The recreation division continues its interest in dancing but now performs largely supportive functions for the clubs and council.

4. The Minneapolis Aquatennial Association sponsors an annual civic aquatic event, including waterskiing activities, parade, fireworks display, fish fry, athletic competition, and cultural exhibits and performances. The program has evolved over the years (since 1934) into a total community event which is underwritten by

17. Diana R. Dunn, "Dynamic Programming: Enabling Recreation Independence," *Leisure Today* (Washington, D.C.: American Association for Health, Physical Education and Recreation, 1973).

interested individuals, business, and industry. The Minneapolis Park and Recreation Board assists the sponsoring Minneapolis Aquatennial Association.

According to Dunn, the enabling role performed by the above mentioned public recreation agencies serves three principal advantages which make it particularly relevant and functional in the 1970s.

> First, this dynamic, imaginative approach has great appeal to innovative citizens and professionals, especially those bored with the reruns of life. When agency programs are not expanding—even when they are cut back severely—the new interests of citizens need not be wasted nor the creative ingenuity of staff inhibited. For as professionals "work themselves out of a job," they have the opportunity to begin new challenges in new program spheres.
>
> Another virtue . . . is that when citizen participants perform the operational details, professional personnel productivity becomes impressive. Output per man hour ratios can achieve incredible levels. Stretching scarce public dollars has long been accepted objective of over-extended, under-financed local recreation professionals, and it is more necessary today than ever before. "Helping people help themselves" toward recreational independence is one way of doing it in these austere times.
>
> Finally, more of . . . these agencies . . . are inexorably committed to the continuation of these programs or events if interest wanes or new opportunities emerge . . . If demand languishes, fads do not become white elephants awaiting retirements or demolition for a decent burial. Even where new facilities were built, as in the case of the Miami Valley Dance Council's Michael Solomon Pavilion in Dayton, they are sufficiently multifunctional to be available for a wide variety of program alternatives.[18]

The standard direct leadership delivery model has served parks and recreation well over the years but has, in many instances, encouraged "robot-like" recreation dependency. It is suggested by the enabling process that recreation agencies give careful consideration to the enabler process which moves away from measuring success in terms of attendance to fostering individual initiative and evaluation of program success in terms of human development.

SUMMARY

The forces of modern technology have resulted in a creation of problems in society that is manifested by a collective groping for identity and

18. Ibid.

meaning. At the same time there is a growing awareness that the leisure domain serves as a significant aspect of life in which an individual may engage in a qualitatively wide range of personally satisfying experiences. The deprivation people experience in other parts of their lives may be overcome in the leisure environment. There is a need for leisure service agencies to be cognizant of this and to provide opportunities for people to realize their own potentialities, through continued self-development.

The individual participant exists within a total environment. The participant and the agency-structured environment represent an *ecological* unit. The primary objective of any recreation and leisure service agency is to provide opportunities for people, individually and collectively, to engage in leisure behavior.

Leisure service agencies may be expected to fall somewhere along three continuums: direct service or enabling service; cafeteria approach or prescriptive approach; or instrumental or expressive activity goals. *Each agency makes a commitment to encourage and facilitate certain kinds of behaviors according to their objectives and philosophy of service.* It is important for each agency to recognize the interests and desires of users and nonusers and to orient its service approaches to meet the needs of citizens in a way which invites participation and a realization of individual goals. Users will have the tendency to repeat the response if the results are satisfying. If, as a result of activity, the participant is dissatisfied, the agency must have an effective feedback system which elicits information in which to modify the service approach and promote opportunities related to participant goals. Occasionally the agency's service approach is not conducive to certain life-style expressions. Hopefully, agencies will not structure their service opportunities too narrowly and overlook certain diverse, less noticeable, groups within the community setting.

chapter SIX
leisure and life-styles:
subcultural expressions

---

what to look for in this chapter...

Definition of Life-Style

Life-Style Types

The Rhythm of Life and Leisure

Alternative Life-Styles
   Youth Subculture
   Counterculture
   Blue-Collar and Working Class
   Minority Group Subcultures

The term life-style has become an important social indicator which is often used to represent group cultural heritage, family life, education, income, and/or occupation. Feldman and Thielbar[1] suggest that life-style (1) is a group phenomenon, influenced by a person's participation in various social groups; (2) pervades many aspects of life and spills over into other areas of social contact—i.e., work, play, school, family, church, etc.; and (3) implies a central life interest in which a single activity (avocational pursuits, religion, work, ethnic heritage, etc.) pervades a person's other interests and unrelated activities.

According to Czechoslovak economist, Filip Hronsky, the term life-style is derived from a way of life category and serves as the functional integration of the life of society.[2]

It is seen as the sum total of life forms conforming to certain criteria which provide basic life security, develop human abilities, and are conducive to the cultivation and humanization of life. Life-style may be viewed as one of the ways of understanding living patterns as a unified expression for various subcultural, interest group, and ethnic ways of life, that would make possible the maximum harmony of individual and social interests, a balance between the development of needs and the way of satisfying them, and that would result in the balanced development of the human personality in all the spheres of human existence.

This perspective views life from a qualitative standpoint and takes into account the whole complex of material, ethical, ideological, and political values that people make on their own on the basis of their needs, interests, and views, and that expresses their aspirations and desires. Hronsky states that: "It is according to these that people take their bearings in various life situations and adapt, within the framework of objective determinants, their relationships to other members of society."[3]

The introduction of large-scale, mass-production techniques in industry led to a widening of choice parameters for workers. As technology has increased our ability to produce beyond marginal survival necessity, a vast range of goods, services, and life conditions, previously unattainable, have become freely available and accessible to most people in our society. The commitment of society in the late nineteenth century to a machine-based production economy, and more recently in the latter quarter of the twentieth century to automated processes, has removed the dependence

1. Saul D. Feldman and Gerald W. Thielbar, eds., "Is There an American Life Style?" *Life Styles: Diversity in American Society* (Boston: Little, Brown and Co., 1972), pp. 1-3.
2. Filip Hronsky, "On the Relationship Between the Socialist Way of Life and the Standard of Living," *Society and Leisure* 4(1972):105.
3. Ibid.

on day/night and seasonal cycles, as well as freed man from geographically limited life locations, and has resulted in the prospect of the human condition characterized by a multiplicity of choice possibilities. Ways of living are no longer constrained by economic necessity.

The choice range of life-styles, locations, and work has been extended, and even more characteristically one's way of life may coexist in several different modes (e.g., work-leisure living) without having to partition them according to the customary sequence—vacation, weekend, work. They are no longer seen as exclusive life spheres. Many new and varied life-styles have emerged with the transformation of obsolete work-skills into leisure-skills, in such areas as surfing, skiing, and skydiving, where previously localized craft survival skills have developed into complex work-leisure techniques which reflect an art-form direction.

There appears to be an emergence of a number of subcultures, a recognition of the many varied cultural, religious, racial, and leisure forms of expression which dominate a group's behavior. The concept of life-style provides a useful understanding of the leisure behavior of people. Life-style provides a total analytic perspective, since various groups in American culture are characterized at the same time by both great uniformity and great diversity. There really is no national character type, but, rather, a great diversity of character types. Such diverse character types reflect differences in beliefs, values, and life-style expressions which all contribute to the establishment of a broad cultural base that influences the behavior of nearly all Americans.

Some life-styles may be seen as reflecting the basic values of people in which leisure represents a central, dominant element around which other elements of living are grouped. Characteristic examples include surfers whose total life often revolves around the beach, waiting until the "surf is up," combing the beaches of the world in search of good "rides," and even seeking employment in surfboard manufacturing plants and surf sale shops.

This total life-style phenomena is also true to some extent of motorized camper enthusiasts. The yearning to get away in the out-of-doors by way of house trailers, tent trailers, truck-mounted "campers," and motor homes is increasing in America. It has been reported that millions of Americans are finding this outdoor nomadic retreat all the more palatable with the convenience of double beds, television sets, and air conditioning.

The desire for a relaxing retreat from the humdrum existence and the pressures of work are driving more and more motorized camping fun-seekers to the mountains, deserts, and river valleys. This motorized camping cult is similar to a growing cadre of houseboat fanciers who appear less inspired by the rugged river life than by their floating palaces equipped with dinghies, family rooms, wood-burning fireplaces, and color TV.

We are often critical of individuals who take to the out-of-doors with all of the paraphernalia associated with modern technological society. But the refuge from cluttered city life by recreation nomads is enough of a break from the ordinary day-to-day experiences that the social relationships, assurance of camaraderie of like-minded "campers," or mere proximity to the natural environment serve as lures to people who seek new experiences to fulfill certain needs.

LIFE-STYLE TYPES

According to Sessoms, life-style relates to activity patterns, association patterns, expenditure patterns, and living arrangements. He states that there are three dominant life-styles which are reflective of these characteristics.[4] First, there are *consumers-collectors*, who represent a majority of Americans. They are seen as materialistic, passive consumers. They tend to be clock conscious and live fragmented lives. They gain pleasure out of purchases, acquisition, and display, not from involvement in living. The second dominant life-style group is the *counterculture*. This group rejects the life-style of the consumer-collector. They are not conscious of clock time but are more bound by their personal, inner sense of time. The third life-style representation involves a small but growing group of people who are identified as *integrators*. They approach life holistically, fusing work-play into a whole, and seeing each sphere as beneficial and rewarding. They are concerned about tasks at work, not the time it takes to do them. Similarly, they pursue recreation experiences regardless of the time involved because they are personally satisfying. These individuals are seen as self-actualizing people, who are not constrained by survival and belonging needs. They are largely professional people who are able to integrate various aspects of their lives.

By noting the particular life-style patterns, recreation, and leisure service personnel could do well to promote, not deter, their particular forms of expressions and plan for their interests. For example, if a number of collector-consumers desire to use community recreation facilities, programs could be developed which encourage stamp collecting, car displays, and dog shows, so that its attracting features would be characteristic of the particular life-style representative of this group of people and would enable them to realize common needs in a desirous setting.

4. H. Douglas Sessoms, "Seminar in Contemporary Issues in Recreation and Leisure Service" (Lecture given at San Jose State University, June 28, 1973).

Research indicates that distinctive styles of leisure are found in various subcultures. Those individuals who live in close proximity to one another, who share common values, racial and/or ethnic backgrounds, and who come from similar socioeconomic conditions are inclined to develop an attachment to one another. The informal but governing relationships of the group upon individual attitudes, values, and aspirations is likely to exercise a powerful influence. While there are common elements prevalent throughout society, subcultures are found to either take the form of variations within a common framework, or develop a completely independent and self-sustained style of life. With the growing increases in subcultures, a partial result of the breakdown in community life and strengthening of leisure interest sects, it is important for leisure service agencies to become more familiar with and understand the nature of subcultures and their application to leisure in American society.

Subcultures, which develop through continuous association, evolve behavioral traits and cultural mechanisms which are unique to the group and are different from the larger society. Arnold states that there may be no national culture at all, no consistent strains throughout society, but only a "hodge-podge" of subcultures.[5] The norms and traditions found within specific communities exercise distinct social control over the leisure lives of people, even to some degree when they seek to use the leisure facilities and service offerings provided by the wider society.

The prevalence of a number of subcultures in American society reinforces the necessity for leisure service agencies to provide alternative means through which various groups within the community could realize their goals and ambitions in the leisure setting.

THE RHYTHM OF LIFE AND LEISURE

Leisure tends to be blended into a common rhythm of life. The rhythm of life in our society is based around the organization of work. The organization and provision of leisure opportunities is geared primarily to this pattern. However, not everyone fits in with society's rhythm of life. "Outsiders" cut off from the normal rhythm of life find it difficult to enjoy a normal style of leisure, which emphasizes the extent to which the leisure of the vast majority of people is geared to a common rhythm of life. The "outsiders" may be the unemployed, retired, hippies, minority groups, and others working on jobs that necessitate unusual hours. The

5. David O. Arnold, *The Sociology of Subcultures* (Berkeley: The Glendessary Press, 1970), p. 83.

conditions of employment, cultural traditions, and other ethnic factors, render "outsiders" incapable of enjoying leisure at all. Roberts states:

> Enjoying leisure in modern society is conditioned upon having a job because, without work, a person's normal rhythm of life and his approach to the daily routine is undermined, and participation in normal forms of recreation and social relationships becomes impossible.[6]

It has been recognized that most people in America have a style of life which is governed by the dominant rhythm, and the deviants—hippies, low-income blacks, retired people, etc.—are for some reason cut off from this normal rhythm of life. It is likely that the size of these groups of "outsiders" will increase in the future as the proportion of old people in society is expected to increase, shift work is expected to become increasingly common, acceptance of divergent subcultural groups will become more prevalent, and growing alienation will frustrate people no longer gaining moral strength from the repetitive tasks of assembly-line work. Leisure service agencies will have an important task of integrating "outsiders" through their offerings.

Leisure service agencies must sort out the most discernible aspects of subcultural life as manifested by "outsiders" and make an attempt to understand their life-styles and values, with a view to assisting them to realize their aspirations as sought through recreation experiences.

Malcolm states that a mass culture can absorb an incredible variety of values and life-styles, but it is reluctant to do so.[7] Many youth, for example, are attempting to demonstrate to adults the dynamics by which a mass culture functions—characterized by experimentation and continual change. Affluent American adults have done precisely what they set out to do: they have liberated their children. They have given them the economic, technological, and psychological bases for self-determination. The values and attitudes that worked so well in the past, acquired during two world wars and the pursuit of economic security, do not apply as much when applied to today's youth. Adults see in their children the things they wanted for themselves—freedom of self-expression, an experimental attitude toward life, a deep moral commitment, and an openness to new and different life-styles. The forces of affluence and technology have reinforced the ability of many young people to achieve an experimental and "open" approach to life.

6. Kenneth Roberts, *Leisure* (London: Longman Group Limited, 1970), p. 13.
7. Henry Malcolm, *Generation of Narcissus* (Boston: Little, Brown and Co., 1971), p. 6.

It is suggested by Roberts that attitudes and values generated during leisure have a generalized influence upon patterns of social life.[8] It therefore becomes increasingly important for the various social institutions to accommodate their own values and structures to the leisure-based inclinations of the public.

The youth subculture or black subculture, are dominant sources of the values, attitudes, and behavior of young people, white and black. There is a need for the leisure service delivery system to adapt itself more to their life-style patterns and rhythms of life.

Leisure has become the part of life to which a growing number of people, particularly youth, attach increasingly great interest and importance. Work no longer provides all of the moral justification it once did. It is paramount therefore that leisure service agencies provide people with satisfying and rewarding experiences, so that they may achieve a sense of identity and worth. That society may become stabilized and alienation reduced will be determined to the extent that man's self-identity and sense of community is achieved in his leisure experiences.

The traditional measuring of satisfaction by an individual's ability to get and hold a job is no longer a valid instrument for estimating an individual's general level of satisfaction. Some members of society have begun to recognize the existence of a conflict between their values and patterns of leisure behavior. Accordingly, leisure has become a manifest problem and, contrarily, a source of tension reduction and self-fulfillment (see chapter 10 for a more complete discussion of the "problem" of leisure).

ALTERNATIVE LIFE-STYLES

Life-style is a term describing the concept of an individual's behavior as it relates to his basic values and purposes.[9] It is an integrating perspective, and the need for integration and synthesis in a postindustrial society becomes paramount when individuals are faced with a multiplicity of choices about activities. Since there are so many subcultures in American society and alternative life-styles, leisure service agencies must be responsive and receptive to a variety of expressions of recreation choice and provide an environment conducive to integration, structure, meaning, and an opportunity for growth, relationships, and creativity for such groups. Eason states:

8. Roberts, *Leisure,* pp. 93-94.
9. Jean Eason, "Life-Style Counseling for a Reluctant Leisure Class," *Personnel and Guidance Journal* 51(1972):128.

Whatever the terminology, basic values may be lived out in a multitude of settings and activities. To the extent that values are actualized, individuals feel satisfied and self-fulfilling. People who do things in consonance with what they believe to be valuable and significant are those who feel whole and integrated. It is . . . valid to expect that leisure activities—volunteer and community undertakings, education for personal growth, and development of full potential, recreation, and play—will be most satisfying when they are pursued in line with the individual's basic values.[10]

Leisure service agencies must provide an environment which will facilitate alternative choices, and in which individuals will have some freedom to become self-actualized and express a life-style reflective of the value orientation of the individual.

Youth Subculture

Youth have evolved a way of life which is a combined result of industrialism and advanced technology, which has prolonged adolescence and created a life sequence divorced from childhood and adulthood. Youth have increasingly created a lot of interest, excitement, suspicion, and even disgust among the general adult population. They have intrigued and disturbed society, and this underlies their importance as a social concern in recreation and leisure service.

The youth subculture provides an alternative source of fulfillment, identity, and meaning for teens and young adults who find they are opposed by or cannot relate to the values and beliefs of the larger society. Many youth are reluctant to be afflicted with the "electric-toothbrush syndrome," of a highly advanced technological society. The nature of the work ethic and its by-product, compulsive consumerism, has been rejected by a large segment of the youth population in favor of a form of community life more conducive to "human" needs.

There is a movement toward "retribalization" in American society. This trend is symbolic of a search for security and stability through close association with other people, through communions with them. There is a change in human outlook and attitude among a lot of youth. "People are weary of the sense of 'aloneness' and they seek meaning and understanding—and they seek a sense of belonging, of brotherhood."[11]

This humanistic movement represents an expression and a desire to establish a way of life and philosophy that will satisfy not only a social,

10. Ibid., pp. 128-129.
11. W. D. Sprague, *Case Histories From the Communes* (New York: Lancer Books, Inc., 1972), p. 44.

but a spiritual (an inner and personal) need. The formation of communal living arrangements is seen as a rejection of the existing type of social life—a revolt against the disagreeable aspects of industrial progress. Communes represent only a small segment of the youth subculture and have commonly designated the counterculture. Roszak suggests that the youth counterculture is characterized by the new "centaurs," who search for individual awareness, consciousness, and new forms of community life and collective action.[12] Roszak's book symbolized the emergence of the counterculture and an ideology of those who opposed objective consciousness and envisioned the need for the development of a new kind of consciousness, new values, new aspirations, and new life-styles—a culture based on subjective, aesthetic, symbiotic, and organic values.

Berger quotes Malcolm Cowley, a noted literary critic, who wrote of the impact bohemianism had in this country during the 1920s, and the similarities between bohemian doctrines and the hippie subculture:

1. *Salvation of the Child.* Each person at birth has certain special potentialities which are slowly crushed and stifled by a standardized society. A relationship is seen between the retention of balloons, flowers, bubbles, and lollypops by hippies and youth to counteract this distinction and retain innocence.

2. *Self-Expression.* The purpose of each person in life is to express himself, to realize his full individuality through creative work and beautiful living in beautiful surroundings—"do your own thing."

3. *Paganism.* The prevalence of eroticism in public by women (bare parts of bodies) and men (symbols of strength, including beards, boots, denim, and motorcycles).

4. *Living for the Moment.* Live extravagantly and seize the moment as it comes—the relationship of personal versus linear time. Where the action is—now.

5. *Liberty.* Any law, policy, regulation, or rule that prevents self-expression or the full enjoyment of the moment should be abolished. The attempt to legalize marijuana, to render ecstasy respectable—dancing in the park, the impulse to turn everyone on, open sexual relations—to demonstrate the absurdity of laws against acts which harm no one and the hypocrisy of those who insist on the enforcement of these laws.

6. *Psychological Maladjustment.* The importance of drugs of "mind expansion" is an outgrowth of repressed, unhappy people who

12. Theodore Roszak, *The Making of a Counter Culture: Reflections on the Technocratic Society and Its Youthful Opposition* (Garden City, New York: Anchor Books, 1969), pp. 42-83.

feel they can overcome that state through a daily dose of hallucin-
ogenic drugs or by the mystic qualities of psychophysical disci-
plinary or by some other meditational means of transcending the
realities that hang one up.

7. *Changing Place.* The wisdom of old and primitive cultures are
   being affirmed by youth—anything to break the Puritan shackles.[13]

Student Views on Leisure

Youth is separated from the older generation partly because the
values which emanated with the Protestant work ethic are no longer seen
as meaningful today. Additionally students remain in the educational
sphere for a much longer time than ever before. The pervasiveness of new
values are manifest because of the expressed dissatisfaction of youth,
particularly white middle-class and black youth, with the traditional society
and its failure to provide adequate opportunities for them.[14] On the whole,
white students desire both immediate and deferred gratification during
their leisure. They are more interested in diversion than creativity. Their
leisure activities are collectively oriented, indicating a preference for to-
getherness more than solitude. Generally, students do not show a need to
achieve; leisure is for fun rather than profit. They tend to be noncompeti-
tive, and achievement is missing from their leisure activities. They believe
that since America is a nation of many ethnic groups, individuals should
be allowed to show pride in their cultural heritage and express their
diversity. Students prefer active pursuits rather than the passive assimila-
tion of messages.[15]

Black student leisure patterns resemble that of whites. They are
primarily attracted by diversionary leisure interests, although blacks do
show more interest than whites in self-improvement activities. While
blacks enjoy spending their leisure with others, they show a strong inclination to pursue their leisure by themselves. Generally black students, particularly women, enjoy more passive, intellectual pursuits.[16]

The value pattern of black and white students in basic social-institu-
tional areas are generally similar. Both groups are oriented more toward
collective pursuits and are not strongly self-oriented. However, there are
some areas of difference. While whites are more involved in the concerns
of society as a whole, blacks see the problem of the poor and the black
community as a special object of their concern. Another area of difference

---

13. Bennet Berger, "Hippie Morality—More Old Than New," *Transaction* 5(1967):
19-20.
14. Mary Lystad, *As They See It: Changing Values of College Youth* (Cambridge,
Massachusetts: Schenkman Publishing Company, Inc., 1973), p. 5.
15. Ibid., pp. 46-48.
16. Ibid., pp. 70-71.

is the emphasis on achievement. More blacks are concerned about personal achievement than whites, and they tend not to want to sit on the sidelines and watch others perform and lead. Both groups see a need to encourage social pluralism—decentralizing government authority and encouraging diversity. But the area of distinction that is an important consideration for leisure service agencies involves the belief by blacks that their responsibilities reside almost exclusively within the black community.

According to Miller there are five significant behavioral changes which have occurred in students, relating to their leisure life-styles, which may ultimately have a lasting effect on American life as a whole.

> First is the increasing shift from the role of spectator to that of active participant. This is particularly true of women. Second is the growing shift away from group to more individually oriented activity. This is to be expected in light of the increasing attention devoted for self . . . A third shift is away from activities of sociopolitical orientation and a return to the more traditional. Sports, beer busts, even dances are back on the "in" list. Fourth, there is a move away from the urban type of recreation to a greater involvement with nature and more rustic activities . . . The fifth shift is in the use of free time not just for play but to learn in the nontraditional setting vis a vis the academic. There is great interest in noncredit instruction in lifetime outdoor recreation activities (tennis, cycling, sailing, backpacking, fitness, etc.), and in the more exotic activities, particularly those that tend to have mystical or religious overtones (martial arts, yoga, and other similar existentialist thought activities).[17]

Life-styles of students in the university setting are important and increasingly central to a student's source of identity, self-understanding and rhythm of life. The university must attach greater significance to the leisure life of students and their activities, as Miller observes, particularly if these major shifts are manifest in the population at large, if it is to really fulfill its total educational mission.

Youth Subculture versus Counterculture

The youth subculture does differ from the traditional patterns as idealized in the Protestant ethic. The differences, however, reflect a new set of priorities rather than a totally new philosophical framework. The counterculture is a movement away from the traditional cultural orientations; it is in essence a new way of life. It is more drastic in its philosophical dissension from the traditional culture but does not indicate

---

17. Norman P. Miller, "Life-Styles in the University," *Leisure Today*, November/December, 1974.

a rejection of democratic government. In all, the subcategories of youth appear to represent one dissident category, although they appear to be dissenting about different things. Lystad's findings indicate that the youth subculture differs from the prevalent culture, characterized by the values of the Protestant ethic, in its assertion of a new set of priorities (revealed in Table 3.1 in chapter 3), described as a humanistic ethic. The differences between the Protestant and Humanistic ethic do not suggest drastic or revolutionary changes in the society, but they do suggest an alteration of the old, established institutional structures. Youth believe man should be valued for his intrinsic worth and dignity. It is in the leisure domain that "youth are most comfortable and successful since it is here that one can really 'do his own thing.' "[18]

Possible future societal patterns are indicated in Table 6.1. The pattern most likely to emerge would appear to be that of the Egalitarian Society. It contains a blend of old and new values and does not involve rapid, discontinuous social change in the direction of new values, nor does it involve repression of old or new values.

The conflict of youth, both black and white, is no longer only over the provision of equal opportunities to bring America's "deprived" and "divergent" groups into the mainstream of American life, the direction of the mainstream itself is being questioned. For blacks the emphasis is not on breaking out of the ghetto, "but on gaining the autonomy of their people within the ghetto, and on claiming for its culture equal legitimacy with the other cultures of America."[19]

Leisure service agencies face the conceivable consequences of persistent attempts by divergent groups to legitimize their subcultures in the face of the disappearance of many of the "middle-class" requirements for social respectability. This would necessitate a major shift in the approach of leisure service delivery in order to accommodate the life-styles of several subcultures. According to Berger there are two reasonable and viable alternatives for coping with the demands of blacks and youth for recognition: "[They are] . . . those that envision either integrating them into the nation as individual first-class citizens, or recognizing their corporate reality as distinctive American groups, and hence honoring their subcultures as authentic expressions of the pluralistic American experience."[20]

18. Ibid., p. 125.
19. Bennett Berger, "Racist Plastic Uptight," *Looking for America: Essays on Youth, Suburbia, and Other American Obsessions* (Englewood Cliffs, New Jersey: Prentice-Hall, Inc., 1971), p. 228.
20. Ibid., p. 231.

TABLE 6.1

SCENARIOS OF THE FUTURE GIVING DIFFERENT VALUE ORIENTATIONS AS RELATED TO INSTITUTIONAL PATTERNS

	Scenario I: Individualistic Society (Rapid, discontinuous social change in direction of new values)	Scenario II: Egalitarian Society (Some blend of old and new values in a continuous manner)	Scenario III: Elitist Society of older tradition-oriented group (repression of new values)	Scenario IV: Elitist Society of young radical group (repression of old values)
(Political Institutions)	Considerable civil unrest with the government unable to achieve consensus on national goals and unable to accede to the demands of numerous small groups.	More civil unrest for awhile, eventually tapering off as large groups achieve satisfactory representation.	Repressive law-and-order measures to quell unrest.	Repressive law-and-order measures to wipe out old institutions.
(Economic Institutions)	Less rapid economic growth because of lack of interest in economic system.	Sustained economic growth.	Less rapid economic growth because of high cost of police state.	Less rapid economic growth because of high cost of police state and lack of interest in economic system.
(Leisure Institutions)	Increase in leisure pursuits. Greater use of individual kinds of escape from reality (such as drugs, alcohol, etc.).	Increase in leisure. Part of leisure spent in process of lifetime education.	Decrease in leisure which is considered somewhat sinful by elite.	Increase in leisure which is considered one of the few legitimate activities by elite.
(Family Institutions)	Appearance of different kinds of family units, such as single parent households, loose communal households, etc. Rise in divorce and separation rates.	Dominance of nuclear family. Less permissive childbearing, with emphasis on responsibility to community.	Family structure of elite classes closely knit, much more tradition-oriented.	Family structure of elite class very loosely knit. Decline in importance of any one kind of family unity for all classes.
(Religious Institutions)	Decline of traditional religious institutions, but proliferation of small, short-lived cults.	Religious institutions oriented less to dogma and more to social-welfare pursuits.	Religious institutions oriented more to dogma.	Appearance of new religious institutions oriented to dogma.
(Educational Institutions)	Rise in nonaccredited study programs. Greater interest in humanities.	Increase in college enrollment. Increase in minority group enrollment in college. Greater interest in humanities.	College enrollment remains static or decreases.	College enrollment remains static or decreases.

Source: Mary Lystad, **As They See It** (Cambridge, Massachusetts, Schenkman Publishing Company, Inc., 1973), pp. 6-7.

Blue-Collar Workers and Hard Hats

While youth do not embrace the Protestant ethic, there is still a relatively high level of working-class consciousness in America among blue-collar workers.[21] In most industrialized societies work represents a major source of integration in society for adults and their families. In urbanized societies the individual's status is dependent upon his production and consumption roles. An individual's occupation, and those aspects associated with it, including income, place of residence, and forms of leisure, is representative of success or failure in society. Work, particularly for the working classes, is the most important influence on the life chances of members of society.

While America is an affluent nation, the styles of life of upper middle-class individuals tend to create the illusion of general opulence. "Yet the central fact of our economic life is that a majority of American families earn less than $9,000 a year. In 1969 the median income of all families, based on the income of all families, was $8,632."[22]

Most blue-collar workers must work forty hours a week or more, fifty-two weeks a year, and not be laid off in order to earn a decent living wage. In a nation where rising expectations and belief in equality exist, most people naturally want something better than they have. "The middle American feels *relatively* deprived, just as blacks feel deprived in relation to others. The average man's *absolute* living standard is low enough to warrant dissatisfaction . . . But his relative standard—relative to the affluence of others—is intolerable."[23]

Leisure is a big consumer item in America. Working-class leisure, however, may be more of a myth than a reality. During the workweek the average working-class person is too busy and too tired to enjoy free time. It is estimated that most of the money spent on leisure in America is spent by the affluent and rich.[24]

It has been noted that most working-class Americans do not take "real vacations," trips which amount to more than five days duration. How does the average man pursue his leisure? The working-class leisure milieu is probably best characterized by television, alcohol, sex, bowling, and card playing. "The workers' tastes, creations, recreation, intelligence, and culture are assaulted by those professionally in the mass media who impose their own style and taste on workers, and by those in the academy who

21. Robert Lejeune, ed., *Class and Conflict in American Society* (Chicago: Markham Publishing Company, 1972), p. 5.
22. Patricia Cayo Sexton and Brendan Sexton, *Blue Collars and Hard Hats* (New York: Vintage Books, 1972), p. 31.
23. Ibid., p. 36.
24. Ibid., p. 44.

cloister art and culture and admit only the elite to their inner sanctums."[25]

The working-class subculture is excluded and ignored by some human service professionals who program and administer libraries, colleges, parks and recreation centers, art institutes, performing art centers, theatres, and museums. There often is a middle-class bias in the management of these services.

Blue-collar workers have a hard life, and it is one which does not share all of the corporate and social benefits enjoyed by many white-collar workers. Lasson states that "28 percent of all blue-collar types receive no medical or hospital coverage, 38 percent have no life insurance, 39 percent are not included in a retirement program, and 61 percent do not have available to them employer-sponsored training programs."[26]

While the working-class work environment is often hazardous and job conditions oppressive and alienating, neighborhood life is not much better. Often blue-collar families live in areas which have been sliced by freeways and are crime pockets. There are usually few neighborhood parks. Those park and recreation facilities that are available are often rundown and poorly equipped.

The hard-working blue-collar laborers achieve little beyond providing the basic necessities for their families. For many, this means forfeiting the opportunity to develop and contribute as individuals to improved neighborhood and community life. They are too often the victims of social change and technological advances. This creates an attitude of despair, discouragement, and disgust. They need to feel that they can make a contribution and use their human talents and not be pushed aside in favor of progress and advancement.

The working-class culture is characterized by a striving for new things; there is not the same revolt against materialism among working-class youth as found among middle-class youth. Workers seek material possessions for the sake of comfort and security rather than for status and power, since they are struggling to acquire the basic necessities.

They want the good life, but it may be characterized less by the over-indulgence of the middle-class and more by material conveniences, an interesting job, a home which will shelter the family, and some extra money put away in savings. Recreation and leisure opportunities are more home-oriented since there is little excess money or time available for travel or vacation.

The differences manifest in the working-class subculture as contrasted with the youth subculture is seen as a cultural chasm. However, the con-

25. Ibid., p. 255.
26. Kenneth Lasson, *The Workers* (New York: Bantam Books, Inc., 1972), p. 6.

frontation will likely lead to a compromise, a synthesis of the two value orientations combined into a life perspective which sees a humanizing of work and decline in individual competitiveness. The two "America's" are not irreconcilable. Additionally, life-styles will increasingly be developed by a rapidly expanding multiplicity of choices—choices made possible by the interaction of affluence and cosmopolitanism.

The acceptance and tolerance of more diverse life-styles, expressions, and growth in material affluence and cultural sophistication increases the likelihood that an individual will be able to pursue a life-style which is tailored more to individual choice. Future life-style modes of working class, lower middle-class and upper middle-class groups are depicted in the following way by Rainwater:

Working Class	Sophistication of the nuclear family base. Traditionally enmeshed in kinship, ethnic, and peer group ties. Movement toward adopting the styles of the lower middle class.
Lower Middle-Class	Traditionally centered its life-style on a necessity to achieve and maintain respectability. Respectability is still a dominant but not as pervasive theme. Affluence has led to an increase in outward experiencing, but as a very solid family-oriented base.
Upper Middle-Class	Push to the outside world has been intensified. Egocentric class. Claims of respectability and membership in clubs, associations, etc., are subordinated to personal goals and desires. Self-sufficiency and pursuit of self-gratification. Increasing resources and knowledge-ability intensify the striving after exploration of fuller self-realization.[27]

It is suggested that in the future, people as they become more affluent, will tend to make choices which will result in their having less free or un-

27. Lee Rainwater, "Post-1984 America," *Society* 9(1972):21-22.

committed time rather than more. However, with increasing affluence, workers do not choose greater leisure rather than more income; the shortened workweek which unions have bargained for has been taken up by moonlighting.

The Harried Blue-Collar Worker at Leisure

While increasing affluence has resulted in people buying more goods and services, they have found that using products and services requires time. People will tend to shift their commitments in the directions of activities that seem to provide *more gratification per time unit* and away from those which seem time-consuming in relation to the amount of gratification they provide. In general, working-class and lower middle-class people will become impatient with routine, instrumental activities which consume a great deal of time and effort relative to the gratification they produce.

"The principal effect of this time/affluence dynamic is to make daily life more 'commodity and service intensive.' That is, people will tend to use more and more products and services in ways that maximize the satisfaction in a given period of time."[28]

It is suggested by Linder that with rising incomes, pure leisure (classical or its modern example, anti-utilitarian) tends to decline because the degree of satisfaction—gratification that is available from goods and services that were previously too expensive—is now greater than the gratification that is available from leisure and from one's own efforts to turn leisure into gratifying activity.[29] "Similarly, activities that are less productive of gratification tend to be given up or the time devoted to them sharply curtailed in favor of activities that are more productive and more expensive."[30] This means the less time goods take per unit of satisfaction provided, the more in demand they will be. They may be indicative of the increased interest in erotic shows and pursuit of activities in more exotic settings as a way of heightening satisfaction.

Leisure service agencies must be aware of the growing interest among working-class and lower middle-class, blue-collar workers for increased stimulation with a minimum of time commitment. The structure of typically operated programs is oriented to deferred gratification through award incentive programs that require an entire summer or whole season to accumulate and then enjoy. Blue-collar families have struggled for years to earn a "decent" wage and meet basic living requirements. With in-

28. Ibid., pp. 25-26.
29. Staffan Linder, *The Harried Leisure Class* (New York: Columbia University Press, 1970).
30. Rainwater, "Post-1984 America," p. 26.

creasing affluency, rising expectations, and growing cultural sophistication among all social classes, recreation and leisure service agencies must attempt to structure their offerings in a way to minimize *long-term* goal-seeking through short-term experiences.

Minority Expressions

America is characterized as a nation of democracy, freedom, and equal opportunity, in which each person according to his own ability, may achieve success and self-gratification. For many racial groups this ideal has not been fulfilled in reality. There has been a moral gap in American culture between our ideals and our practices.

There has been a reawakening among racial minority groups in America, particularly blacks and Chicanos. The urban unrest of the 1960s served to underscore the weakening moral fiber of the nation and bring the recreation movement back to human welfare concerns in which the social ends of human development are central.

Several studies undertaken during this period of turmoil revealed that recreation and leisure facilities and opportunities were an important need among urban minority groups, particularly the inner-city poor. A study of New York City neighborhoods by Jenkins, which examined recreation needs and services, revealed that there was a deficiency of group work and recreation facilities in the areas of greatest need.[31] The need for public and voluntary youth-serving leisure opportunities was considered to be important in the lives of deprived groups, particularly impoverished blacks, Puerto Ricans, and Chicanos.

Jenkins' study of New York City found that the neighborhood with the highest degree of socioeconomic need and community disorganization had far less public and voluntary agency group work and leisure services and resources than more affluent groups. Her findings were later expanded to almost every urban community in America following the aftermath of the violent disorders, in which President Johnson's National Advisory Commission on Civil Disorders found inadequate recreation facilities and leadership to be the fifth most important cause of the riots.[32] The Commission examined ghetto grievances and identified those complaints which were most casual. Of the twelve most significant grievances, poor and insufficient recreation facilities and leadership ranked fifth behind police practices, unemployment, housing, and education.

31. Shirley Jenkins, *Comparative Recreation Needs and Services in New York Neighborhoods* (New York: Community Council of Greater New York, 1963), p. 13.
32. *Report of the National Advisory Commission on Civil Disorders* (New York: Bantam Books, Inc., 1968).

In 1968 studies by Kraus of the five boroughs of New York City and twenty-four suburban communities in New York, New Jersey, and Connecticut, and the National League of Cities investigation of fifteen major cities shown that public recreation and leisure service for blacks and other minority and disadvantaged groups was poorly conceived, extremely inadequate, underfinanced, and in demand by inner-city residents.[33] Kraus' study led to the formulation of a new concept of leisure service as a social instrument, in which recreation opportunity provides an entry to other forms of service in the community setting and to the actualization of social needs.

Minority groups require a special approach to the delivery of leisure service, particularly low-income and deprived minority groups. They have been found to be almost entirely dependent upon public recreation service offerings and require an approach to program which will relate to their social and cultural needs and desires. Recreation and leisure service is most successful when applied to deprived minority groups which incorporate a comprehensive approach to providing needed services. This principle embraces the belief that leisure service is most meaningful when job, education, health and welfare, and recreation opportunities are embodied in a single approach to make leisure a positive and constructive reality. The concept is strengthened by decentralizing the control and implementation of recreation in the communities affected by the provision of leisure service.

Successful restructurings of recreation and leisure service programs aimed at paralleling the new thrust of black and Chicano pride and dignity, have been oriented to local community needs, and have been organized and administered substantially by the neighborhood residents affected by service. The development of productive cultural enrichment and self-help programs (acquisition of skills and knowledge which will enable a group to meet many of their own basic needs in terms of food, housing, clothing, education, and recreation) oriented to indigenous neighborhood need has contributed to the democratization of recreation and enhanced the value of the program.

The provision of recreation and leisure service which recognizes the determination and validity of the black and Chicano subcultures, and incorporates a program consistent with the life-style and self-determination of these groups, appears to be the most relevant approach to assist in

33. Richard Kraus, *Public Recreation and the Negro: A Study of Participation and Administrative Practices* (New York: Center for Urban Education, 1968); *Recreation in the Nation's Cities: Problems and Approaches* (Washington, D.C.: National League of Cities, 1968).

the elimination of racism and inappropriately designed facilities and activities. Other minority groups have similar problems and desires which will require that the recreation and leisure service field be responsive and sensitive to their needs.

The investigation of several large, urban, community park and recreation systems by Kraus revealed a changing role of leisure service in the form of social service and public responsibility. According to Kraus leisure service agencies must recognize:

> . . . that the major urban problems of the 1950s and 1970s—crime and vandalism, economic constriction, physical blight, racial militance, and flight of the white middle class to the suburbs—have all made parks less usable and reduced their base of popular support. And they recognize the corollary of the development, that unless park and recreation departments can contribute effectively to the healthy redevelopment of cities, they are likely to decline still further in support.[34]

SUMMARY

Life-style provides a *total* analytic perspective in attempting to understand the leisure behavior of people. It is seen as the sum total of life forms conforming to certain criteria—cultural heritage, family life, education, income and/or occupation—which provide basic life security, develop human abilities, and are conducive to the cultivation and humanization of life. Examples of life-style types are: consumer-collectors, integrators, and counterculturists.

There are an increasing number of subcultures in our society. Leisure service agencies must be responsive and receptive to a variety of expressions of recreation choice and provide an environment conducive for such groups, including youth, students, blue-collar workers, and minority groups, to have an opportunity for growth, relationships, and creativity.

The concept of life-style is a relatively stable but flexible concept which must be viewed with greater concern by recreation agencies in the future as it provides a framework for understanding how and why various subcultures and groups make choices throughout a life-span. By using this concept, recreation will necessarily alter its service offerings to focus more on enhancing self-development and personal gratification, since it springs primarily from *within the individual* rather than from others, and promotes an acceptance of self-responsibility and a feeling of worth and mastery. It is seen as a unifying perspective because it brings considerable

34. Richard Kraus, *Urban Parks and Recreation: Challenge of the 1970s,* (New York: Community Council of Greater New York, 1972), p. 68.

clarification and satisfaction to participants who previously were drifting aimlessly from one experience to another and gives them a sense of purpose and meaning. It also provides the leisure agencies with a service approach in the areas of leisure choice which will conceivably be more relevant to the participant.

chapter SEVEN
contemporary issues and value conflicts

---

what to look for in this chapter...

Value Formulation in a Technological Society

Race Relations — Leisure and Civil Unrest
  Special Responsibility to Minority Deprived

Ecological and Environmental Concerns
  Energy and Natural Resources Crisis

Urban Planning and Community Development
  Total Needs Assessment

Life-Styles and Urban Community Living
  Social Worlds of Community Members

New Dimensions in Sport

Urban Renewal—Self-Renewal
  Improving and Developing a Mutual Life Support System

The Meaning of Place

The Goal of Leisure Expression — Self-Actualization

Achieving Stable Mental Health — Developing a Flexible Life Pattern

The Dynamics of Aging

Our society has developed a myth of a unified national culture. It has been an effort to bring together diverse elements from a culture fragmented by class, region, religion, and ethnicity to formulate an American way of life. However, as Berger relates, it hasn't occurred. "Despite the hope that a unified American culture might emerge from the seething cauldron, it didn't happen; instead, ghettos and other ethnically homogeneous communities helped the immigrants preserve large segments of their culture."[1]

There are still attempts made to create an image of the typical or representative American or his community, "Attempts which have succeeded only in creating stereotypes—usually a caricature of one or another variety of *Our Town,* white, Anglo-Saxon, Protestant, and middle-class. *Saturday Evening Post* covers, white picket fences, clapboard houses, maple hutches, and such have historically played an important role in such attempts."[2]

It is not surprising that it is extremely difficult to abstract from American life a system of values which can be described as representatively American. An interest in value formulation has occurred in recent years. Studies have been undertaken to determine the preferences of social groupings and to match these with the main institutions in society in order to facilitate service. Basic values often attributed to Americans include achievement, success, work, efficiency, practicality, progress, material comfort, freedom, and secular rationality. While these values have played an important role in creating equality and fostering participation in American life, various segments of the lower and working class do not share them, and elements of the upper class do not need them. The above mentioned values do characterize a majority of white, middle-class Americans.

As our society has moved into a technological age, profound confusion and groping for American "ideals" has occurred, particularly among the young, women, and minority groups. Work has traditionally served as the *core* of the American way of life. In recent years there has been a shift away from work as the sole determinant for individual and collective meaning and purpose in life. The quest for new sensations, new expressions, and new leisure identities is a process which involves the questioning of traditional behavior, morality, and sexual norms. It is suggested that the growth and identification process of minority subcultures, exotic cults, acceptance of protest and rebellion as a way of life involves a rejection of

1. Bennett Berger, "Suburbs, Subcultures, and Styles of Life," *Looking for America* (Englewood Cliffs, New Jersey: Prentice-Hall, Inc.), p. 172.
2. Ibid., pp. 172-3.

the traditional view that work (whether enjoyed or endured) is the center of our way of life.

REDEFINING THE GOOD LIFE

People appear to be seeking a new focus, a redefinition of the "good life." Carl Rogers notes that the "good life" has had different meanings for different groups throughout recorded history.[3] For some it has meant a life of achievement—gaining wealth, status, knowledge, or power. For other people it has meant a strict adherence to a creed, a set of principles emanating from the Bible, the Koran, or a religious leader. For some it has been the indulgence of every pleasurable appetite. Rogers believes that such approaches to life cannot be perceived as some known, fixed, timeless goal. Rather, an increasing number of people identify life goals with a *process*, continual change being the essence of such goal formulation. A second change noted by Rogers involves a movement toward greater trust of one's own self. "The emerging modern individual places his confidence not in society's norms, nor religion's rules, nor parent's dictates, but in his own changing experience as it occurs within himself."[4]

The guide to human conduct is increasingly seen as an ever-changing flow of inner experience. This occurrence is an optimistic statement for recognizing the evolution of recreation as a humanistic service field, as the person is seen as gradually developing an increasing thrust in his capacity for making choices. What threatens all institutions, including recreation and leisure service, is that the good life is no longer defined for people by institutions. Also the ingredients of community life no longer provide the security, a sense of place and permanence, they once did. The changing fabric of social relationships, the disruption of neighborhoods, and the dehumanization of a highly technological society have moved people to seek a new sense of community, one based on shared interest, mutual compatibility, and trust.

In summary, the good life for many involves the shedding of traditional societal values for more personal, individually determined ones. The good life is seen as a process of becoming; as a movement toward greater openness to what is, within and without; as a greater trust in one's own self, one's own experiencing, even if that puts the individual at odds with our institutions; and as a thrust toward deeper communication and intimacy with one's fellows.

3. Carl R. Rogers, "Good Life Is Being Redefined," *San Jose Mercury News*, 25 November 1973, p. 30.
4. Ibid.

CRISIS IN VALUE FORMULATION

The technological transition of American society from a predominant-ly agricultural society to a postindustrial society has left most social groups unprepared for the cultural changes which have affected our ways of be-having, values, and interpersonal relationships, and which have literally destroyed the social foundations. The traditional value system in America was predicated on a work ethic and a shift from economic security to non-occupational, consumption spheres has exacerbated these values associated with productive concerns.

> The social structure of the industrial society, governed by an eco-nomic principle of rationality, clashes with the emerging values of the culture, an anti-utilitarian, hedonistic, pleasure-seeking rationale based on openness, choice, flexibility, change, and spontaneity. This incon-sistency has resulted in the development of a host of subcultures and subcommunity deviations which view life primarily from the perspec-tive of free time.[5]

Doug Sessoms relates that we are presently in the third stage of the industrial revolution.[6] The first period was characterized by the mechani-zation of the work force, which allowed man to extend his own powers. Work was seen as an integrative activity. The second stage gave birth to the corporate society with its organization for mass production. "In it workers no longer used machines as an extension of themselves but became like machines, elements of the assembly line . . . Workers became specialists, with the accompanying loss of identity as the rhythm of work became the dictate of the production manager, not the laborer."[7] In effect, as work became time-structured, man's work was no longer integrative, his life was divided between work and nonwork activity.

The third stage, cybernation, brought the possibility of more changes in our life-styles. The shift in work from mining and manufacturing to service-related industries brought about worker interest in his free time and self-expressive behavior. "We are literally creating new time blocks, new residential patterns, new consumption behaviors and new approaches to life."[8] The third stage of the industrial revolution has resulted in a value conflict and the need by contemporary societal members for activity and meaningful existence, found in both work and leisure. The perceptions of

5. James F. Murphy, *Concepts of Leisure* (Englewood Cliffs, New Jersey: Prentice-Hall, Inc.), p. 10.
6. H. Douglas Sessoms, "The Meaning and Significance of Leisure," *Journal of Medical Association of Georgia*, July 1973, pp. 255-260.
7. Ibid., p. 256.
8. Ibid.

an American style of life and self-esteem are no longer solely based upon work, but also upon finding satisfaction and meaning in all aspects of life experience. "We are coming to accept that both leisure and work are the same: avenues of man's expression and fulfillment. One is not subservient to the other nor the result of the other."[9]

Values are patterns of behavior and beliefs we hold important to our way of life. Each new generation determines the type of life-style and sources of gratification that lend meaning to life. Leisure expression is a part of our value structure; leisure activities we choose result from that value structure. Traditionally, psychic fulfillment has been derived from work. Now, however, work is being viewed as just another source of fulfillment and people are increasingly turning to other forms of expression for achievement, mastery, self-worth, and pleasure.

> The challenge to postindustrial society seems to be to *provide moral reinforcement for people to express and act out leisure attitudes and behavior whenever they desire, during free time or at work, and the opportunity to be identified by their leisure life-styles and cultural tastes rather than by their occupations.*[10]

The rapid technological changes in our society have raised basic issues in the values we embrace. Significantly, leisure is being identified as a system of new human experiences which represents the whole life of a person and how he wants to live, not just as his income, housing, or other physical conditions.[11] This is seen as a trend toward ego-conscious as contrasted with class-conscious symbolism. Status symbols and life-styles are becoming expressions of individual taste rather than reflections of economic position or social class. The growth of individual self-awareness underpins the movement toward ego-conscious symbolism. As people become more aware of themselves as separate individuals, the process of choice becomes a conscious one, and they are less guided by what is "appropriate" than what expresses their own self-image and style of life.

Accordingly, recreation and leisure service agencies need to restructure their approach to recognize this new psychology of leisure (which is guilt free) as being reflective of man's desire to become whole. Kaplan suggests two guidelines that would facilitate leisure life-style expression.

1. Provide the *individual* with information about—and access to—the new choices. Help him understand what they can mean to his

9. Ibid., p. 258.
10. Murphy, *Concepts of Leisure,* p. 13.
11. Max Kaplan, "Towards Improving the Quality of Life," *Clipper,* November 1973, p. 18.

development as a whole person. Anything that helps the individual to know himself, to feel confident in himself, is useful. It builds his internal security.

2. As a matter of *public policy,* the community should provide a variety of *alternatives*—not just a library, but a sports stadium too; not just housing to *stay* in, but roads and other transportation for getting *away;* not just indoor but outdoor facilities."[12]

RACE RELATIONS: LEISURE AND CIVIL UNREST

The twentieth century has been witness to a sharpening of conflict between blacks and the dominant white population in this country. The fundamental inequities of education, employment, housing, health care, and recreation opportunity have stirred blacks, particularly since the landmark *Brown v. Board of Education of Topeka* (1954) Supreme Court decision banning segregation in public schools, to respond to these deficiencies and basic civil rights infringements in the form of increasingly violent protest action.

Prior to the establishment of the various Office of Economic Opportunity summer "crash programs" and community self-directed recreation programs beginning in 1964, the delivery of leisure service was still largely outside the sphere of the relatively powerless and unorganized slum dwellers. Public servants have generally assumed that all groups of people are equal in their need for recreation and that it is universally a voluntary experience. An equalitarian philosophy, or "recreation for all" concept, was propagated in the early 1920s and was considered to be viable administrative policy for the ensuing five decades. This approach, however, has not worked for most minority groups.

Blacks and most other subordinated groups are not able to participate the way the advantaged citizen does because of discriminatory practices directed against them and the accompanying lack of sufficient values and skills necessary to take part in middle-class oriented public leisure service programs. The problem is compounded among the disadvantaged population for several reasons:

1. Coping with sustenance difficulties produces a pragmatic orientation . . . leisure rewards must be relatively immediate and concrete; and they must accompany income security, or else futility is reiterated.
2. Restricted childhood play experiences . . . implies an underdeveloped recreation repertoire. The disadvantaged population seldom

12. Ibid., p. 20.

has the opportunity to gain leisure "know-how" in the realm of the dominant society's positively sanctioned leisure and play activities.

3. Disadvantaged neighborhoods are distinguished by their lack of recreation services—whether they be public, semi-public, private or commercial.

4. Disadvantaged populations, though often residentially mobile within their own neighborhoods, infrequently travel outside this context on their own volition . . . this factor considerably lessens the extent and degree of potential recreation experience and resources.

5. Cultural differences may be the source of leisure habits that are inappropriate to the urban setting, or contradictory to values and norms of the larger society.

6. Minority membership may deter participation in available leisure activities because of social pressures and discrimination by other groups of the society.[13]

Leisure service has special responsibilities to minority disadvantaged populations because of its orientation and close proximity to the people. The urban community is laden with problems of unemployment, substandard housing, illiteracy, school drop-outs, etc., and demands particular attention. These deleterious conditions tend to *deter* voluntary recreation participation. A lack of special or compensatory approaches to recreation and leisure service for deprived minority groups has greatly hindered their involvement in recreation, particularly public recreation, on a voluntary, willful basis.

Not only is recreation and leisure service recognized as a basic cultural and social need, it is also viewed as a means of correcting these inequities and providing a "threshold" or entry to other forms of social service in the community setting. It may even serve to improve the quality of life, reduce social pathology, build constructive values, and generally make communities a better place to live. The recreation experience contributes to individual growth and fulfillment and to social development. The negation of recreation as an essential component in the cluster of community services necessary for human well-being contributes to social disorganization; continued deprivation of public and youth-serving agency recreation for black people has been linked to urban rioting and civil unrest.[14]

13. Vel Moore, "Recreation Leadership with Socioculturally Handicapped Clientele," *Recreation and Leisure Service for the Disadvantaged,* ed. John A. Nesbitt, Paul D. Brown and James F. Murphy (Philadelphia: Lea & Febiger, 1970), p. 167.
14. *Report of the National Advisory Commission on Civil Disorders* (New York: Bantam Books, 1968).

The National League of Cities study report of recreation in several American communities revealed the importance of the provision of leisure service for deprived citizens:

1. Residents of deprived urban neighborhoods are almost entirely dependent upon public recreation facilities, whereas residents of more affluent neighborhoods have a wide range of recreation alternatives. Adequate recreation programs and facilities are considered a high priority item among the deprived.

2. Residents of urban slum neighborhoods frequently charge that too much effort is directed toward middle and upper income groups, and that recreation planning is being performed by persons having no real knowledge of the needs and desires of the deprived. To overcome this charge, planners should encourage the participation of a wide spectrum of the community in the planning process. To be successful, recreation programs must be what the people want, not what the recreation department believes to be best for the people. Increased emphasis on citizen participation can be an essential component for the development of meaningful programs.[15]

The remoteness of most large bureaucratic human services necessitates a realignment of their delivery approach, particularly with respect to deprived minority groups. Various racial subcultures represent distinct and unique ways of life which often require a separate and specialized service delivery approach. It was suggested by the National League of Cities in their investigation of urban recreation that "the special needs of the poor require more neighborhood recreation facilities in inner-city areas and more person-oriented recreation programs in which supervisors can work with small groups in meaningful interpersonal relationships."[16]

A study undertaken by Staley determined that there were measurable *social characteristics* (juvenile delinquency rate, density of population, youth population, and median family income), and *neighborhood recreation resources* (number of full and part-time professional staff hours, and the acreage and number of recreation centers) which together indicate a comparative need for recreation in given neighborhoods.[17] It was his estimation, after analyzing the recreation services and social needs in south central Los Angeles neighborhoods, that *priorities* in community subsi-

15. *Recreation in the Nation's Cities: Problems and Approaches* (Washington, D.C.: Department of Urban Studies, National League of Cities, 1968), p. 2.
16. Ibid., p. 17.
17. Edwin J. Staley, *An Instrument for Determining Comparative Priority Need for Neighborhood Recreation Services in the City of Los Angeles* (Los Angeles: Recreation and Youth Services Planning Council, 1968), 15 pp.

dized recreation services should go to those experiencing maximum social pressures. The greatest deprivation in municipal recreation was found in hard-core districts in Los Angeles.

The data from these studies clearly revealed insufficiencies in the quantity of recreation facilities and opportunities as defined by the needs, criteria, and relative deprivation of black and other economically disadvantaged groups as compared to more affluent populations. More importantly, these investigations of urban recreation in the late 1960s developed the concept that deprived communities require relatively greater staff-to-clientele ratios, altered value orientation and service delivery approaches, more specifically educated recreation workers, as well as certain program adaptations to effectively meet the needs of disadvantaged racial minority groups.

Urban riots have been particularly significant by increasing the sensitivity and awareness on the part of white American citizens of the day-to-day suffering and degradation exemplary of ghetto life in the lives of black people and other minority groups. The riots of the 1960s have pointed rather directly to the need for increased and improved recreation and leisure service delivery approaches in meeting the needs of urban minority groups. Many of the conventional approaches and traditional recreation activities and services do not apply to the central and inner-city urban residence "because of a vast difference between user and supplier goals, objectives and values. Supplier goals often encourage nonuse and do not provide the measure of social service possible in the area of leisure."[18]

Service delivery at the neighborhood level requires a planning approach and the determination of recreation opportunities which takes into consideration the expressed *goals* and *objectives* of the residents. Gold suggests that public resources for recreation are a direct reflection of *resident values.*[19]

The concern for the provision of minority group recreation opportunities is seen as an essential guidepost for the future. Increasingly America will be characterized by a multitude of subcultures whose life-styles and leisure patterns will be markedly varied and distinct. The goal and value differences between the supplier (recreation directors and leaders) and user (participant) serve as a barrier to leisure expression and contribute to nonuse of parks and recreation areas. It appears that leisure behavior will be marked by increased spontaneity, choice, and diversity in the future. The recreation movement will be challenged to meet diverse leisure

18. Seymour M. Gold, *Urban Recreation Planning* (Philadelphia: Lea & Febiger, 1973), p. 260.
19. Ibid., p. 208.

expressions in the future as it has traditionally emphasized "organization, program leadership, and scheduling of activities."[20]

NEW DIMENSIONS IN SPORT

America's attempt to utilize sport and physical education as a technique for keeping fit has largely failed. Even more interesting, perhaps, is the fact that there has been a low correlation between success in athletics and success in life in general. Largely because of the efforts of the Esalen Institute and former professional and amateur sport performers and critics, including Jim Bouton *(Ball Four)*, Dave Meggyesy *(Out of Their League)*, Harry Edwards *(The Revolt of the Black Athlete)*, and Bernie Parrish *(They Call it a Game)*, athletics and sport in general is going through a reconceptualization. There has been a growing interest in viewing sport as a self-actualizing process and consciousness exploration.

Increasingly, sport is being studied and practiced with an aim not related to performance per se, but to the education of the body in general. This includes (a) *sensory awareness*, experiencing the body very carefully in meditative attitude; (b) *structural integration*, reviewing through manipulation the natural and energetic alignment of the body with gravity; (c) *structural patterning*, studying perferences in movement and noting the enormous cumulative energy wasted; (d) *body relaxation*, learning an elementary method of physical survival and protection against psychogenic illness; and (e) *expressive movement*, getting to know one's body in full motion. These concepts are related to the holistic, humanistic perspective in other facets of life. For example, the notion that the body can be used as a vehicle for the education of the whole person is implicit in a number of ancient Asian disciplines, including Tai Chi Chaun, meditation-in-movement; aikido, the modern Japanese martial art that emphasizes centering and becoming aware of physical energy in and outside of oneself; and hatha yoga, a basic Indian preparation on the path toward the highest.

These aspects of the *new* sport philosophy attempt to realize an integration of the body with emotions and the mind. It has been suggested that some traditional sports appear to hinder this basic integration. Various monotonously rhythmic sports, such as swimming and long distance running serve to detach the body from the mind in the interest of endurance and rhythmic perfection. A surge of interest in such an activity as mountain climbing, for example, has proven to be popular with the new

20. Ibid., p. 107.

sport cultists, who find that it requires instantaneous sensory awareness as well as continually renewed decisiveness and planning.

Whether or not these new transcending sports and movement education will realize any better quality of participant or lead to positive personality development is still to be determined. However, it does appear that these new directions in sport are providing insight into the multi-faceted potential of man's involvement in sport. Similar to recent occurrences in play research (outlined in chapter 2), sport is increasingly being recognized not as an end in itself but, like so many other human endeavors, as a means to the full development of the person.

The Esalen Sports Center was established for the purpose of developing new concepts, practices, and teaching methods in athletics and physical education. The sports center attempts to take a more comprehensive view of the athletic experience, including the mental, emotional, spiritual, as well as physical dimensions of the individual, which can elicit greater potential for human growth within athletics. Esalen Institute has for many years been exploring pioneering work involving human potentialities. The sports center may well serve as a guidepost which will lead to a transformation of groups and organizations by synthesizing traditional sports and physical education methods with approaches such as the Japanese and Chinese martial arts and new Western techniques of body awareness, movement, and energy flow.

Dave Meggyesy, a codirector of the Sports Center, indicates that the athletic experience can be made richer and more rewarding by linking athletics with play and recreation expression:

> One dimension of the Sport Center's [Esalen Sports Center] work is to develop strategies for changing the misconceptions which surround Sport generally. It seems we lack a great deal in our understanding of the purpose of play, leisure, and sport for human growth. . . . Possibly two avenues for evoking sport and body movement activities are through the creation of new environments for some as well as other leisure activities. Organized recreation activities, particularly activities oriented toward the athletic experience, could be done in environments which are central to community life. For example, aikido classes in store fronts sponsored and funded by Park and Recreation Departments.[21]

Meggyesy's ideas have been instituted by several recreation and leisure service agencies and educational institutions. The University of California, Santa Cruz, is an example of an educational institution which has

21. Letter from Dave Meggyesy, codirector, Esalen Sports Center, Esalen Institute, May 10, 1973.

abandoned intercollegiate athletics in favor of "participant activities," such as parachuting, scuba diving, sailing, jogging, yoga, dance, surfing, mountain climbing, horsemanship, archery, and aikido. The program conceives of education as preparing students for life and, therefore, has designed its physical education and recreation offerings to meet the total needs of the indviidual.

The absurdity of rigid and inflexible rules, master plan schedules, lined courts, diamonds, and fields reduces and even contradicts the *essence* of sport. Too often the materialistic and emotional factors of man have exploited athletics. It is suggested by Slusher that America's obsession with ends and goals, and almost complete avoidance of means and process, has resulted in a situation which has caused us to miss the real value of sport and focus on outcomes as the human answer.[22] He suggests that *process*, and not results, is the essence of true humanity. "To involve oneself in the *real* of sport is to engage in the process. To look *within* ourselves and to ask questions of *process* is to recognize the basis of sport."[23]

One must be aware of the total situation. Such a realization invites man to participate in sport as a whole organism. In this way, man humanizes sport—its basis is within man. "The use of the body transcends this inward sensation into time and space orientation. In the awareness of the act man's existence stands before him."[24]

The process of being through sport occurs when the conditions of man and nature are perfected and meshed into a unitary configuration and outlook of the world. Man becomes aware of his existence because of the inherent value in comprehending the universe as an interrelated whole. The value of sport lies in the individual's awareness of and exploration for a meaningful existence—of becoming what he is.

THE RAVAGED ENVIRONMENT

There is a great need for parks, playgrounds, wilderness areas, beaches, forests, and other recreation areas. The combined effect of population increase, expanding incomes, shorter and more flexible working hours, and greater concentrations of people in metropolitan communities and sprawling suburbs has resulted in an unprecedented demand for outdoor recreation opportunities. A paradox exists in outdoor recreation planning and development. On the one hand, increased demand requires expansion of

22. Howard S. Slusher, *Man, Sport and Existence* (Philadelphia: Lea & Febiger, 1967), p. 139.
23. Ibid., p. 139.
24. Ibid., p. 140.

areas and facilities to make them more accessible to people, and contrarily, a concern for a quality environment necessitates limiting use of certain overcrowded recreation areas to preserve the aesthetic value of outdoor amenities for future use.

Ecological concern for the natural environment is not only manifested by biologists, scientists, and population experts, but is also growing in importance among recreators who find that increasing outdoor recreation usage requires their attention. But the erosion, pollution, and despoilation of the environment means that more and more people seeking satisfaction and fulfillment out-of-doors will be deprived if something is not done to preserve and protect recreation places. At the same time the unique and attractive features of parks and outdoor areas must be enhanced to facilitate positive and enriching experiences for people, particularly in urban centers where these encounters are often infrequent.

Kraus reports that ecology and environmental concerns are now a conscious part of public recreation and park departments.[25] This new role includes a profile of promoting public awareness and knowledge as well as stimulating community action in the areas of conservation and environmental protection. This concern involves cleanup and antilitter campaigns, recycling drives, various historical restoration projects, as well as recognition by leisure service agencies of the impact of park and recreation programs upon the environment. According to Kraus the following guidelines are suggested for leisure service agencies as they relate to physical preservation and aesthetic development of their communities:

a. Park and recreation departments should directly sponsor a variety of ecology-oriented activities, such as waste, recycling programs, antipollution and antilitter campaigns, conservation education courses, sponsoring nature centers, bicycling and walking tours through natural areas, and closing park roads to auto traffic on given days. Efforts should be made to involve large numbers of young people as participants and volunteers in such programs, in order to build a solid base of support for environmental protection.

b. Park and recreation authorities should, both individually and through their departments, assume leadership in promoting community programs to preserve green areas (including nature preserves, marshes, wildlife sanctuaries, tidelands areas, or simply open space) and generally prevent pollution and protect vegetation and wildlife. They should help to mobilize individuals and organizations with similar concerns into team efforts and, when this can be done without compromising their position as civil employees,

25. Richard Kraus, *Urban Parks and Recreation,* pp. 36-37.

promote needed social action or legislative drives to protect the environment.[26]

We have at our disposal the means to improve the quality of the environment. How and where we make these changes should be based on a knowledge of how the environment functions to provide for human needs. Gray states: "A central purpose of community recreation programs is to help improve the quality of living. A great many recreation people have not made the connection between recreation and the environment or recreation and the quality of life."[27]

The energy and natural resources crisis of the 1970s reflects the demise of an economic posture which saw the consumption and waste of exhaustible resources. There is a need for the economy to be built on a steady-state situation, and similarly, the leisure sphere must be seen as an opportunity complex in which an individual should not feel prompted to be recognized by his material acquisitions and consumption pattern. Certainly, the environment is at stake. Additionally, the free-and-easy life of more abundant times may have to be considerably tamed down in the future. More home-centered and reduced energy leisure patterns may again emerge for awhile, similar to the era of the Depression.

The emphasis on economic growth as a goal of the individual and society was derived from the Middle Ages, as Western man came to believe that his ability to produce material goods was equated to personal fulfillment. With the depletion of fossil fuels and degradation of our natural environment there is increased recognition that the concentration on economic growth must be replaced by a more balanced-growth, quality-of-life perspective. There is an imperative need for reordering national priorities to enable members of society to enjoy what they produce and to grow in ways harmonious with the natural environment. Increasingly people are realizing that gaining great wealth is not synonomous with contentment, that there is a difference between wealth and the good life.

It is suggested by a balanced growth pattern that in the future, man will need to *economize time and space*. He will have to reduce many of his superfluous material expenditures that do not compensate him for the time spent in achieving or enjoying them, while society will be forced to limit certain types of expenditures and costly programs that consume or destroy excessive amounts of space. The value system which perpetuates economic man and the Protestant ethic is expected to decline in the future and be replaced by a more humanistic and complete view of *homo sapiens:* a view

26. Ibid., p. 15.
27. Gray, "Inner Space," p. 19.

which recognizes society's task to build an environment in which man can develop himself to the full.

The environmental and energy-saving controls placed on America's abundant society in the early 1970s began to alter recreation use patterns, as gasoline shortages and rationing effected power boat and snowmobile fanciers, and reduced use of electricity and lighting cut down the use of parks and community centers in the evenings and weekends. The challenge the energy crisis posed to recreation officials necessitated renewed thinking and judgment of its value as a basic human need.

There were some efforts made to curtail nonessential community activities to conserve energy. Recreation and leisure service was equated by some national leaders to be "nonessential," other congressmen, senators, and government officials pointed out that recreation is most often viewed as a basic public service. Recreation opportunities, particularly in times of stress and national emergency, have always been viewed as providing one of the few meaningful outlets and forms of expression for the young and elderly.

A study report which investigated the national energy problem, outlines three possible scenarios for the future, based upon different assumptions about energy growth patterns our society might adopt in the years ahead.[28] Under a "historical growth" scenario, the U.S. would need to aggressively develop all of its major domestic energy resources in order to continue the growth in our standard of living; this would require putting energy-saving technology to use. The "technical fix" scenario would serve the U.S. almost as much energy as our present total energy consumption, through energy conservation measures, without causing changes in life-styles. The "zero energy growth" scenario, in which the economy would continue to grow, and then curtail in demand after 1985, would occur following gradual changes. Through greater efficiencies, people would be able to enjoy more goods and services. This would result in an improved quality of life and a potentially more enriching and satisfying leisure experience without an unnecessary degradation of the environment.

Recreation and leisure service is an opportunity system which can promote individual fulfillment and lend meaning to life. Increasingly, our awareness of a despoiled natural environment and the energy crisis reminds us that an important source of enjoyment will be eliminated in the future. Synthetic and plastic environmental substitutes may serve as alternatives to more natural forms of appreciation. If park areas are reduced to artificial outdoor settings, important aesthetic and social needs will be

28. *Exploring Energy Choices* (Washington, D.C.: Energy Policy Project, 1974).

substituted by environments serving stereotypic population groups. The natural environment is a *process-dynamic*—an everchanging mosaic of relationships involving human beings and environmental conditions. A planning method must be developed based on the needs and goals of potential users which creates an environment that encourages direct and spontaneous use.

URBAN PLANNING: TOWARD SOCIETAL AND SELF-RENEWAL

Most plans for community development focus attention primarily on commercial, industrial, health, and residential users of the land. City planners have traditionally given second priority to cultural, educational, and recreational interests of the community. Planning here involves provisions for civic or community centers, public libraries, schools, and parks and playgrounds. Increasingly planners are devoting more of their attention to the total needs of the community. Paralleling this development has been a growing acceptance of community responsibility in providing and regulating recreation facilities. "The development of public parks and recreation areas has become an important aspect of community planning."[29]

Cities serve several purposes, including commercial, residential, manufacturing, and recreational needs. Attention for the functional and aesthetic aspect of community life has been articulated by Lewis Mumford, while several sociologists have emphasized the role of cities in fulfilling cultural and social homogeneity. The organic form of the city serves to unite town and country through an interdependent and complimentary design, and to provide a balance of urban and rural opportunities. Mumford suggests that city planners must design communities utilizing an architectural form which yields a "compactness that is needed to make daily encounters and mixtures between people and groups not merely possible but inevitable."[30]

LIFE-STYLES AND URBAN SPACE

The spatial complexity and the social diversity of any community should be engineered to promote the integration of human and physical components within the city milieu. According to Strauss, the social worlds of members of community life are linked by some sort of shared symboliza-

29. Noel P. Gist and Sylvia F. Fava, *Urban Society* (New York: Thomas Y. Crowell Co., 1964), p. 586.
30. Lewis Mumford, *The Urban Prospect* (New York: Harcourt Brace Jovanovich, Inc., 1968), pp. 151-152.

tion, through effective channels and avenues of communication. Each ethnic group and subculture circumscribes certain social worlds, a mixture of neighborhood and larger community social space, as well as certain sociopsychological images which are not rooted in space. Strauss states:

> The important thing, then, about a social world is its network of communication and the shared symbols which give the world some substance and which allow people to "belong" to "it." Its institutions and meeting places must be rooted somewhere . . . The experiences which the members have in those areas stem from, and in turn affect, their symbolic representations of those areas.[31]

A SENSE OF PLACE

Subcultural groups are most often identified with specific areas or *locations* where they tend to cluster and congregate. A location is an area occupied largely by a single social grouping, such as a completely ethnic residential block. Physical segregation (and often cultural differentiation) is at a minimum. People indulge openly in ceremonial and ritual gestures, and the outsider knows he is out of place. Affluent groups are more likely to abandon a particular location with ease if it becomes uncongenial. This is contrasted with poor people who have the greater stake in their particular "turfs." Certain sections of communities may be in between a location and a *locale* (a site for many differing activities carried out by members of varied social groups, as exemplified by a downtown street, theatres, restaurants, and shops). Physical segregation is at a minimum here.

Lee notes how certain social groups function in a transitional zone of *social orbit* (the range of locations and locales used by individuals living according to their life-styles):

> Local territorial definitions of place were observed in a small neighborhood park situated in a Chinese district of Pacific City. Community service workers report that the primary users of the park are propertyless low income residents, who use it as a place to join others for conversation, games of chance, or to observe local social life. Higher status residents use the park only as a pathway or a setting for local ceremonies. Territorial use varies both spatially and temporally.. From daylight until 7:30 A.M. the park is used as a training ground for the Chinese martial arts. From 8:00 to 11:00 A.M. elderly men slowly gather on the upper level to play games and visit. Activity is greatest between 11:00 A.M. and later afternoon. Between midmorning and

31. Anslm L. Strauss, "Images of the American City," *Studies in American Urban Society*, ed. Frank L. Sweetser (New York: Thomas Y. Crowell Co., Inc., 1970), p. 23.

later afternoon mothers bring their small children to play in the children's playground, which is located at the northeast corner of the lower level of the park. When the weather is favorable they are joined in the late morning by elderly women who come to sit in the sun and visit. Adult women seldom use other sections of the park except as a pathway. At noon Caucasian white collar and construction workers occupy benches throughout the park to eat their lunch. A group with similar spatial orientations, the tourists, use the park as both an attraction and a pathway from midmorning until evening. In the late afternoon and early evening Chinese men, who had been working earlier in the day, come to visit and play games. Throughout the day both black and white Skid Row indigents wander about the park, begging from tourists, sleeping, and drinking.[32]

Middle-class property owners tend to regard their neighborhood locations as places to reside not live. They often emulate a life-style which is diverse and not bound by space because of their high mobility. Friends are typically widely dispersed, and places of employment may even be situated in a different county. "Space outside the dwelling unit, including hallways, streets and open spaces, is public and anonymous. It is perceived as belonging to everyone, and as such belongs to no one."[33] This is contrasted with working-class neighborhoods where boundaries between dwelling units and public spaces are highly permeable, and the people often feel at home on the streets. Streets are not just parks but have become bounded places to which residents feel they belong.[34] At times recreation settings become places of conflict and strong identity, particularly in more homogeneous areas where individuals venture "outside" their location into another. "The widening network of communication and shared symbolism has resulted in social orbits becoming increasingly more diverse and oriented toward nonwork concerns. This has meant that leisure, not work, is responsible for . . . important changes and conflicts in our society."[35]

Recreation settings such as parks, community centers, and playfields, particularly in specific locations of a community, are perceived in widely differentiated ways by people who frequent them. Gray comments on the functions of a prak in an urban locale:

32. Robert G. Lee, "The Social Definition of Outdoor Recreational Places," in: *Social Behavior, Natural Resources and the Environment*, ed. William R. Burch, Jr., Neil H. Cheek, Jr. and Lee Taylor (New York: Harper and Row, Publishers, 1972), p. 77.
33. James F. Murphy, John G. Williams, E. William Niepoth, and Paul D. Brown, *Leisure Service Delivery System: A Modern Perspective* (Philadelphia: Lea & Febiger, 1973), p. 47.
34. Lee, *Outdoor Recreational Places*, p. 76.
35. James F. Murphy, *Concepts of Leisure: Philosophical Implications* (Englewood Cliffs, New Jersey: Prentice-Hall, Inc.), p. 220.

A downtown park may be viewed as a physical environment, an institution, a society, an ecology, or as a system with subsystems and interfaces with the surrounding city. From one point of view, a downtown park is an island in the paved urban world; it is conditioned by the physical environment and the social system of the surrounding territory. The park is a subsociety of the neighborhood and the neighborhood is a subsociety of the community and so on.[36]

Gray surveyed a downtown park in Long Beach, California and determined that there was a dynamic relationship between a park and its neighborhood. He observed that the relationship may be friendly, where people move with ease from their social roles in the park society to ones they maintain in the neighborhood or they may be hostile with park people and neighborhood dwellers harboring deep mutual suspicion with little exchange of social interaction. Similar to Lee's observations, Gary noted a well-developed social system in Lincoln Park, a mixture of cliques, class, and groups of various kinds.

> The lower class, made up largely of indigent men—the homeless, "winos," and the like—occupy the older section of the park. They are more argumentative and more radical in their politics. Their conversations may erupt into oratory. They have a well-defined territory which is seldom visited by any of the other regulars. Here some pass the time of the day, look for a handout, and sleep in the bushes at night. For a few, the park is 'home' between visits to jail. They look to the park for satisfaction of their biological as well as their social needs. The upper class—composed for the most part of elderly retired middle-class men and women—belong to the recreation clubs and occupy the redeveloped section of the park. They play cards, shuffleboard and roque, sit on the benches in the sun and carry on endless discussions. They avoid contact with the lower-class individuals whenever possible. Generally people of their class are clean, well dressed, and orderly. They look to the park primarily as a source of satisfaction for their social needs.[37]

Urban parks are particularly successful in serving a variety of clientele when they provide a diversity of opportunity, an attractive physical and aesthetic environment, and a design which fosters amenable social groupings. Urban locales, as distinguished from neighborhood locations which serve more homogeneous needs and interests, must provide a diversity of settings in order to attract the diversity of users who seek "sun and

36. David E. Gray, "The Un-Hostile Park," *Reflections on the Recreation and Park Movement,* ed. David E. Gray and Donald Pelegrino (Dubuque, Iowa: Wm. C. Brown Company, Publishers, 1973), p. 235.
37. Ibid., p. 236.

shade, openness and seclusion, . . . activity and contemplation, places to walk and to sit, grass and pavement."[38] The large city must greatly enlarge its range of leisure selections for residents, particularly since there has been a rebalancing of work and nonwork alternatives available to the urban dweller. Kaplan comments:

> Historically, the city has always been attractive for leisure purpose through its variety of persons, its range of potential experiences, and its possibility for excitement. The variety of persons stems naturally from the variety of work, from diversities of ages, museums, races, religions, tastes, educational backgrounds, and values. . . .[39]

URBAN RENEWAL

Programs of slum clearance and public housing programs were begun in the 1930s in an effort to revitalize aging and decadent cities and provide a method for rehabilitation of cities. The effort to improve community life by replacing deteriorated physical structures and stimulating favorable recreation and working conditions has been an important part of the American scene for the last forty years. While significant urban rehabilitation programs have alleviated deleterious physical and social decay pervasive in many districts of cities, urban renewal has not always been conducted in concert with citizen goals. Community restoration has often ignored the wishes and desires of those residents uprooted and relocated by the rehabilitation process.

SELF-RENEWAL

It is not hard to defend the need for better housing, more beautiful neighborhoods, improved public services, and more efficient land use. However, the process of human renewal (change) is just as important and must out of necessity, in a fast-paced society, be conceived as a continuous process whereby an individual becomes competent in directing his own self-interests. The social forces of urban living necessitate his own self-interests. The social forces of urban living necessitate that an individual be able to cope with the many social changes which occur and adapt himself to the altered environment.

Leisure service agencies may serve as "filters" to diffuse the shock of too rapid change. Communities, primary groups, and environment are

38. Ibid., p. 238.
39. Max Kaplan, "The Urban Framework for New Work and Leisure." (A paper presented at the Conference to Commemorate the 600th Anniversary of Krefeld, Federal Republic of Germany, September 4, 1973), p. 19.

torn apart by the rapidity of social change and the temporariness of structures and institutions in society. Since encounters and relationships are of shorter duration and often lack intimacy and stability, man's relationship to people and things is increasingly temporary. Individual competence in a transient and disposable society necessitates creating an environment in which temporary encounters may be enriching and satisfying while they last.

Since larger group experiences (except for spectator events) are more difficult to arrange, and the processes of self-development and mutual support are only available in a small group, leisure service agencies must, out of necessity, focus on the small group as an important and vital unit of life support. Old forms of small groups are being eroded in our society and being replaced by new ones. Gray states:

> Groups based on family, work, and friendship decline. New forms like collectives, communes, liberation groups, "growth centers," ecology and consumer action organizations, and liberation units have evolved to replace them. These groups are not random; they are attempts to bring people together in an organization capable of coping with the world influx. If we are to help mitigate the human toll of transience, it is our task to develop nuclei around which small groups can form, and speed up group process so that the benefits of group membership can be experienced before transience tears it apart again.[40]

In a world of constant change, descriptive words such as plastic, quick, instant, fast, turbulence, stress, intensity, overchoice, accelerate, anxiety, and instability, are all part of a society which experiences "future shock," or too much change in too short a period of time. Recreation centers and neighborhood playgroups may increasingly serve as mediums for people to gain the benefits of group membership experiences before they are obsolete. They may also serve as opportunities for people to assess their individual goals and practice their implementation, utilizing institutional means and methods to provide instant feedback. These newer forms of small group collectives are processes to promote self-actualization and to serve as mechanisms for social control and integration within relevant neighborhood units.

LEISURE AND SELF-ACTUALIZATION

As our affluent society continues to generate and accumulate greater amounts of material wealth it removes itself from the urgent necessities of

---

40. David E. Gray, "Put the World on Hold," (Speech delivered at Twenty-fifth Annual Conference of the Washington Recreation and Park Society, Yakima, Washington, October 25, 1972).

satisfying basic wants and needs. Leisure may be seen increasingly as an opportunity complex which will provide experiences for people to realize certain "higher" goals and aspirations. Recreation and park departments, therefore, may become service centers for helping an individual to become self-actualized and fulfill higher order needs that will assist him in realizing his own potentiality, finding opportunities for continued self-development, and being creative.

According to Farina, self-actualization is the goal of leisure.[41] Leisure is seen as the condition of being free from the urgent demands of the lower-level needs—food, shelter, protection, and need for belonging. Leisure is visualized by Farina as a personal response, which promotes self-realization. One engages in leisure in order to express oneself, whether that experience involves an intellectual, spiritual, or physical activity, in order to strive toward his full potential as a human being.

Farina's notions of leisure and self-actualization correspond with Maslow's theory of human motivation.[42] In a highly materialistic society, individuals are deprived of certain intrinsic values and may be frustrated by a society which mistakenly focuses its goals on only extrinsic materialistic concerns. Many young people have felt alienated and uncommitted to certain national priorities because they did not see the "value" of many of the more materialistic goals of the larger society. Increasingly, as individuals are able to satisfy certain basic needs, they will pursue higher level needs. Maslow has indicated that self-actualizing people are able to transcend the dichotomizing of work and play, and such a perspective may be of great importance in the future as our society becomes oriented to nonwork concerns.

While America is essentially an affluent society, it also includes a sizeable population which is less fortunate. Of necessity, the numbers of poor people, some thirty million Americans are primarily concerned about meeting their basic needs. While recreation programs must increasingly provide environments conducive to self-actualization, they must also provide clientele nutrition advice, counseling service, and well-baby clinics, to aid disadvantaged groups in meeting primary needs and having an opportunity to achieve self-fulfillment.

LEISURE AND MENTAL HEALTH

The provision of recreation opportunity has been linked to the maintenance of sound mental health. The potential of a more flexible life pattern

41. John Farina, "Toward a Philosophy of Leisure," *Convergence*, 2 (1969): 14-17.
42. Abraham Maslow, "A Theory of Human Motivation," *Psychological Review* 50 (1942):370-396.

in the future may help individuals adjust to the stress and tension of a highly technological society. In the past, the somewhat rigid and inflexible life patterning was characteristic of a work-oriented society. Martin states:

> Unfortunately, our culture perpetuates conditions unfavorable to the natural, rhythmical functioning of these capacities [effort and relaxation]. They become suppressed and perverted by the pressures, demands, and inappropriate values which characterize a world oriented exclusively to work. The glorification of work results in the early and continued suppression of our capacity for relaxation, and our capacity for effort, from childhood on, becomes completely subordinated to practiced demands. It loses psychological value and has only social value. It becomes outer-directed and wholly utilitarian. It is encouraged and developed, but only in the service of the gods of work.[43]

It is suggested by Martin that a leisure ethic which embraces a variety of life-style expressions is more conducive to individual growth in leisure and will promote the kind of experience which will provide for physical and emotional satisfaction, relaxation, and restoration of energy. The play of the child is often interrupted at an early stage, normally at the time of entry into school, when his natural interplay and interaction with the physical environment is curtailed and refined to reflect adult expectations. The process deprives a child of healthy, refining friction with the environment. Brightbill states: "The frictionless pattern alienates him from others, and inwardly he avoids inner conflicts by alienation from himself. Soon he avoids leisure because he feels helpless to control his inner conflicts which result in further avoidance of leisure and alienation from his creative self."[44]

The leisure domain is often best characterized by fantasy, in which the individual is free to act out certain daydreams, anxieties, tensions, and frustrations. This enables the individual to more capably cope with outside pressures and demands. However, organized recreation often does not allow, and even discourages, fantasy in play because it is not seen as "productive" use of leisure. This appears to be an erroneous approach to service. Brightbill acknowledges the value leisure pursuits may provide in revitalizing, rejuvenating, and refreshing the individual seeking a respite from the compulsive pressures of the outer world:

> It is not only that we can find in leisure socially acceptable outlets for our aggressive, regressive, and sadomasochistic desires, unconscious as we may be of them, but also because we can find in it the

43. Alexander Reed Martin, *Leisure Time—A Creative Force* (New York: The National Council on the Aging, 1963), p. 9.
44. Charles K. Brightbill, *The Challenge of Leisure* (Englewood Cliffs, New Jersey: Prentice-Hall, Inc., 1960), p. 87.

opportunity for belonging and for retaining our self-esteem. Add to this the chance to make our lives exciting, and we see its potential in emotional balance.[45]

Recreation serves as a way to maintain one's equilibrium, to counteract the often alienating forces of work and the biological requirements of the human organism to meet certain instinctual needs. Recreation serves to synchronize man's interaction with the environment, by providing a balance between ego-syntonic and ego-dystonic sensory input.[46] Syntonic percepts are those that the personality finds congenial, pleasant, and rewarding. The opposite are said to be dystonic. Recreation provides a balance and personal life rhythm which has the potential of integration, of giving man "complete instinctual, emotional, intellectual, and social coherence."[47] The recreation experience is seen as an enjoyable pursuit. Recreation and leisure service may serve as one of the few opportunities in a highly technological society for spontaneous, growth-stimulating activity. Work may be a pleasurable experience too. However, recreation and leisure service may be seen as aiding people to realize their own potential, or refine their own specialized needs, and develop self-affirmation through fun. Haun recognizes the role of professional leisure service in maintaining individual mental health.

> Having fun is a basic human need, present in everyone, sick or well.
> For the sick, this need is not met by the medical profession or by any of
> the supportive hospital disciplines other than recreation. To this need
> recreation specialists properly address themselves as a professional
> group; in this area they develop and refine their skills; to this end they
> make their unique contribution.[48]

THE DYNAMICS OF AGING

There are more than twenty-million people over the age of sixty-five in America, and it is expected that there will be over thirty-two million by the year 2000. The elderly represent the last social grouping of the human development sequence, and for the most part they have been cut off from the mainstream of society. They have been forced to retire from their work careers; placed in a convalescent home, residential care treatment facility, board and care home, or nursing home; confined alone to a one room tene-

45. Ibid., p. 86.
46. Paul Haun, *Recreation: A Medical Viewpoint* (New York: Bureau of Publication, Columbia University, 1965), p. 48.
47. Ibid., p. 37.
48. Ibid., p. 19.

ment in a decaying, delapidated part of town; or are living with their families under adverse conditions. Townsend comments:

> They wander aimlessly down busy sidewalks, so the rest of us push them aside. Bus and train stations are crowded with them, though they rarely buy tickets. They huddle in doorways in full view of the public. They are America's aged. . . . Most of them, fortunately, are invisible most of the time. Only one million are permanently invisible in institutions; others are afraid or unable to leave the rooms where they live. But the ones who do venture into the streets are an unpleasant reminder of a serious national problem.
>
> Since they are forced to retire at sixty-five, and since only a few have enough money to live on, most of the aged depend upon their families or the state for their welfare. . . . Most families cannot keep their old parents at home because of social and economic pressure, and many old parents will not accept public assistance because of pride or ignorance. If they do accept funds from the state, they are rarely able to eke out an existence on their meager allotments. At least one-third are forced to spend the remaining years of their lives alone or with strangers, of no use to society or themselves.[49]

The elderly find when they reach sixty-five that they no longer fit into society. Psychic fulfillment, for example, has traditionally been derived from one's accomplishments of work. The work ethic has degraded life in America for the individual following retirement or when one is no longer productively useful. Because of their alienation, seculsion, and loss of a productively useful occupational role, the elderly have less power and efficacy to influence socially defined roles and alter the thrust of social change in community life. It is suggested that an adoption of a holistic, fused work-leisure pattern of life, will make the transition from full-time work to retirement (disengagement) an easier and hopefully anticipated process.

The aged who are ill represent only 5 percent of the total number of elderly in America, and it's unfortunate that all of this age category are typically classified as being infirm, senile, productively useless, and are disenfranchised from the mainstream of society. While there is an eventual, natural deterioration of physiological functions in all human beings (and it does vary from person to person), the aging process is *normal, universal, and variable*. While death is inevitable, older people can lead productive, useful, and self-directed, meaningful lives. Society has labeled the elderly as an unviable age group, and members of families, institutions,

---

49. Claire Townsend, *Old Ages The Last Segregation* (New York: Bantam Books, Inc., 1971), p. xiii.

and the government have generally sought to exclude them from full participation in community life.

Leisure Service for the Elderly

As mentioned earlier in the text, the organization and delivery of leisure service should be viewed within the total configuration of social, educational, health, environmental, and transportation services.

> The concerns of poverty, urban squalor, malnutrition, illiteracy, and alienation must be considered to be part of the related concerns of recreation workers and which affect the ability of the individual to participate in organized recreation offerings. For the elderly, these psychological, social, physical, and medical concerns impinge on their ability to take part in recreation programs and realize certain personal goals.[50]

The central tasks of leisure service agents of change must be to ensure accessibility and to provide a comprehensive recreation program. For the elderly a series of factors influence the leisure milieu. They include the following points: (a) The time at their disposal is continuous time; it is not fragmented as in the work life; (b) the elderly are often poor, particularly as a result of economic inflation and loss of full-time work income; (c) psychic problems stemming from loss of a full-time production role result in the elderly questioning their usefulness and value system, also a product of their work life; and (d) the elderly's subordinated position, from indifference or rejection, challenges whether the content of leisure can provide a life-style of sufficient meaning to replace the contribution of work to one's identity and self-worth.

According to Kraus there are eight areas which can contribute to helping the elderly make such adjustments successfully:

1. Provision of economic security, an element essential to all other aspects of aging
2. Health assistance, including both community-based and hospital medical care—readily available and nondemeaning
3. Practical assistance with housing and maintenance problems—living units for aging persons are today being included in larger, low- or middle-income housing projects, along with plans for assisting older persons who live by themselves in such developments
4. A sense of importance and contribution to society, to supplant the loss of past work
5. The opportunity for meaningful relationships with others

50. James F. Murphy, "The Dynamics of Leisure Service Delivery and the Elderly," *California Parks and Recreation* 29-8. December 1973/January 1974.

6. Interesting and challenging physical and mental activities, appropriate for their age level
7. A position of respect and dignity in society
8. Direct help to those who are able to maintain their living independence in the community, and carefully planned programs of maintenance and treatment for those who cannot[51]

Program opportunity in these areas may take the form of direct or referral-coordinated service. The implication of a comprehensive, integrated (ecological) framework of leisure service delivery and agency organization for the elderly views recreation opportunity as a dynamic configuration, not a static given, which serves to promote interrelationships among the primary elements of the delivery system (the physical environment, social environment, recreation agencies, other human service organizations, and participants). The establishment of an integrated service approach to recreation agency delivery makes leisure expression a more viable and meaningful opportunity for the elderly whose social, psychological, physical, and medical needs are complex and interrelated.

Institutionalized leisure provisions differ from such programs in retirement communities. It was found in a study by Bultena and Wood that residents of four retirement communities in Arizona were oriented toward a leisure life-style and were attracted to these age-graded communities partly because of the leisure opportunities available for an active social life in their old age. It is suggested from their research that the retirement community provides both the facilities and psychological atmosphere for the type of consummatory-oriented leisure expression they are seeking. Most individuals moving to retirement communities surveyed increased their level of participation and involvement in recreation pursuits and some had taken up new activities. In contrast, retirement in their home communities tended to expose them to social norms which affirmed the value of work and the importance of older persons remaining in productive roles.

While physical concentration of retired persons in separate communities tends to remove them from the rest of society and further alienate them from younger groups, it appears to perform three important functions in easing their adaptation to the retirement role:

First, these communities provide a group of age-peers whose orientations toward leisure are compatible and who collectively constitute a reference group which legitimizes behavior that might be defined as improper or excessive in other settings.

51. Richard Kraus, *Therapeutic Recreation Service* (Philadelphia: W. B. Saunders Company, 1973), p. 146.

Second, age density permits the development of programs which generally hold only limited appeal for the aged population. These communities were able to offer their residents such diverse activities as an organ club, hiking, bird watching, painting, jewelry making, ceramics, and discussion groups, activities which in many age-integrated communities would not have attracted enough interested participants to sustain them.

Third, the age-grading and status-grading in these places produces a relatively homogeneous population and thereby enhances the likelihood of residents developing viable friendships."[52]

There is a growing interest among middle-age individuals in leisure. A number of people are seeking self-fulfillment outside productive activities or instrumental roles commonly associated with work or home-centered obligations. The legitimacy of leisure appears to be gaining greater acceptance among individuals nearing retirement age, and is particularly enhanced in retirement communities for those who have an inclination toward leisure expression. Such communities, however, may prove dysfunctional to the personal adjustment of older persons imbued with the work ethic, due to the overemphasis accorded leisure in retirement communities, and for those seeking a less involved social existence who may be resentful of instrusions on their privacy and pressures directed toward participation in social affairs.

Leisure service personnel should be cognizant of the need differences among the elderly and should recognize that efforts must be made to integrate certain older people within the social structure of the general population while also making separate provision for retirees who may best be served in settings in which they are physically separated from younger persons and insulated from values which differ from their own orientations toward the retirement role.

SUMMARY

In the future the task of leisure service catalysts-change-agents will be to blend their spectrum of delivery approaches and maximize the life-styles and values of people seeking their services through a variety of opportunities designed to meet diverse human needs. Leisure agencies should not dwell on a segment of the population and ignore the critical and pressing needs and issues (including race relations, ecological con-

52. Gordon Bultena and Vivian Wood, "Leisure Orientation and Recreational Activities of Retirement Community Residents," *Journal of Leisure Research* 2:3-15, Winter, 1970.

cerns, urban planning, self-renewal, and mental health) of another portion
of the community. Eventually they may alter their direct service approach
and provide a free-reign leadership profile in which people will articulate
their own needs, and the enablers of leisure service will aim to "nourish the
individual's potentialities so that each, according to his capacity, could
find his own solution."[53]

If our society continues to become more and more affluent, the previous dominant drives of food, shelter, and belonging will be more easily
satisfied. The future may well reflect an environment in which intrinsic,
higher level needs will become preeminent. Man will be driven by his
internal necessities to discover and develop his own capabilities. We are
nearing the saturation point with security and material gain as the guiding
motivations of our work effort. The humanistically oriented leisure milieu
is one which should be conducive to self-fulfillment and self-development
but which seeks a harmonious work-leisure fusion. Overly rigid participation requirements and excessive standardization of programs will deter
certain individuals and groups from participating. On the other hand,
broad and loosely structured programs will serve to frustrate other potential participants looking for more guidance. We are approaching a stage
in our historical evolution which will require new concepts of work and
leisure. It is suggested that people desire a better, more holistic, style of
life which will ultimately lead to a search for a more integrated sense of
work and leisure to fulfill the needs and aspirations of our total existence
rather than solely out of limited economic concerns. Essentially this also
means the reaffirmation of work as a human activity directed at the fulfillment of real and total needs.

53. Stanley Parker, *The Future of Work and Leisure* (New York: Praeger Publishers,
Inc., 1971), p. 139.

chapter EIGHT
leisure
as a path
to learning

---

what to look for in this chapter...

Optional Learning through Leisure

School's Responsibility for Leisure Education

Leisure and Learning

A Personal Experience

Leisure Studies — A Humanistic Discipline

Integrating University and Community
Preparing Dynamic Community Catalysts for Leisure Service

A New Age of Learning and Living

Four Levels of Learning

The occupational focus of education, with its stress on the acquisition of knowledge and learning of skills appropriate to job related functions, is no longer the only meaningful objective of education. It represents only one-fifth of an average person's life sequence. Education for leisure, which represents an opportunity for self-fulfillment and realization of one's own potential and life rhythm, should not be dictated solely by the work cycle. Educating individuals throughout their lifetime is a goal of leisure-centered society. Education for leisure implies educating (a) for a full life, (b) the whole person, (c) the free and liberated person. The whole concept of self-fulfillment is an objective of education which has heretofore taken place primarily during work, but which may now occur in leisure as it has traditionally in work.

OPTIMAL LEARNING THROUGH LEISURE

The entire environment can provide opportunity for learning, and it is paramount that leisure service catalysts encourage and foster the mesh of school and community to increase the transfer of learning to subsequent human actions. This process encourages an interest in a receptiveness toward the environment, recreation experience, adult education, health, and a variety of human concerns, and increases the likelihood that they will be treated as compatible and interrelated goals for education in terms of their impact on the quality of life.

The central purpose of an education-for-leisure development program must be the promulgation of self-expression and self-development through human involvement. Involvement need not be limited to the schools in the future, but can be extended to all phases of living, adopting the attitude that by *integrating* all of man's experiencing, people will be freer, better prepared, and more interested in pursuing knowledge and learning to live and adapt to a culture oriented to nonwork concerns. Society's task (developed early in the home and supported by all allied community agencies, including schools, recreation and day-care centers, social work services, city hall, etc.) is to educate man so that every phase of living, including leisure, can have meaning for him.

Our environmental and energy crisis, decaying slums, and unstable race relations, are examples of the genuine need for a change in present behavior. These problems which confront an emerging leisure-centered society require our urgent attention and a reorientation and development of a whole new set of attitudes, skills, and behavior which will ameliorate these aberrations and constructively support elements necessary for the maintenance of a vital environment.

Brightbill, perhaps the most articulate spokesman for the importance of educating for leisure, noted several reasons for the failure in using leisure wisely. They provide us with an understanding of why we often have a narrow and rather disjointed perspective of the value and scope of leisure's potential.

1. We have the wrong values, equating our success with the amount of material things we possess.
2. Many of us lack the appreciations and the skills to use our leisure to best advantage.
3. We have not made the machine serve our own best ends. Witness the motor car wiping out the city as the expressways wipe out the country.
4. A decrease in work hours does not always mean time for self-fulfillment. Sometimes the nonwork hours are not long enough in one stretch; people spend much of this time going to and from work.
5. We may lack the right opportunities as the resources may be unavailable at the time we are off the job.
6. Monotonous jobs may leave some workers incapable of shaking their fatigue.
7. Our energies are drained by family, political, and social pressures.
8. Many of our off-the-job pastimes lack depth and holding power.
9. Our work concepts infiltrate our leisure patterns. 'Work, oh work, for the night is coming.'[1]

The recognition of the total environment and the potential and use of man-made and natural resources is necessary for the maintenance of a life-support system. A leisure-centered society or a humanistic postindustrial society not only requires that people be prepared for using their personal time but also is predicated upon appropriate attitudes, values, interests, and competencies.

While forecasted increases in free time, or at least nonwork time, have struck a variety of responses from the population, its virtues and its pitfalls have remained largely unchanged for 10,000 years. Time connotes pressure and tension to some, freedom and flexibility to others. Time is for living. While work time has chopped up moments and fragmented the lives of most industrial nations, it remains unscheduled, cyclic, and whole in other preindustrial and folk cultures. A more spontaneous, uninterrupted, and flexible time orientation, reflective of a postindustrial social order, would help to reintegrate fragments of time; such an orientation would guarantee respect for individual dignity, autonomy, and self-deter-

1. Charles K. Brightbill, *Educating for Leisure-Centered Living* (Harrisburg, Pennsylvania: The Stackpole Company, 1966), p. 102.

mination according to one's personal rhythm of time. This perspective reinforces the concept of leisure service personnel as community catalysts who help the individual gain an understanding of himself, thereby increasing the possibility of him being able to actualize his own needs. Brightbill states:

> He [community catalyst] comes to know the personal and inorganic elements, the impediments, and the forces which bear upon leisure and its uses. He relates one to the other and has the capacity for bringing them together at the appropriate time to meet the need. He is the leader who welds interests and appreciations to skills and opportunities. While recognizing diversity of interest and the essentiality of self-determination, he views all as a whole toward the end of enabling the individual to get the best from himself in leisure. The catalyst-leader expedites relating the recreative life to the wholeness of life and human resources to natural resources. The emphasis is upon generating self-expression through human involvement, preferably self-propelled.[2]

THE SCHOOL'S RESPONSIBILITY FOR LEISURE EDUCATION

The idealogy of work, which encompasses jobs, vacations, and clock-time, is of central importance to the process of education. The present structure and culture of American schools is oriented toward the preparation of people for a job-oriented society. American society is at present in a cultural transition. We are passing from an industrial to a technological or postindustrial society—from an era in which production of goods was a primary concern to one dominated by services and the generation and use of new knowledge. The shock of change poses some particular problems for education.

Conceivably, if American education is not reversed or modified, we may find ourselves approaching a leisure society with a system of education that is inappropriate and no longer suitable. Green suggests that schools should make teaching and learning a fun experience, in which the process of learning provides its own inherent motivation and is not controlled by any certification procedure. "The value of teaching and of learning, in this view, is like the value of play: it is intrinsic and immediate and directly related to the characteristics of leisure."[3]

During earlier eras, schooling served as one of many alternatives for people to acquire skills, knowledge, socialization, and entry into adult

2. Ibid., p. 157.
3. Thomas F. Green, *Work, Leisure, and the American Schools* (New York: Random House, Inc., 1968), p. 157.

society. Now it has become nearly the sole path for entry into the techno-logically-based job market. On the whole, the educational process, with its emphasis on jobs, work, and productive results, is not appropriately oriented to nonwork concerns and preparation for life fulfillment. The certifying, sorting, and selecting process of education for technical com-petence involves preparation and training for a specific occupational func-tion. The outcome is more important than the process. However, in a society characterized by constant change and temporary structures, educa-tion should provide its own intrinsic rewards and focus on play. In this sense play and leisure are seen as interrelated by Green. "Play and leisure are related to each other in precisely the respect that distinguishes them both from work—namely, they both involve activities that are done for the sake of some remote and terminal result or product."[4]

Education in a postindustrial society should have its own immediate motivation. It cannot be controlled by some standard of certification, rather learning should be engaged in for its own sake. The connection be-tween an education in a technological, postindustrial society devoted to preparation for living and leisure is fundamentally different from school-ing in a work-oriented society. Free time in the latter society is viewed as time for rest, relaxation, and recuperation from work. In a society which increasingly is oriented to nonwork, free time may be viewed as an essen-tial, creative part of life. Michael questions education for free-time use which involves values and goals of a work ethic.

> Is the goal of self-fulfillment through creative free-time activity at all compatible with the requirements of an economy which depends upon the voracious consumption of leisure-time gadgets, mobility, and all those other things which one gets now and pays for later? Actually, the careful cultivation of self through hobbies, avocations, and any other activities involves the cultivation of technique and insight much more than it involves the steady acquisition of things.[5]

The task of education is to impart the value of free time, to provide students with a sense of alternatives on how to adopt styles of life for free-time use (including those of tranquility, appreciation, reeducation, etc.). As our society becomes leisure-based and individuals internalize the qualities and values associated with their leisure lives, education must be revised to reflect this change in roles and expectations, and in accordance with leisure-centered self-concepts. As the self-consciousness of man be-

4. Ibid., p. 160.
5. Donald N. Michael, "Free Time—The New Imperative in Our Society," *Automation Education, and Human Values,* ed. William W. Brickman and Stanley Lehrer (New York: Thomas Y. Crowell Company, 1966), p. 301.

comes based upon the interests and activities which are associated with leisure, institutions will have to adapt to these new value and behavioral changes. Roberts notes how institutions must change to respond to individuals. "In order to function effectively other social institutions have to accommodate their own values and structures to the leisure-based orientations of the public. Thus leisure, as the source of man's sense of self-identity, becomes the basis of all social life."[6]

The leisure milieu must be perceived in its totality, in which the individual can explore and take advantage of all possible opportunities for satisfaction and self-fulfillment. According to Leonard, the total environment must be the central theme of education. "It is only when the learning environment is viewed and acted upon as a whole that education can become truly efficient and joyful."[7]

LEISURE AND LEARNING

The purpose of leisure takes form in the attitudes, knowledge, skills, and behavior which must be altered or cultivated. Kraus provides a framework for perceiving the goals of leisure education.

> *Attitudes.* It is essential that students develop an awareness of the importance of leisure in society and a recognition of the significant values that it may contribute to their lives. . . . Essential too is the inculcation of a keen sense of taste and discrimination, and the ability to make sound judgments and rational choices with respect to all kinds of leisure participation.
>
> *Knowledge.* Through direct experience and exposure, the student learns about recreational opportunities on many levels and comes to realize how he may become involved in them, and what kinds of outcome may be derived. He gains information about recreation resources in the community, and learns to make full use of them.
>
> *Skills.* The purpose of teaching skills is not to have a student master a number of specific activities with the thought that he will necessarily participate in them as the core of his recreational life in later youth and adulthood. It is, rather, to provide him with certain basic skills directly related to recreational opportunities presently available, so that he may participate in these activities with a degree of competence, success, and pleasure.
>
> *Behavior.* The outcome of leisure education must be *behavior* which is marked by good judgment in the selection of recreational pursuits; a

6. Kenneth Roberts, *Leisure* (London: Longman Group Limited, 1970), p. 94.
7. George B. Leonard, *Education and Ecstasy* (New York: Dell Publishing Co., Inc., 1968), p. 182.

diversity of leisure interests that meet physical, emotional, and social needs; and solid competence in participation. This means that the school has a responsibility to provide a laboratory experience, either by directly sponsoring, or by cooperating with other community agencies that do sponsor recreational programs that implement its program of leisure education.[8]

Leisure is most statisfying when it comes naturally. It is an attitude, a state of mind, a condition which is freely sought. But to reap the richest harvest from leisure, one must be conditioned and ready for it.

Education for leisure must place far more emphasis on a balanced life than has education for work. The challenge to recreation and leisure service personnel is to help alter the image that only work provides the central values for people and that free time is more than an opportunity to recuperate from labor or to be filled with endless household chores or vicarious hours of spectation.

Hawkins notes a series of objectives for community education in a leisure-centered society:

Objective 1.   To conceptualize and to catalyze education and action efforts designed to produce a quality living environment.

Objective 2.   To design intervention strategies which bring leisure services to diverse populations, particularly those handicapped by social or economic inequities.

Objective 3,   To serve as an advocate for the leisure client through effective liaisons with leisure commodity and service producers.

Objective 4.   To utilize social experimentation and evaluative research to influence leisure service planning and decision making.

Objective 5.   To educate the total citizenry for the worthy use of leisure.

Objective 6.   To develop avocational counseling programs designed to diagnose leisure behavior problems or needs and prescribe therapy and solutions.

Objective 7.   To act as an exemplar for public/private cooperation in providing leisure services.

Objective 8.   To analyze and develop comprehensive leisure service systems.

Objective 9.   To concentrate on career development and manpower utilization stressing career lattice approaches and differentiated staffing patterns.

8. Richard G. Kraus, *Recreation and the Schools: Guides to Effective Practices in Leisure Education and Community Recreation Sponsorship* (New York: The Macmillan Co., 1964), pp. 85-86.

Objective 10. To encourage environmental design conducive to the multiple use of open space, physical facilities, and natural resources for educational and recreational purposes.[9]

In order to construct a curriculum which will provide a learning environment conducive to the flowering of the self, the curriculum must be built around the individual learner. So too, must the leisure setting construct an environment which will foster self-realization. It is suggested by the foregoing that leisure service personnel provide minimal organization and maximum flexibility. Stainbrook states: "The emerging self must be allowed to define its experience in the very act of creating, and not be coerced by the structure, the value system, or by the preconceptions of those in recreation and leisure planning who expect only certain kinds of self-fulfilling behavior to happen."[10]

The leisure setting should provide opportunities for the individual to engage in a full range of possible experiencing which will allow for spontaneous and direct use of the environment. It must also provide for diverse expressions to allow each subculture an opportunity to meet its needs through participation in leisure which is meaningful to them. Leisure service agencies may appropriately recognize their delivery approach to fall along a continuum which ranges from self-actualization and self-development to unconditional pleasure and satisfaction.

A PERSONAL EXPERIENCE

The thrust of leisure education must be toward recognizing the worth of the individual. Recreation is seen as a personal response, which grows out of personal experience. In the future, our task must apparently be to provide the individual with the necessary attitudes, knowledge, skills, and behavior in which *he* can make relevant leisure choices to realize personal goals. Typically, recreation opportunities have been designed by individuals lacking personal and immediate contact with participants.

In the future, Gliner suggests a reorientation of recreation to make it more relevant to the individual participant and consonant with the rapid pace of change, characteristic of a technological society.

In order to change recreation, to break the cycle caused by the acceptance of *a priori* rules and values, and the "entertain-me," "win-lose" ramifications which inevitably result, "recreation" must be taken at its

9. Donald E. Hawkins, *Community Education in a Leisure-Centered Society* (Washington, D.C.: AAHPER, 1970), pp. 10-26.
10. Edward Stainbrook, "Man Happening in a Leisure Society," *Leisure and the Quality of Life*, ed. Edwin J. Staley and Norman P. Miller, (Washington, D.C.: AAHPER, 1972), pp. 177-78.

word meaning: to *re-create*. Children on playgrounds would be permitted, or situations set up, whereby they could *create their own games and rules*, where games and rules could constantly be brought under fresh examination and altered, where the process of creating games and rules would take precedence over preserving outmoded forms of recreation. Emphasis would be on flexibility, on constant change, rather than bolstering up an already shaky status quo.[11]

LEISURE STUDIES: A HUMANISTIC DISCIPLINE

The college and university has only a minimal effect on the development of the whole personality. The family plays a significantly greater role in forming the attitudes, values, and beliefs of the growing child than any other institution. However, higher education does serve to build a foundation for a student's entry into society with respect to certain social and occupational roles. Colleges and universities must realize that even their institutional goals cannot be effectively achieved unless they assume some responsibility for facilitating the development of the total human personality.

A student is not a passive digester of knowledge elegantly arranged for him by superior artists of curriculum design. He listens, reads, thinks, studies, and writes at the same time that he feels, worries, hopes, loves, and hates. He engages in all of these activities not as an isolated individual but as a member of overlapping communities which greatly influence his reactions to the classroom experience. To teach the subject matter and ignore the realities of the student's life and the social systems of the college and community is hopelessly naive.

The simple reception of information by the student is no guarantee of learning. The student's *intellect* and *feelings* must both be engaged if learning is to occur. To engage his intellect is not too difficult. To engage his feelings, however, means communicating a relationship to him between the subject matter and quality of his own life. The task of the teacher should be to serve as a facilitator of the learning process and advance the student's perception of these relationships, to engage him *wholly* in discovery.

Goals of Humanistic Education

The following are four goals of humanistic education which serve to advance a student's receptiveness to the world around him and provide opportunities for self-enlightenment.

11. Robert Gliner, *American Society as a Social Problem* (New York: The Free Press, 1973), p. 331.

The first goal—self-esteem—refers to those feelings of competence or incompetence which derive from a person's subjective perceptions of his own experiences. An individual's self-esteem is an important beginning, because it forms the base of support for further behavioral development.

. . . the second goal [is] self-actualization—that is, growth toward fulfillment of his special potentialities and talents. Any individual's potentialities span a wide range of abilities . . . Growth toward self-actualization may take place relatively early in life and become part of the individual's special memories and feelings, or it may be an ongoing process which the individual experiences throughout life.

[The] third humanistic goal [is] self-understanding. If an individual's feelings and abilities are unique to him, he is in a better position, at least hypothetically, to determine what and how to learn. To profitably engage in this kind of introspection, however, requires considerable attention to the question "Who Am I?" beyond those early efforts to establish a base of self-esteem ("Am I competent?"). He must be able to identify his needs and their sources (such as cultural values), his abilities, his interests, and the interrelationships among these variables. By understanding these components on the self, he can more readily integrate them into a meaningful life-style which will bring him closer to social and emotional well-being.

The fourth and final humanistic goal moves beyond the self to social considerations . . . the adoption of such values as sensitivity toward others and cooperation should further upgrade the quality of interpersonal relations, especially if the first three goals have already been met.[12]

Leisure Resource Awareness Center

Students should be provided with a flexible and expansive learning environment to pursue independent study, self-paced programs, work-study programs, student-prepared video casettes, travel-study, computer assisted learning, community-based instruction, intensive group experiences, and many other efforts which foster human development and encourages an individual to be inquisitive, sensitive, and open to alternatives. Leisure Resource Awareness Centers, such as operated by Oregon State University's Department of Resource Recreation Management, serve as personal assessment centers. Such service centers may be equipped to include: (a.) information relative to all facets of recreation and leisure studies and services, (b) space available for a discussion area for both

12. Donald R. Hellison, *Humanistic Physical Education* (Englewood Cliffs, New Jersey: Prentice-Hall, Inc., 1973) pp. 110-112.

faculty and students, (c) a professional library, and (d) resources available for use (not restricted to recreation majors) that foster total university goals. Additionally, the personal assessment center provides counseling services which help identify a student's self-image, personal insight, interests, developed talents, undeveloped potential, personal goals, and professional aspiration. Throughout a student's stay in the university community his personal inventory would be updated periodically to reflect the student's maturation and learning growth. A series of learning experiences can be designed which might include a variety of self-paced media programs, community involvement, group interactive experiences, skill training, laboratory work, apprentice relationships to a practicing professional, and seminars.

As the activity concept of recreation programs is no longer suitable to the design of a contemporary leisure service delivery approach, similarly educational programs must be altered from an activity-skill-information orientation to a process orientation. This latter approach in recreation and leisure studies combines the insights of such root disciplines as sociology, psychology, anthropology, cybernetic systems, and communications with an effort to understand and assess the nature of recreation experience and how positive human results can be stimulated by it.

It is suggested by this new design that the context of the curricula be shifted to emphasize group process, human ecology, the character of urban and natural environments, organizational behavior, public affairs, management, the taxonomy of recreation outcomes, avocational counseling, community organization, social movements, informal educational methods, contemporary philosophical movements, program development, human growth potentials, environmental design, and other suitable topics which center on interrelationships of life roles and experiences and which focus on human development potential.

This process is vital to facilitate the transfer of learning from the classroom to the community. As the college must perceive the totality of the student's potential for learning, the organization and delivery of leisure service must be viewed within the community's total spectrum of social, educational, health, environmental, and transportation services. The preparation of students for work in contemporary society assumes a new urgency in which such vexing and pervasive concerns as poverty, racism, urban squalor, malnutrition, and illiteracy must be considered to be part of the related functions of recreation and leisure service personnel, and which affect the ability of the individual to participate in organized recreation offerings.

INTEGRATING UNIVERSITY AND COMMUNITY

Colleges and universities have traditionally prepared students for work as facility managers. They were taught the fundamentals of the conduct of games and activities, rule formulation, scheduling, safety inspection, and grounds maintenance, with a minimum consideration for the *effects* of activity and environment upon individual participants. Twenty years ago this was not a major concern, in fact, most recreators were vigorously attempting to increase the short supply of facility personnel in order to maintain the strength and durability of the "chain-link fences" that surrounded and protected their investments.

The "isolationist" perspective is no longer valid. Two-and four-year colleges and universities must begin to prepare students to serve as dynamic *community figures,* which will enable them to move beyond the protective confines of the "chain-link" fences and out into the streets and neighborhoods where the development of people, improvement of the community, and concern for the social problems of our time will be embraced within the leisure service delivery system.

The *humanistic* consideration of recreation and leisure service personnel as being *encourager-catalysts* (as defined in chapter 5) of the poor, disabled, indigent, and able-bodied, represents an essential thrust for *all* human service fields. The design of such curricula suggests that students need to be prepared to be placed in positions which will require them to serve as agents for community change. The traditional role of the community recreation worker as primarily a facility manager is no longer applicable and is largely dysfunctional with respect to societal needs and its demands for leisure service. What is the worth of medical science, progressive civil and human rights legislation, humane and just Supreme Court rulings, and technological advancements, if we are unable to learn, or have access to, the necessary requisites to live an enriching and full life?

The entire environment can provide opportunity for learning, and it is paramount that we encourage and foster the mesh of university and community to increase the transfer of learning to subsequent human actions. Environmental awareness, recreation, adult education, health, and a variety of human concerns should be treated as *compatible* and *interrelated* goals for education in terms of their impact on the quality of life. The task of two- and four-year colleges and universities should be to educate students to serve as community *encouragers-catalysts* who can interpret to community members that every phase of living, including leisure, can have meaning for them.

Several communities have developed philosophical statements which embrace the concept of outreach and a human service advocate perspective of recreation and leisure personnel. The city of Long Beach is an example:

> Recreation serves as a catalyst within the community to create a climate for developing leisure-time activities that enhance the quality of life and meet the basic needs shared by all human beings—the need to belong, to achieve, to be recognized, to have status, to acquire and use skills, to have a creative outlook. Recreation develops sportsmanship, leadership, physical fitness, appreciation of the cultural arts, conservation of the environment, and education for leisure. Recreation creates opportunities to promote family units and develop understanding and positive interaction among people.[13]

One of the goals of the city of Long Beach's Recreation Commission is to "be alert and responsive to current and changing recreational needs and interests in the community." Accordingly, the Commission enacted a series of objectives to carry out the intent of the goals. In order to fulfill the objectives, the Commission outlined a series of evaluative criteria for the staff of the service area.

A. Establish an advisory council within six months of the adoption of these objectives.

B. Identify formal and informal recreation-related interest groups in the service area and determine potential relationships with the department program by defining goals and objectives within six months of the adoption of these objectives.

C. Identify within six months of the adoption of these objectives, socioeconomic characteristics through demographic data of the service area with particular reference to those characteristics which have relevance for program planning.

D. Visit a minimum of three different community/leisure serving agencies within the service area, per quarter, to assess areas of mutual cooperation and accomplishment of similar agency objectives.

E. Visit with a minimum of five homeowners and a manager of at least one business within the service area each month, to discuss and explain the objectives of their recreation programs and to ask for suggestions for providing better service.

F. Visit or communicate with a minimum of one public, private or commercial recreation agency per quarter to assess new, workable, or successful program ideas.[14]

13. "Statement of Philosophy," the Coordinated Plan of Municipal and School Recreation, Recreation Commission, Long Beach, June 11, 1970.
14. "Proposed Statement of Objectives," Coordinated Municipal and School Recreation, Recreation Commission, Long Beach, N. D.

PREPARING COMMUNITY CATALYSTS

The intent of two- and four-year institutions of higher learning must be approached in such a way, using developmental principles, to educate students to be able to improve the capability of individuals and organizations to identify and evaluate alternative courses of action. It is suggested by this perspective, the concept of leisure service delivery, that the traditional organizational approach to meeting the needs of people must be altered, and with it, a restructuring of the content and learning process of educational institutions.

For curriculum reform to be effective in preparing the student to serve as community catalyst, it must have as its reference point the student and his developing personality. Each student:

1. Needs to acquire a positive and realistic conception of his own abilities in the world of higher learning and in the world at large
2. Needs to reach the point of being able to see the structure and interrelations of knowledge so that he may being the process of forming judgments on his own
3. Needs to see the relevance of higher learning to the quality of his own life and to see that life in relation to the new kind of judgments he will have to make

A NEW AGE OF LEARNING AND LIVING

People are no longer seen as being apart from the natural world but a part of it. However, there are still many fragmented elements in the world which tend to deter human growth, including, population and food supply, changes in the biosphere, poverty, and the developmental gap, biological and psychological alternatives through human and civil rights.

> The problem is not to be solved through "progress" of the civilization in which it is inherent. The "Great Refusal" of youth to go along with the system has provided not only a retarding force, but a whole range of positive, educational leisure modes (from meditation to militancy) directed at creation of alternatives [including participation in scheduled classes to self-directed, mind expanding experiences in leisure service programs] .[15]

We are on the threshold of a New Era, similar to the Protestant Reformation, as we are experiencing a rapid shift in basic, previously unquestioned cultural premises, and seeing its pervasiveness impinging

---

15. Judson Jerome, "Radical Premises in Collegiate Reform," *Let the Entire Community Become Our University,* ed. Philip C. Ritterbush (Washington, D.C.: Acropolis Books, Ltd., 1972), p. 203.

upon every aspect of social institutions and custom.[16] It should be the goal of educators at a national level to take such actions as will foster the peaceful transition to the "New Age" premises and values (which are compatible with the founding values and the overarching national purpose) and which are uniquely suited to preserving the planet's habitability and to creating a society conducive to the individual's achieving the highest degree of self-fulfillment. They include, preeminently, an image of man as part of a whole, potentially capable of an awareness transcending ordinary awareness, in which his identity with the whole and his role as chooser of the experiences that happen to him become apparent. Thus man is viewed as a part of nature, partner in the adventure of evolution.

We are moving at an ever-increasing rate toward the breakdown of conditions requisite to human dignity through fragmentation, perceptual change, ideological and aesthetic bankruptcy, and increasing depersonalization of experience. A massive change of consciousness has resulted in a revolution of awareness, of values, of life-styles, as a counter to alienation and dehumanization of life; indeed it is broader than cultural change, it seems to be part of the evolutionary development toward mass self-enlightenment. Writers such as Theodore Roszak, Margaret Mead, Robert Theobald, Philip Slater, and Lewis Mumford have described this *total* revolution, simultaneous on all fronts, which is occurring around us. In this transitional period, leisure service and leisure studies institutions are mainly serving the process inadvertently—by providing gathering places for young people and intellectuals, communities of concern and collections of resources to be recycled for new purposes, purposes to which the very structures of the institutions are antithetical.

Various efforts providing for open admissions and external degree programs are all devices for giving credit for life experiences. But the continued pressure is for economic attainment, not essentially for education, and the drive for unlimited economic betterment is, in the long run, an ecological and psychological cul-de-sac.

> Circa 1972 the American utopian dream is for each nuclear family to have a private home, probably on about a quarter-acre lot, within easy reach of a metropolitan center, with air-conditioning, central heating, a complex set of appliances, a couple of automobiles, telephones, television sets, expensive (mostly packaged and barely nutritious) meals, free (compulsory) schooling through the bachelor's degree, high quality medical, police and fire-protection services—

16. Willis W. Harman, "Some Implications of 'Alternative Futures' Research for Education Policy" (Stanford, Calif.: Education Policy Research Center, Stanford Research Center, July, 1970).

and so on. The demand is for "conveniences" such as most middle-class people enjoy, if that is what they do with them. We class social groups as "'disadvantaged" until they achieve that level of consumption, and other nations are merely "developing" until they have attained it.[17]

The values of the New Age are in many cases the reverse of those which go into present definitions of standard of living (an anti-GNP, no-growth throught consistent with ecological concerns and New Age values). People who have not experienced firsthand the well-advertised "advantages" of American middle-class culture, who have not suffered the anomie of life in *Better Homes and Gardens,* are not likely to be aware of the wealth around them. "We are conditioned to be blind to the girl next door and to pursue at great expense the plastic Bunny in the store window."[18]

The mass changes in consciousness are not likely to be motivated by appeals to self-denial and reincarnation. The task will be to remove the plastic wrapping from the natural world around us, a nature which includes our own bodies and one another. Those who have not yet been involved in the aspirations promoted by the system have a great deal to teach us concerning the necessary redefinition of personhood and wealth. For example, the kind of consciousness Harman refers to depends upon an understanding of human nature which extends beyond the materialistic, economic, reductionist definition which was a convergence of the industrial age. Other cultures than the dominant Western one ("other" including subcultures within the latter) have kept alive the conceptions of spirituality and soul and psychic awareness which are in disuse to a great degree in our own society. The New Age defines wealth in terms of nature, of process and experience rather than acquisition. Jerome warns us that there is a need to consider the value system of the New Age or we may face destruction.

> The new scarcities are of unobstructed sunlight, clean air and water, uncontaminated foods, honesty and love in human relations, and the body, with all its riches. These commodities are abundant in the world at large and will be so in our own culture when the hang-ups, perversions, and unnecessary exploitation of the old culture are eliminated.[19]

FOUR LEVELS OF LEARNING

Presently most institutions of higher learning perceive their primary task as laying down a host of facts for students who are expected to retain

17. Jerome, *Collegiate Reform,* p. 205.
18. Ibid., p. 206.
19. Ibid., p. 207.

them and regurgitate them on an objective examination. If they successfully handle this assignment students may be expected to grasp the meaning of their education. This is the *first* level of learning. A *second* level of
learning occurs when two facts are interrelated. Some colleges and universities find this approach more appropriate. The *third* level of learning
occurs when an individual improves his performance within an existing
system of understanding. The *fourth* level of learning, as articulated by
Robert Theobald, evolves when one is able to perceive the nature of the
present system and to reexamine it with a view to discovering how the total
structure can be modified and changed.[20]

TWO TRACK LEISURE STUDIES CURRICULUM

As mentioned earlier in the text we have seen a fusion of life roles.
David Gray comments on this phenomenon.

> The old pattern of division of life experience into work, leisure, educa-
> tion, civic, and family roles with a life-style, value system, schedule,
> set of expectations, clothes, language, and other characteristics to
> match each role, has declined substantially. The effort to improve
> life experience and to integrate a stable personality in a secure physical
> and emotional environment, led by the social psychologists, has dem-
> onstrated that division of life into a series of roles inhibits development
> of a secure personality. Many people no longer try to decide whether
> they are working or enjoying a leisure experience. The primary focus
> now is on improving life experience whatever the character of the
> activity of the moment.[21]

Gray's invitation to learning and living to be synthesized by educational institutions serves as a basis for the development of a two- or possibly three-track recreation and leisure studies program. The first track,
the traditional and dominant recreation and leisure service professional
preparation with a supervised, residency internship, provides students
with a sufficient background to enter the field, equipped to handle first-
line supervision jobs. As indicated earlier in this chapter there is a need
for recreation educators to realign their service programs to focus more
specifically on the needs and developing personalities of students to meet
their growth expectations while they are pursuing a professional degree.
The second path, a studies in leisure and human development program, is
a proposed nonoccupational track, which emphasizes exploration in self

20. Robert Theobald, *An Alternative Future for America II* (Chicago: The Swallow
Press, Inc., 1970).
21. David E. Gray, "Looking Backward From 2001: Notes on the Education of Recreation and Park Professionals 1975-2000" (Paper presented to the Society of Park and
Recreation Educators on Recreation and Park Education in the Fourth Quartile, 1973).

and individual growth potential, with either an independent senior growth experience project or expanded curricular exploration in an area of interest which is pursued in the community or at the university. There might be a core selection of courses pertaining to the relevance of leisure in American life, and additional areas of study grouped under (a) skills for personal growth, (b) skills for group awareness, (c) skills for community-societal awareness, and (d) special group interest/sensitivity (such as handicapped, elderly, minority, and ethnic groups, etc.). The senior project might involve such areas of personal growth experience as (a) research and writing; (b) site exploration, observation, participation and reporting (pertaining to nursery schools, day-care centers, cooperative programs, and tiny tot programs, for example); c) initiation of a community service program (half-way house, board and care home, convalescent hospital, etc.); (d) service as an aid/intern to legislative advocate, assemblyman, senator, etc.; (e) development of a project related to aesthetic experience (in poetry, music, photography, dance, etc.); and (f) participation as a community organizer for effecting change. A third possible leisure studies curricular track might include graduate studies in recreation and leisure, with an internship emphasizing research, education/teaching/counseling and guidance and/or consultation. This latter approach may well be crucial if leisure studies curricula expect to generate the respect and impact they seek on campus and in the community in general.

The study of leisure is a multifaceted educational concern. It requires drawing upon many disciplines for insight and focus. The measure of humanity increasingly rests on the ability of all areas of society to willingly integrate in order to better support and nurture human development. This is precisely the reasoning that prompts directors of leisure studies curricula to focus their curricula upon an interdisciplinary approach and allow for more students to select a path which provides meaning and growth potential to their lives, whether it be vocational or avocational. Members in society in the future may well have to select a work or non-work path for a major part of their lives. Others may not have a choice. If educational institutions are to provide innovative preparation for life-long learning, then there is a profound need to make available curricular alternatives which mesh more realistically with human needs.

SUMMARY

The aim of a humanistic perspective is to develop new patterns of goals which will enable people to begin the process of overcoming their weaknesses and thus develop their own human potential. Our task in recreation and leisure education should be to create problem-centered courses which combine study of the problem with action to deal with it. Students, then will come to perceive their own capabilities and learn to contribute where it is most relevant. This is the realm of the community catalyst-encourager, who seeks to help people come to identify and solve their own problems and realize their full potential.

Education is now seen as a lifetime process. The entire environment can provide opportunity for learning. It is important that leisure service catalysts encourage and foster the mesh of school and community to increase the transfer of learning to subsequent human actions. The central purpose of an education for leisure development curriculum must be the fostering of self-expression and self-development through human involvement.

chapter NINE
leisure
and work:
a forward
look

what to look for in this chapter...

The Outmoded Work Ethic
Poverty of Abundance

Historical Meanings of Work

Changing Human Goals of Life and Work

Emergence of Three and Four-Day Workweeks
Flexibility and Adjusted Work Patterns

New Worker Options

The spread of automation in industry has led to speculation on the replacement of the role of work as central to our culture. The depreciation of leisure expression as justifiable only as it relates to its release from work time relegates off-the-job living to second-rate status. However, there has been a shift in the status of leisure, primarily as a result of the demeaning and unfulfilling work opportunities found in the assembly line, but also due to monotonous, repetitive work elsewhere in business and industry.

Workers are looking for alternative sources from which they can derive status, role, and identity, since work has lost much of it ability to influence and command their moral identification and loyalty. They are challenging basic assumptions about work and looking for a broadening of worker responsibilities, rotation of job assignments, shift to four-day and even three-day workweeks, and opportunities to determine their own hours of work. The humanization of the work setting and conditions of employment reflect a recognition on the part of people that they desire a balanced life, a meaningful job, and a fulfilling and satisfying life away from work. Work, as we know it, is not expected to disappear, but the newly emerging knowledge-service worker desires a more autonomous, less routinized work situation than has been characteristic of the assembly-line and some industrial settings.

POVERTY OF ABUNDANCE

Work has served as an important source of moral integration. It has also made America the most affluent country in the world. America continues to manufacture and produce goods at a tremendous pace. However, there are signs that all of this production is not needed, primarily from a standpoint of economic individual necessity. Work has been the center of our lives, but it no longer is a meaningful expression for a growing number of people. The accumulation of material possessions has been the primary motivating force for a large number of workers. There has been no saturation point to acquire what one does not own.

The necessity to acquire things resulted in a mania to consume what was produced, even though primary subsistence needs were satisfied. The Puritan work ethic, once a dominant force in our society, has been challenged by some who feel that there are other values to be derived from work and nonwork. Additionally, many social, economic, and political theorists and policy makers have explored the consequences of the lack of need for workers and of its potential impact upon a population uncommitted to a work tradition. The consumer orientation which marks contemporary society reflects a population which desires to use up goods. If one were not to be employed, it would be difficult for that person to buy goods at the current rate of production-consumption, and *this could* conceivably result in a highly disruptive situation.

While our Gross National Product has continually expanded, it seems that our society's sense of purpose and direction has increasingly become unclear and muddled. Affluence has not led to a "heaven on earth." Therefore, people are desiring more fulfilling experiences outside of work. Alienation and boredom are pervasive aspects of contemporary work life. Manual work is said to be boring because of its monotony and repetiveness, while white-collar work is boring because of its bureaucratic character, which leaves little responsibility to the individual.

The average American worker's attitude is changing with respect to work. He now desires an opportunity to do meaningful work and to achieve and grow on the job. While leisure affords the worker a chance to realize personal goals and ambitions not realized in work, satisfaction may also be gained through the humanization of work. Studies have shown that the work situation would be vastly improved if jobs provided more automony, interesting work, and an opportunity for the individual to be active, to grow, and to achieve.

HISTORICAL MEANINGS OF WORK

The concept of work has generated many and varied meanings throughout history. C. Wright Mills has noted several interpretations of work.[1] Work has meant a mere source of livelihood for some, the most significant part of one's inner life, an expression of self, boundful duty, or the development of man's universal nature. Historically most views have ascribed to work an extrinsic meaning, holding little or no internal value.

To the ancient Greeks, where mechanical labor was done by slaves, work brutalized the mind—it made man unfit for the practice of virtue and enjoyment in higher, intellectual pursuits (leisure).

In primitive Christianity, work was regarded as punishment for sin. It also was seen as serving the ulterior ends of charity, health of body and soul, and warding off the evil thoughts of idleness. However, work was of no worth in itself.

In the time of St. Augustine, work took on organizational forms. For monks, work was obligatory, although it was to be alternated with prayer, and even then it was to engage them only enough to supply the real needs

1. C. Wright Mills, *White Collar: The American Middle Class* (New York: Oxford University Press, 1951), pp. 215-23.

of the monastery. The church elders gave priority to pure meditation on divine matters, above even the intellectual work of reading and copying in the monastery.

Under Luther, work was first established in the modern mind as "the base and key to life." It was believed that all who could work should do so. Idleness was regarded as an unnatural and evil evasion. It was seen that to maintain oneself by work was a way of serving God. During this period work was first valued as a religious path to salvation.

Calvin's idea of predestination prodded man further into the rhythm of modern work. It was necessary to act rationally and methodically in the work, and continuously and hard, if one was to be among those who would be elected. Strong-willed, untiring work based on religious conviction, not contemplation or retreat, would ease guilt and lead to a good and pious life.

The Renaissance concept of work saw it as a spur rather than a drag on the development of man. By his own involvement and activity, man could accomplish anything.

The Protestant sects encouraged and justified the social development of a type of man capable of ceaseless, methodical labor. The psychology of the religious man and the economic man thus coincided. Burgeois man lived in and through this philosophical premise.

During the nineteenth century there were several reactions against the utilitarian meaning assigned to work. Ruskin believed that the total product of work should go to the worker. He glorified what he supposed was in the work of the medieval artisan. To Marx, the essence of human beings rested upon their work, both what they produced and how they produced. Essentially, both men drew upon the Renaissance view of man as a tool user.

There have been two dominant philosophies of work: (1) The various forms of Protestantism have been the most influential on the philosophy of modern industrial work. Work is seen primarily as an activity which derives meaning from religious sanctions. Work justifications are not intrinsic to the activity and experience, but are religious rewards. (2) The Renaissance view of work ,which sees it as intrinsically meaningful, centered on the technical craftsmanship—the manual and mental operations—of the work process itself. It identifies the reasons for work in the work itself and not in any ulterior realm or consequence. This humanistic view of work as craftsmanship values the technical processes of work as gratifying, not income, status, power, or any other extrinsic form of enticement.

The craftman's pattern does not involve a split between work and leisure. The simple self-expression of leisure and the creation of ulterior value of work are combined in "work-as-craftsmanship." The craftsman or artist expresses himself at the same time and in the same act as he creates value. *He is at work and leisure in the same act.* The craftsman perspective of work provides a possible future model for work in a highly technological society (similar to Johnston's "turquoise" concept of work expressed in chapter 1) where such activity may only be needed for essential survival goods and a few "extras," because automation will assume most of the production responsibilities. The worker's livelihood in technological society, as with the craftsman during the Renaissance, may well be determined and infused in his entire style of living.

Primitive man does not separate basic economic from aesthetic and religious needs. Herzberg, Mausner, Synderman relate how primitive man engages in work which produces the food he consumes, the clothing he wears, the dwelling in which he lives.[2] He is motivated because his tasks are integrated and are related to his immediate needs.

> There is no doubt, for example, that the builder of a primitive canoe, who is fulfilling aesthetic as well as economic needs, probably shows a high level of motivation . . . Similarly, the carver of a totem pole, who is fulfilling religious and social needs, probably has an equally high level of motivation.[3]

The opportunity for individual growth distinguishes primitive man from modern man. While there often is little opportunity for primitive man to break tradition and develop unique modes of behavior, he has an opportunity to be fulfilled through responsibility and skills of his craftsmanship. The worker on the assembly line and in large organizations no longer experiences a direct relationship between work and biological needs. He has substituted indirect relationships in a society *based on* division of labor and a consumption-oriented economy. While our highly technological society cannot return to primitive life characterized by folk communities, it can return to a sense of responsibility and pride in work through increased worker recognition, achievement, advancement potential, responsibility, and enrichment of work itself.[4]

Living An Integrated Life

Individuals are no longer motivated primarily by materialistic goals. There is a yearning to realize "higher" level needs—personal growth, self-esteem and self-actualization—whether it be at work or leisure. Work and

2. Frederick Herzberg, Bernard Mausner, and Barbara Synderman, *Motivation to Work*, 2nd ed. (New York: John Wiley and Sons, Inc., 1959), pp. 121-122.
3. Ibid.
4. Ibid., pp. 59-83.

leisure, as previously noted in chapter 7, are purposeful human activities which may be directed toward the satisfaction of human needs and desires. Human needs are *not* limited exclusively to the acquisition of material wealth. Technology has enlarged the range of options available, and people are increasingly choosing to pursue satisfaction of nonmaterial needs rather than to continue the production and acquisition of traditional economic wealth.

As more members of society move to the point of satisfying security and material needs, it is reasonable to "expect not only a widespread tendency to give up additional material goods in favor of nonmaterial goals but also a desire to integrate and balance our lives."[5] The net effect of the pursuit of self-actualization is a desire to avoid the compartmentalization of our lives, evidenced by the impact that industrialization had on the dichotomizing of work and free time. Best states: "As our social, self-esteem, and growth [self-actualization] needs become more important to us, we will be less likely to endure interpersonal alienation, repression of our individual dignity, and the absence of growth opportunities in our work situations."[6]

It is reasonable to expect that the activity of work will become a positive and valued part of the human experience. Its orientation will have to be altered as we have neared the saturation point with security and material gain as the guiding motivations of our work efforts. The desire for a more holistic style of life by some will necessitate the integration of work to fulfill the needs and aspirations of our total existence rather than solely of our limited economic concerns. "Essentially we must reaffirm the meaning of work as a human activity aimed at the fulfillment of real and total human needs."[7]

Changing Human Goals

A contention of several futurists and economists is that man will define and express his future existence by the style of life he desires. Accordingly, the table "Types of Society and Changing Human Goals of Life and Work," illustrates the changes in human needs that have occurred in the twentieth century.

Mitchell suggests that security, belongingness, and ego levels are "deficiency" states, that is, specific and satiable need patterns arise from internal or external deficiences. The growth level is *not* a deficiency state

5. Fred Best, *The Future of Work* (Englewood Cliffs, New Jersey: Prentice-Hall, Inc., 1973), p. 3.
6. Ibid., p. 3.
7. Ibid., p. 16.

TABLE 9.1

TYPES OF SOCIETY AND CHANGING HUMAN GOALS OF LIFE AND WORK

	Security (1900-1930s)	Belongingness (1940-1950s)	Ego—Self-Esteem (1960-1970s)	Growth—Self-Actualization (Future)
Dominant Value Patterns	Concern for surviving All nations experience emergencies which threaten life-giving essentials	Conformity to group norm The sense that there is a "right" and "wrong" way of looking at things	Achievement "Success"—typical American Frequently expressed as visible, even ostentatious	Concern for living up to one's inner potential thru full expression Emotionally mature person is able to express himself fully, tapping full range of his abilities
Psychological Traits	Insecure, fearful, ruled by appetites Little moral sense, uncooperative, dependent, rigid, seek familiar, few social contacts, status quo orientation, afraid of new, intense	Conforming, mass-oriented, puritanical, conventional, conservative, needs praise, segmented, nonexperimental, outer-directed, rewards virtue, "togetherness"—way of life	Upwardly mobile, Materialistic, "I" world, ambitious, hard working, power-oriented, status seeking, competitive, "better than" syndrome Winner/loser approach	Individualistic, expressive, accepting of self and others, spontaneous, problem-centered, inner driven, creative, unhostile, flexible, self-reliant, likes unexplored, motivated by ends
Typical Origins	Socially deprived Extreme poverty Lack of opportunity to grow Failure to get the usual rewards	Conventional mores in family Dependency and conformity cultivated through differential reward Criticized for unusual ideas	Keeping-up-with Joneses Family values Wealth, status-conscious background Rewards given in terms of pay-off	An upbringing that reacts to experimentation without censoring
Typical Groups	Minorities Poor Disenfranchised Marginal farmers Small businessman	The organization man Middle-class Speciality cults Routine teachers Happy tract-dwellers Hero worshipers	Business executives Political leaders College professor Noveau riches Professional and technical workers	No typical groups, only individuals

Source: Adapted from Arnold Mitchell, "Human Needs and the Changing Goals of Life and Work," **The Future of Work**, ed. Fred Best, (Englewood Cliffs, New Jersey: Prentice-Hall, Inc., 1973), pp. 32-36.

—the individual is merely trying to express himself to his fullest potential. As a person grows from one need level to another, one would expect his values and attitudes to shift—thus influencing the type of society he would seek to build. Note the chart on page —— (a graph developed by Arnold Mitchell) which depicts various types of alternative societies for 1990 and

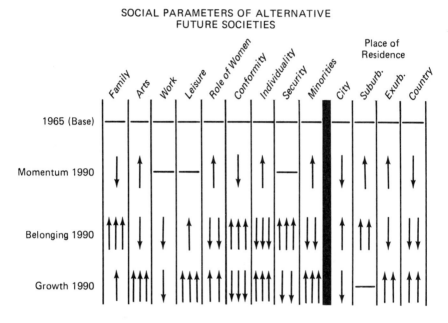

Figure 9.1. "Social Parameters of Alternative Future Societies," taken from Arnold Mitchell, "Human Needs and the Changing Goals of Life and Work," **The Future of Work,** ed. Fred Best (Englewood Cliffs, N.J.: Prentice-Hall, Inc., 1973), p. 42.

the future. The Momentum Society depicts the society we expect to evolve by 1990 if present trends continue. The Belonging Society indicates the movement of society from a survival and security orientation to a more collective mode of life. The Growth Society would yield a nation of self-actualizing people, an extremely difficult projection to make. The expectation would be that such a society would be highly efficient, utilizing every technology to improve output per man-hour, so that all could be well cared for with fewer working much shorter hours.

The desire for a holistic pattern of life and Maslow's theory of total human need relates to the importance of *integrating* our need-satisfying efforts (work and leisure) into balanced lives and synergic work situations. Best relates: "As human beings, we have important needs that extend far beyond the mere satisfaction of our material wants, and truly humane work must integrate these needs in a way which gives our lives balance, completeness, and purpose."[8]

New approaches to work must be developed to meet the changing demands of a population increasingly characterized by service and knowledge work, involving more autonomous, less routinized conditions which have created new goals and options for future human endeavor. In the future, it will conceivably be the *totality* of our human needs which will guide and shape the evolving conditions of work and leisure.

While leisure service agencies are not primarily concerned about work, they must be oriented to the needs and interests of community members who are looking for opportunities for fulfillment and realization of personal goals through leisure. Work influences other attitudes and behavior. A society of alienated, groping, confused people, poses serious leisure problems—as it is in their uncommitted time that the pressures of personal and institutional life bring about confusion, disorder, and chaos.

The challenge of the future for leisure service agencies involves the need to restore in the individual, a sense of purpose, an opportunity for achievement, challenge, mastery, and the freedom to set one's own pace. While the humanization of work may result in individual self-realization, it must be recognized that increasingly, the nonwork environment will serve as an important source of fulfillment and meaning.

THREE- AND FOUR-DAY WORKWEEKS: TIMEWEALTH

While the greatest gains in leisure, as a block of discretionary time, have occurred largely as a result of labor union demands, the most recent reductions of the workweek have been initiated by management. It is recognized that the shortened workweek is a new recruitment device. However, the flexibility of life-style patterns in a postindustrial society necessitates that workers be given options in their nonwork hours to allow opportunities for self-paced living. There is increasing recognition that people should be allowed to exercise greater control over their work and leisure lives and pursue subsistence requirements according to their *own* particular life regimen.

Riva Poor's book, *4 Days, 40 Hours* reports on a trend of industry, particularly small companies, to reduce the workweek into four days.[9]

8. Ibid.
9. Riva Poor, ed., *4 Days, 40 Hours: Reporting a Revolution in Work and Leisure* (Cambridge, Massachusetts: Bursk and Poor Publishing Co., 1970).

The sacred forty-hour week is undergoing a serious reconsideration as employees in both the private and public sectors are beginning to receive the benefits of technology. The worker is beginning to *maximize* his potential in both work and leisure according to a schedule which agrees with his personal rhythm of life. The new work schedules afford the individual worker an opportunity to seek creative and service-oriented outlets not ordinarily possible with only two days off work. With an increase in the proportionate amount of free time needed to recuperate from work generated from a reduced workweek, employees will have new opportunities for self-expression and satisfaction not possible with the rigid five-day, forty-hour schedule. As a result of four-day workweek patterns most workers studied by Poor and Steele report they spend their time differently.[10] The shortened workweek provides an opportunity for bunching leisure, and opens up new possible forms of expression with the extended weekend. Changes in leisure activities involved increased spending; resting, relaxation, and loafing; creative activities, such as hobbies, reading, and educational endeavors; yard work and more time for family involvement. Poor and Steele report on the most significant theme of the increased leisure, which indicates that workers of all occupational classifications, choose unorganized, relaxing activities over organized or disciplined ones.

> The most striking increase is reported in the category or participant activities (travel, fishing and hunting, other hobbies, athletics, swimming, and boating). More than half of the workers state that they travel regularly now, compared to one fourth beforehand. The vast changes that would result from increased travel if the 4-day week were to become widely accepted are difficult to imagine. One can only speculate that the demand for recreational facilities and travel services would mushroom beyond our wildest current imaginings.[11]

The four-day workweek serves as a kind of salvation. The erosion of work and declining Protestant work ethic is being replaced by a humanistic ethic which places value on individual fulfillment and realization of personal goals in concert with societal goals. The reduced workweek serves as a gateway to flexible new experiences not previously available to the workingman and only partially realized through once-a-year vacations accrued from a year's labor. Now he is able to pursue personally motivated goals more often. Additionally, speculation on the eventual adoption of the year-round school program suggests that members of the family may have an opportunity to share this new found leisure—timewealth—together.

10. Riva Poor and James L. Steele, "Work and Leisure: The Reactions of People at 4-Day Firms," *4 Days, 40 Hours,* op. cit., pp. 105-122.
11. Ibid., p. 116.

According to Millard Faught the creation of a three-day workweek, ten hours of work for three days, yields four days of usable leisure, and results in timewealth, a new form of wealth previously unavailable to the worker.[12] In highly industrialized societies, the work rhythm of life is highly routinized. In postindustrial societies the need for such rigid pattern is unnecessary. More flexible life-style patterns are possible in a highly technological society like the United States. The fusion of work and other segments of institutional life results in an integration and synthesis of all segments of community life. A reduced workweek and more flexible life-style pattern allows the individual to perceive the environment in its totality, and eliminates the fragmentation and rigidity of participation in society.

The steady reduction of the workweek has led workers to be more conscious of leisure and increased the demand for professional recreation and leisure service workers.[13] Future work and schooling arrangements will necessitate more diverse and flexible leisure provisions. In a postindustrial society where people will have several options, several approaches to patterning leisure service opportunities will be required to meet the varied demands, life-styles, and cultural tastes of people.

In a study of senior union blue-collar employees of Kaiser Steel Corporation who receive a thirteen week's paid vacation, Klausner found contrary to expectations, that the workers reported strong, favorable reactions to the extended leisure experience and indicated greater personal and family integration as a result.[14] This study and others have consistently shown how work serves a means, not an end for the employee. When workers are freed from the requirement of work, they happily pursue family activities and individual hobbies and pastimes. Nonwork time is increasingly being recognized as an opportunity for self-growth and a source for individual and family integration.

TOWARD A LEISURE ETHIC: NEW WORKER OPTIONS

As work loses its influence as a central life interest among many industrial and service workers, leisure is emerging as a primary source of fulfillment and identity. A holistic work-leisure relationship has been articulated by Stanley Parker, in which an individual recognizes that all parts

12. Millard C. Faught, *More Timewealth For You* (New York: Pyramid Books, 1969).
13. J. D. Hodgson, "Leisure and the American Worker," *Leisure Today* I (1972).
14. William J. Klausner, "Extended Leisure and the Family," *Educating for the New Leisure* (Conference Proceedings, February 2-5, 1969, University Extension, University of California, Riverside).

of his life are integrated. This social pattern does not seek to maximize work over leisure or vice versa, rather, it seeks to develop a *fusion* of work and leisure spheres in the society as a whole. According to Parker:

> In this fusion, work may lose its present characteristic feature of constraint and gain creativity now associated mainly with leisure, while leisure may lose its present characteristic feature of opposition to work and gain the status—now associated mainly with the product of work— of a resource worthy of planning to provide the greatest possible human satisfaction.[15]

The separation of work and leisure in most industrialized nations resulted in people having to give up some opportunity for personal expression to satisfy family subsistence needs. Greater value is placed on the sanctity of work, diminishing leisure to "spare time" status. The work ethic—a quantitative, utilitarian view of man's purpose and role in life—has negated purposeless expression as a viable activity.

By some accounts we are on the *threshold* of an abundant age where most Americans already have access to extensive amounts of free time, a result of a shortening of the workweek, longer vacation periods, earlier retirement, longer life-span, increased discretionary income, etc. However, as noted by Staffan Linder, while one would expect most sectors of the community to have an abundance of unobligated time at their disposal and be enjoying their leisure, we observe to the contrary that there is a scarcity of time and more hectic life tempo.[16] The scarcity of time results from persistent consumption pressures requiring man to work overtime or "moonlight" resulting in a cancellation of expanded free time.

In advanced technological societies it becomes increasingly important for the emotional, symbolic, and affective aspects of life to be integrated into everyday life to overcome the stultifying forces of the industrial work cycle which provide little gratification. The movement towards three- and four-day workweeks is seen as an opportunity for American workers to free man from his humdrum existence and begin to liberate him for wholly new forms of experiencing, which he is free to choose himself.

Additionally, Maslow's theory of human needs relates to the importance of integrating our need-satisfying efforts into balanced lives and a fused work-leisure relationship. As human beings, we have important needs that extend beyond the satisfaction of lower-level security and ma-

15. Stanley R. Parker, *The Future of Work and Leisure* (New York: Praeger Publishers, Inc., 1971), p. 122.
16. Staffan Linder, *The Harried Leisure Class* (New York: Columbia University Press, 1970).

terial wants, and truly fulfilling work and leisure must integrate all our needs in a way which gives our lives balance, completeness, and purpose. Work is not expected to disappear in the future. The new knowledge and service workers are expected to work under more autonomous, less routinized conditions, to create new goals and options for future work endeavors.

SUMMARY

As our society becomes more leisure-centered, the opportunity is presented for people to unite the values of personal work fulfillment and contemplation into an *integrated, life-enhancing experience.* An age of leisure may provide the individual with an opportunity to select work schedules and allow for the spontaneous execution of personal desires at the moment they occur. The humanization of both the work setting and the conditions of employment is concrete evidence of the desire of people for a balanced life, a meaningful job, and a fulfilling and satisfying life away from work.

The shortened workweek offers a new variety of choice to the modern work who has traditionally had few personal options. While workers are relatively free to spend the money they earn, the modern industrial regime has typically denied the worker similar freedom in choosing the work routine schedule by which he earns these dollars. The increased recognition that people differ in their needs and rhythm of life has led to the belief that individuals should be permitted to pursue work and leisure according to their own particular life-style regiment. In the future, it is the *totality* of our human needs which will guide and shape the evolving goals and conditions of work and leisure. We are not one-dimensional, economic men. Rather, as a result of humanistic psychology, we have discovered that we have powerful, complex "higher needs" which are identified as social belongingness, self-esteem, and personal growth. Technology has enlarged the options of choice, and it may be the synergistic fusion of work and leisure which will foster human use of these options to pursue self-fulfillment and avoid compartmentalization of our lives evidenced by today's dichotomy involving work, leisure, and community life.

the future
of leisure

---

what to look for in this chapter...

Social Change and Leisure
Fragmented Life Pattern
Integrated Life Pattern

The Impact of Leisure on Culture
Fusion of Work and Leisure

The "Problem" of Leisure

Leisure and the Quality of Life

Utopian Forecast of Society—Cyberculture

The Value of Leisure—An Ecological Perspective

The Future of Leisure
A Concern for Human Development

Photograph by Harold M. Lambert

SOCIAL CHANGE AND LEISURE

Social change has become part of the human condition, although some people have operated on the assumption that society is relatively static. The pace of change affects every part of our social lives, including personal values, morality, religion, and leisure, all seemingly remote from technology. Alvin Toffler has espoused a concept of "future shock" which pervades all aspects of life and is disruptive to values, families, and institutions.[1] The rapidity of social change, combined with the inability of people to comprehend and adapt to it, causes social maladjustment in the lives of almost everyone unable to keep up with the impact of change. This is future shock.

Traditionally institutions were created to serve as instruments to preserve some change that was felt to be good and slow down unwanted new developments. With fast-paced change the established order has been unable to control it at the rate at which it affects our lives. Now, institutions must plan for the future by absorbing the impact of change, by altering its operation, and by learning to control change. Recreation and leisure service agencies may help the victims of future shock by diffusing change at the interface where technology and social and cultural developments collide. At present work is loosing its hold on the moral attachment and commitment of men, and it is leisure which is producing the most important innovations.

Fragmentary versus Integrated Life Adjustment

According to McLuhan we have accustomed ourselves to life in a world that was fragmented into little pieces.[2] Now we suddenly find ourselves considering a world that is all one piece, because we can experience any part of it instantaneously. Electric technology is a process which is reshaping and restructuring patterns of social interdependence and our personal lives, in which print technology formerly "'encouraged a fragmenting process, a process of specialism and of detachment. Electric technology fosters and encourages unification and involvement."[3]

The confusion and profound feelings of despair created in periods of cultural and technological transition have caused a great deal of anxiety. Youth, who are not as committed to the system their parents adopted, have evolved a participatory style of life based on involvement and integrated patterns of behavior which foster a unified, fused way of life. The demands

1. Alvin Toffler, *Future Shock* (New York: Bantam Books, Inc., 1971).
2. Marshall McLuhan, *The Medium is the Massage* (New York: Bantam Books, Inc., 1967), p. 8.
3. Ibid.

of youth, minority groups, women, and the elderly are natural extensions of an electric information environment in which social and political participation is direct and universal. The ability of disaffected, deprived, and alienated groups to achieve recognition and solve personal problems in a centrifugal environment, in which the total organism could move from experience to experience, is now being replaced by another process. A centripetal milieu (an integrated environment) which is a reverse movement process, representative of the increased ability of our technology to move the experience itself to the human nervous system, has developed which allows less mobile and powerful groups participation and inclusion in the system.

This holistic process (see "The Impact of Leisure on Culture") is reshaping the nature of leisure opportunity and recreation expression. The standardization of parts, assembly-line operation used for mass production, the separation of the arts and sciences, compartmentalization of education, and overspecialization in our economic lives generated a philosophy of segmentalism and a discretionary time concept of leisure which was valid only after obligatory functions had been satisfied. The holistic philosophy recognizes a continuous, flowing interaction between organisms and their environments in which man's senses are combined and react to the society as a whole. A new consciousness is created in which there is no static point—everything is seen as a process. This means the death of permanence and a resultant acceleration of social events in which people find themselves increasingly disoriented and incompetent to deal with their fragmented environments, because high mobility has created a transient and rootless society.

If man were to continue to embrace a segmentalist philosophy he would view the parts of his life as distinct, separate segments relatively unaffected by each other. The contrasting pattern, the holistic philosophy, conceives that the parts of man's life are integrated, in that each aspect of his life affects and is affected by the other. Such an *ecological-holistic* leisure pattern recognizes an integration and fusion of the work and leisure spheres in the society as a whole.[4]

THE IMPACT OF LEISURE ON CULTURE

The holistic-integrated conceptualization of work and leisure is not seen as an attempt to maximize leisure per se but to *fuse* it with a uniquely satisfying form of work according to Parker:

4. Parker, *Future of Work and Leisure*, p. 102.

In the fusion, work may lose its present characteristic feature of constraint and gain creativity now associated mainly with leisure, while leisure may lose its present characteristic feature of opposition to work and gain the status—now associated mainly with the product of work— of a resource worthy of planning to provide the greatest possible human satisfaction.[5]

Essentially, segmentalists view work and leisure as separate, contrasting and oppositional compartments of life, while holists see an interrelationship between work and leisure. Work is no longer the central life interest for most people living in the approaching postindustrial age. Historically, life-styles have been defined by economic class and occupational status. In the future the traditional factors which ordinarily determine one's role and life-style will no longer be relevant. Man and his social and physical milieu will be increasingly seen as interdependent, with emphasis placed upon coexistence. Therefore, it will no longer be meaningful to conceive of various societal components as separate, compartmentalized sequences. "The overlapping of work/vacation/weekend living is also accompanied by the flexible adoption of appropriate styling for the many different social roles that the individual now occupies."[6]

The provision of leisure service, to have relevance in the future, must merge with other human service offerings to create an environment serving a central goal of human development. The use of the full environment represents the merging of all of man's experiences into what amounts to the *new* leisure. Beck states that "as man is freer to integrate experience and ideas, he is more able to develop his total being."[7] The newly evolving postindustrial man will conceivably seek integration rather than a segmentation of experience. In postindustrial society people desire total *involvement* and reject fragmented, specialized goals or jobs.

THE PROBLEM OF LEISURE

Leisure has emerged as a "problem" in American society. Certain forms of leisure behavior are identified as a problem because they conflict with the values of other members of society. Since leisure has evolved its own set of values, beliefs, and patterns of relationship, it is seen as an institution, which means it must be viewed within the total context of society's value system. Roberts states: "When the members of society

5. Ibid., p. 122.
6. John McHale, *The Future of the Future* (New York: Balantine Books, Inc., 1969), p. 320.
7. Bertram M. Beck, "Recreation and Delinquency," *Recreation and Leisure Service for the Disadvantaged*, ed. John A. Nesbitt, Paul D. Brown, and James F. Murphy (Philadelphia: Lea and Febiger, 1970), p. 67.

recognize the existence of a conflict between their values and patterns of leisure behavior, leisure becomes a manifest problem."[8]

When there is a discrepancy or inconsistency between people's values and their leisure behavior, a state of anomie or confusion, occurs between the goals that society urges its members to aspire to and the means that society makes available to people for legitimately pursuing these goals. There is an assumption that the value systems (which specify the ends which people shall pursue) and the means (rules) by which these ends may be legitimately obtained are congruent for all people. For some segments of the population there are limited means to satisfy leisure expression, or there may be a lack of clearly defined goals or values around which to organize their leisure. If people are frustrated by their inability to find legitimate forms of leisure expression they may be forced to adopt a deviant solution. According to Roberts, individuals may respond to an anomic situation in their leisure "by attempting to derive satisfaction from pursuing an unending series of fads and fashions. Alternatively, they may adopt a ritualistic approach to their leisure, adhering rigidly to conventional forms of recreation despite the fact that they may not be completely satisfying."[9]

With expected increases in free time to continue in the future, people will be faced with a variety of possible ways in which to use their free time, but will be equipped with no coherent set of standards to direct the choices that they have to make. Often deviant leisure behavior is misconstrued as a problem related to family life, peer groups, or work. While they may be the root for deviancy, the problems of leisure are too often not recognized. The source of frustrations should perhaps be investigated in the field of leisure itself, instead of always implicating other aspects of people's lives. The need for change in the leisure field is no less paramount than in the other segments of the larger society.

The value system of the larger society has not conferred honor on leisure as a separate, distinguishable component of the social structure. Society as a whole, and leisure service agencies, do not recognize the problems of leisure posed by various subcultures, as the strains and tensions of these problems do not provoke demands for social change in the field of leisure itself. There is a need for a set of standards which people can use to guide their leisure interests—pluralistically determined—to curb the problems of anomie and equip the public with a set of values and achievable means for satisfying their interests.

8. Kenneth Roberts, *Leisure* (London: Longman Group Limited, 1970), p. 103.
9. Ibid., p. 113.

LEISURE AND THE QUALITY OF LIFE

The failure of American society to develop a leisure ethic which can blend harmoniously with and support the natural environment and bring about an improvement of the quality of life, stems in part from the singular and rather narrowly defined discretionary time reference assigned leisure (refer to chapter 1). It is a by-product of the antiquated Protestant work ethic which was generated from an industrializing nation, but which is still a dominant view in a *post*industrial society.

The creation of a more harmonious leisure quality of life ethic appears to be possible only through the opening up of various options represented in the various concepts and dimensions of leisure (refer to figure 1.1). The sequential-linear temporal reference assigned leisure, with respect to discretionary time, forces the postponement of exhilarating moments, events, and experiences until retirement, after work, or until next season. A more natural, rhythmical, cyclical, and personal pattern of leisure reference, involving play, education, work, and retirement would allow man to exist in a freer, more meaningful time reference.

Leisure may be seen as an opportunity for life enrichment and self-development. However, the prospect for human fulfillment is seriously curtailed within a temporal reference dictated by the industrial time clock, particularly since man's own psychological "time clock" functions independently of mechanical time, activity, and cultural antecedents. Clearly, we must have some understanding of time and its effects on our own life pattern. Only by controlling and adjusting our own time can we begin to consider leisure as a personal opportunity for self-enhancement, mastery and pleasure, and develop a humanistic ethic which will foster a qualitative environmental attitude.

The interrelationships of people in a postindustrial society suggest that one should be able to come into "an association of possible, potential experiencing and be free to arrange the experiencing as it develops without the coercion of organizational structuring and restriction."[10] It is within this reference that leisure's essential properties effectively correlate with man's natural, instinctual play behavior and allows his developmental, self-enriching qualities to emerge and flourish. The milieu in which opportunities for leisure present themselves must be cultivated. The ultimate goal is to preserve and create an environment in which leisure may be engaged in spontaneously. The key ingredients are the mutual competence of ourselves and the environment to interact and our ability to choose and to change our course so that we may maximize our human potential.

10. Edwin J. Staley and Norman P. Miller, eds., *Leisure and the Quality of Life: A New Ethic for the 70's and Beyond* (Washington, D.C.: AAHPER, 1972), p. 178.

CYBERCULTURE: VISIONS OF UTOPIA

Any future discussions of society must conceive of the totality of community life and how each component serves the whole process. In a postindustrial society man's way of life increasingly is based upon the application of cybernetics, the science of relationships. Alice Mary Hilton provides a definition of cybercultural society. "A cybercultural society is . . . an integrated society that affords human beings the opportunity to live human—i.e., purposeful and civilized—lives. In such a society, human beings are free and responsible because they are free."[11] In a cybercultural society individuals assume responsibility for their own action, and all people are motivated to act in harmony with others. One is conscious of his attitudes and behaviors and their impact on fellow human beings. It is important for an individual to give up some autonomy for the collective good of the community, but in advanced technological societies human beings have the opportunity to exercise more judgement, are freer to determine courses of action, and are not enslaved to the mechanization of industry. "It is the duty of a human being to choose his way of life, but it is a duty one may perform only at a high pace in our society. And yet, the individual who ignores his duty to choose his way of life, the individual who permits his personal conscience to be deposed as the supreme arbiter of right and wrong is abdicating his essential humanity."[12]

While an individual assumes more personal responsibility for his actions, he does not forsake his responsibility to others and participates as a cooperative and responsive partner in community life. In such a cybernetic society, leisure and affluency move the individual away from immediate survival needs to higher, more intrinsic forms of motivation. The role of leisure service personnel must be to provide a flexible environment, which allows for spontaneous, multifaceted and diverse leisure opportunities. Hilton comments on leisure service's role: "Abundance and leisure makes the individual free and, therefore, responsible for the way he lives his life. When he is not encumbered with the chores that assure his biological survival, the individual is free to build a civilized society. And each is responsible not merely for himself but also for his fellow men."[13]

A cybercultural society views leisure as an opportunity to fulfill meaningful human tasks, and to construct a life-enhancing community based on purposeful and responsive social relationships. *Leisure service agencies have an important task of developing an opportunity framework and inte-*

11. Alice Mary Hilton, "Individual Responsibility in a Cybercultural Society," *Quest,* Monograph 5(1965):37.
12. Ibid., p. 39.
13. Ibid., p. 45.

grated system founded on the premise of choice and individual determination. The provision of leisure service must merge with other human service offerings in the future to create a total environment serving a central goal of human development. The use of the full environment represents the merging of sensate and intellectual experiences, which is the hallmark of the electric age and, therefore, of the *new* leisure.

Leisure service agencies must be responsive to the needs and desires of those the agencies were created to serve. Recreation and leisure's role is inextricably related to the development of people. The cybernetic era compels commitment and participation and fosters and encourages unification and involvement. The synchronization of experiences as a result of cybernation requires that organizations must be designed to respond to the community as a whole. As such, leisure service cannot isolate its service approach and must develop a holistic perspective in meeting community needs and solving leisure related problems. Theobald comments: "Disciplines are fragmentations of gestalts and totalities: one can only meaningfully analyze totalities."[14]

While the integrative, holistic perspective appears to be most appropriate for dealing with the issues and problems pervasive in community life, it may well be replaced by a synergistic perspective. *Synergistics,* is the process of combining and utilizing the component parts of a system to produce an overall result that exceeds the sum of the parts. Presently, value-oriented concerns which incorporate a functionally integrative perspective to predict, plan, and implement are the most popular approaches to program development. This approach may well be replaced by synergistic patterns which are oriented to quality of life values designed to achieve meaningful grass-roots participation and action. This process recognizes an *organic* blending of knowledge, education, attitudes, and living patterns, with the goal of enhancing the quality of life and experience.

THE ECOLOGY OF LEISURE EXPERIENCING

Leisure is an inseparable aspect of life and, therefore, must be treated as a part of the total environment. Appropriately, "the quality of leisure is an inseparable part of the total quality of life."[15] This ecological perspective recognizes how interrelated all aspects of the environment are and that no part can be identified or understood except in relation to the whole.

14. Robert Theobald, "Thinking About the Future," *Technology, Human Values and Leisure,* ed. Max Kaplan and Phillip Bosserman (Nashville: Abingdon Press, 1971), p. 32.
15. G. Douglas Hofe, Jr., "Environmental Resources," *Leisure and the Quality of Life,* Staley and Miller, eds., op. cit., p. 129.

A postindustrial society is evolving in which, either by recognition of holism or synergism, the interaction of work, leisure, family, religion, education, politics and the economy have become related to each other. No one institution can be isolated from the other. Each element of the leisure service delivery system is therefore interrelated and seen as interdependent.

MEASURING THE VALUE OF LEISURE

In a highly technological society performance should no longer be gauged by its economic worth. While we tend to use elaborate machinery to measure the directions of change with respect to a set of economic indicators, we fail to note human value through use of social indicators. We have no measures for the quality of life.

Quantitative, cost-benefit analysis is an inappropriate and misleading financial tool used for estimating the value of personal goals of people seeking to fulfill themselves through the provision of leisure opportunities. Such an approach appears to be a defective device for estimating value joined from participation in leisure service programs. Rein and Miller state:

> There is danger of sliding into the position that the only goals with merit and legitimacy are those that are quantifiable and convertible into money. Quantitative reasoning may lead to stressing productivity (return per unit of expenditure) over total results. Productivity can be high while total return may be less than in some other kind of activity which has a high relative cost per unit of expenditure.[16]

While cost-benefit analysis provides some important kinds of information, it does not provide the leisure service community catalyst with assistance needed to resolve the issues of values, direction, purposes, and feelings. By incorporating an ecological, holistic (or synergistic) perspective, leisure service personnel will come to realize the conflict of competing interests, values, and programs to better determine priorities which will enhance the quality of living in a pluralistic society. No one group, class or racial strain need be jeopardized by narrow-minded or naive community leaders when an ecological perspective is operable. By definition such an approach recognizes that the various social, psychological, organizational, and management components of the leisure service delivery system are

---

16. Martin Rein and S. M. Miller, "Poverty Programs and Policy Priorities," *Social Science and National Policy*, 2nd ed., ed. Fred R. Harris (New Brunswick, New Jersey: Transaction, Inc., 1973), p. 204.

interrelated and all fundamental to the successful implementation of a viable, meaningful program.

It is the task of the leisure service to recognize this ecological relationship and ensure that each individual is allowed to pursue self-enhancing and pleasurable goals within an interdependent community network. It is also the task of leisure service personnel not to impose a uniform pattern of acceptable social relationships on people but to respect individual diversity, uniqueness, and goals by providing community members with a series of alternatives for self-actualization and self-development from which to select. The value of leisure experience is diminished if leisure service agencies attempt to direct people's energies into specified channels in advance of participation. "We should aim instead to nourish the individual's potentialities so that each, according to his capacity, could find his own solution."[17]

THE FUTURE OF LEISURE—A SUMMARY

This text has endeavored to shed some new light on the recreation and leisure service field. It has underscored the essence of the value of a humanistic perspective in viewing the complex of leisure opportunity; of recognizing the interrelationship of the social, psychological, and organizational components of community life; of the necessity for respecting and elevating diverse subcultures, ethnic, class and racial groups; and of initiating a leisure service delivery approach which utilizes a process orientation, enabling agencies to be cognizant of the social, technological and cultural changes which periodically occur. By understanding the depth and interrelation of all life experiencing, the prospective leisure service community catalyst will make an enormous and significant improvement in the realization of human potential.

Human development is a combination of biological and environmental forces. The human being comes to realize his full potential by the contribution of a complimentary and life-enhancing support system. The previous fragmentary approaches used in attempting to satisfy people are inappropriate in a cybernated era.[18] The synchronization of each part of the environment is made possible by the interdependent aspects of the life support system. The supreme specialist of an industrial era, both in work and leisure, has only marginal value in a postindustrial society, in which each element contributes to an organic whole. The social processes of

17. Parker, *Future of Work and Leisure*, p. 139.
18. Refer to Alvin Toffler, ed., *The Futurists* (New York: Random House, Inc.), 1972, for an enlightening discussion of the future by many noted "Futurologists."

integration, synergism, holism and humanism respond to human behavior through an overall consideration of human unity that enriches the potential fulfillment of each person. The leisure service field must recognize its role in the future to be a part of the total community process in which every human experience is interrelated.

EPILOGUE

redefining leisure:
an action plan for the recreation and park movement

PART I ● **Yesterday and Today**

PART II ● **The Future of American Society**

PART III ● **An Action Program for the Recreation and Park Movement**

This material was originally prepared for the National Council of the National Recreation and Park Association to indicate the future direction of the Recreation and Park Movement. It has since been adopted by the NRPA and many leisure service agencies as a philosophical statement and operation guideline for the provision of recreation opportunity.

PART I ● **Yesterday and Today**

Perhaps we should introduce this paper by saying we predict that in the year 2003—thirty years from now—Germaine Greer will be starting her second term as President of the United States and Eldridge Cleaver will be Vice-President. Probably not likely you say, but not impossible, we say.

The reader can play an interesting fantasy game—choosing an unlikely President/Vice-President duo for the United States of 2003—and the choice will be no more right, or wrong, than our attempt to provoke an instant response of interest. What we're really saying is that our readers, from the very beginning, must share with us the reality that in our world of 1973 it is most presumptuous for anyone to try to make specific, accurate predictions of what will emerge in 2003 in our country, and our profession. 1973 is very different from 1972, and 1972 represents a difference of light-years from 1966 to 1960. In truth, Alvin Toffler's world of "future shock" is probably the only dependable prediction that can be established as a basis for our thinking; there will be rapid change, and the rate of change will accelerate and society will adjust cultural patterns, norms, and value systems to accommodate a process that is dangerously close to becoming an end in itself.

But we—like others—will continue, rightly so, to plan for what we can best speculate about a future that requires anticipation of time blocks of a month, a year, a century; and in our case, thirty years. To not plan is to reach the ultimate in Hedonism; to not plan is to "cop out." But to plan in 1973 is to plan with a realization of the permanence and swiftness of change.

We start with our own concept of America in 1973. It is, admittedly, an America which is perceived quite differently than the America of 1900 by its citizens and by people around the entire world. We are a country that no longer is preeminently shaped by the Frederick Jackson Turner vision of a never-ending physical or geographical frontier. What remains of that type of frontier is in the main peripheral to the mainstream of America, and no amount of nostalgic yearning for the past in the form of citing moon, space, and undersea exploration can obliterate the reality that is confronted today with frontiers of preeminent consequence, they are social frontiers—not matters of geography.

In the 1930s, we suffered a debilitating economic depression; a combination of war and near-war, and tinkering with our free enterprise, sometime Keynesian, economic system has since dimmed the memory of

Prepared by Sy Greben, Director, Department of Parks and Recreation, Los Angeles County, California.

that horrible, degrading period by providing a kind of inflationary near-prosperity for a relatively large percentage of our people. (This should not be read as a walking away from the truth of large, continuing poverty pockets in our populace; more about that later.) Only the "old" people in our society still remember the Great Depression and even they no longer make major life-style decisions of the basis of those memories. If the Great Depression of the 30s is of importance to us today, it is probably so for two primary reasons:

1. Experiencing it, or not having experienced it, represents one of the consequential symbols of our generation gap.
2. The Depression period marked the beginning of a realization that government shall, and will play, a major role in confronting the chronic problems of specifically identifiable groups within our midst. Government became involved with social reality—and quite definitely will remain involved in spite of temporal rhetoric of 1973 to the contrary.

Since the Depression we've experienced war and near-war as a way of life, and as a by-product (fringe benefit?) our economy has received a continuing, substantial governmental stimulus and control. We've been clearly established as a major world power with all the attendant pragmatism, self-righteousness and virtues that are bequeathed to nations of this status. We have sallied forth from an isolation stimulated by a two-ocean separation to involvement in everyone's affairs throughout the world, and now we are flirting again with a probably unattainable goal of semi-isolation. We've begun to explore the solar system and will continue to do so, and we've become somewhat titillated with the bottom of the sea. We've become obsessed with anti-Communism, unfortunately not usually counterbalanced by pro anything of substance, and now we're doing business with the "worst" Communists—and we're pleased about it.

The social historians tell us, probably accurately, that we've been involved with things and accumulation, not ideas or matters of the spirit. Those of us who are of the forty or above age group are mystified and often angry with those who don't seem to understand and appreciate what we feel we've accomplished. Just when we start to feel proud, they "kick us in the ass" (that's how *they* would say it), and they say we're selfish, self-centered, and inconsistent.

It's the *they* that may be a dominant theme of 1973—and the future; *they* are all the American people who no longer can be fitted under the traditional umbrella of American majority opinion and culture, the ones who've been shaking us and threatening us and challenging us and *changing us* these last ten to fifteen years.

In 1973 in our America, we are visibly affected by the reality of old people, hippies, blacks, teenagers, women, American Indians, migrant poor, Chicanos. It's true that at this moment it's becoming stylish to say that the antiwar movement, and the youth movement, and the women's rights movement, as examples, are all passing fancies. They have won no elections, they have had no long-term effect on our national thought process, and they will pass on like dance marathons, goldfish swallowing, Green Chip Stamps, and other fads.

In our opinion, this is patent nonsense, a kind of wishful thinking to go back to a stability that never really existed. The "movements" which we have experienced, and they can all be recognized as social movements, have truly revolutionized our society; they have brought about profound, lasting change, and they continue today. Their rhetoric, their style, have infuriated us at times, but we mustn't lose sight of their deep significance because we're distracted by their noise and fervor. Who among us can deny the reality and permanent significance of these changes?

1. Government cannot any longer tell the people (dictate) what is right and desirable. Government, at all levels, is absolutely dependent upon maximum citizen participation if it is to succeed in accomplishing the classical functions of a democratic government.
2. Ethnic, religious, and other minority cultures must participate equally in the mainstream of life. Abject, unadulterated bigotry cannot and will not be tolerated, legally or socially, and the more socially sophisticated forms of intolerance are passing from the scene.
3. None of our public institutions can function on the basis of a dual standard, i.e., this is what we say we stand for, but it has no relationship with the way we operate (Example: American colleges and universities teaching about democracy, but in the minds of their students and faculty functioning as an oligarchy, or worse, a dictatorship).
4. No longer can industry or government or individuals plunder our physical environment in the names of development and progress and growth. The new laws that are now on the books, and more important the attitudes of our people, will simply not allow for further despoiling of our environment. Perhaps the most astounding reality of 1973 is that somehow industry does accommodate itself to newly formulated controls which protect our environment; industry continues to survive in spite of new zoning laws and legislation which control utility placement, billboards and signs, and which establish standards for open space and park dedication, and even people-passed laws which say when and what can be developed and what cannot be developed.

5. Our conscious and acknowledged attitudes toward social behavior, particularly relationships between the sexes, have taken a whole new dimension, perhaps most typified by a beginning of a diminishing of hypocrisy. Many of us would disagree as to which of the many changes in this category is most significant and lasting, but the changes are real and positive. Largely, they have been inspired by young people's insistence on honesty, and acknowledgement of what is real. Again, this is not to be confused by the distraction of style and rhetoric, or four-letter words, when the main value is one of shock therapy.

6. Recognition that to be old, or to be a female in American society provides a separate experience, a separate environment from all of us who are not old or female. Recognition by the old, the female (and how many other groups?) that no longer will they allow themselves to be despised or ignored or legislated against.

7. Recognition by the majority culture that the job of creating a healthy society requires a conscious and ethical responsibility to share with all of the minority cultures the equal opportunity to participate in our mainstream.

This, then, is a partial selected view of the America of 1973, the America in which our recreation and park profession functions and serves. Our task, now, is to attempt to define figuratively the "State of the Nation" of the Recreation and Park Movement—today, so that we can evaluate our potential to provide productive services to the America which will emerge in the year 2003.

Unfortunately, even as late as 1973, recreation and parks attempts to remain all things to all people. We have many spiritual parents, and perhaps our most honorable parentage stems from the fact that some of the thinkers who caused us to come into existence conceptualized our role as a part of the total quest for the "good life." Early day progressive movements in America—the historically significant ones that dealt with pure food and drug laws, limitations of hours of work and other working conditions, and humanized immigration laws, also paid attention to matters of protection of natural resources and productive use of leisure time. Since early in the twentieth century, these recreation and park issues have been a part of the total Progressive Movement and ethic in the United States. As a result, government throughout the United States has come to accept recreation and parks as a basic in the list of services which citizens should receive, and all facets of local government—city, county, and special purpose district—share the responsibility for the function.

With this acceptance has come the development of a formalized Recreation and Park Movement. We have tended to emulate other governmental services in formulating our sets of goals, organizational patterns, and symbols of professionalism. Nationally known leaders have emerged (at least they are nationally known in our own recreation and park world) and to simplify communication and understanding in our world, we have created our version of a party line complete with words and phrases which are defined with consistent meaning by most of our colleagues. We have, in the best traditions of our country, formed a variety of different professional groups based upon political subdivision, geographic regions, specialized interest, and profession. And we attempt regularly to evaluate ourselves.

Therefore, in attempting to chronicle what we might aspire to in the future (next thirty years) for recreation and parks, it doesn't seem unreasonable that Gray and Greben should attempt to evaluate the Recreation and Park Movement today. How we've functioned historically, our perceptions of the world about us, should be reasonable insight as to what might be expected in the future.

Unfortunately, based upon a measurement of leadership in social movements, there isn't much reason for optimism. This isn't to say that the Recreation and Park Movement has not made important contributions to the well-being of America, nor that certain individuals within the movement haven't made singularly brilliant contributions which are viewed in an aura of great public acceptance. Rather, what we're saying is that our contribution has been somewhat minimal in terms of providing a leadership for the main current of social progress in America and somewhat marginal to where the action is.

It is 1973, and in terms of what is important in our world (achievements, problems, etc.), it appears that we are not yet in the foreground of dynamic change and typically we have been followers, not leaders. How do we arrive at this conclusion?

1. In most cities of America, recreation and park publicly supported budgets are an embarrassingly small portion of the total—at a time when many, perhaps most, Americans would agree that the dual tasks of preserving and protecting our physical environment and providing constructive useful leisure time experiences rise to the top of our national lists of needs. This conceivably results from our own inability to define our role beyond narrow, often parochial boundaries.

2. In most American cities, it is difficult to identify any great overall community interest and knowledge of our movement or of our local leaders. (Compare with concern for law and order, public education, etc.)

3. During the past ten years when change has symbolized our American life, we have not kept pace and hardly ever have we led. Examples?
   (a) *Relationship with Minority Communities*
       There are few or no examples of our movement introducing innovative, constructive ideas which would lead to a greater sense of equality of opportunity. Within our own national organization, we have been publicly embarrassed by the emergence of first a black caucus and later a minority caucus as an expression of disappointment on the part of minority groups and individuals that we are not responsive. If we fail to make an appropriate place for minorities in our own organization, how can we presume to succeed in our local minority communities?
   (b) *Relationship with Environmental Organizations*
       There are exceptions to the statement, but generally we have rejected or have been unreasonably slow in establishing common cause with the Environmental Movement. Hardly ever have we provided substantive leadership for this vital movement which should, in truth, be our natural ally.
   (c) *Relationship with Women*
       A vital, new movement has emerged in America and its existence until now has had little consequence to our own movement and received no creative leadership from us. We still announce jobs for which only males can qualify (although we don't know why), and we continue to announce program offerings such as *Girls' Dance Class* and *Boys' Craft Classes*—even though quite obviously these specially distinguished classes serve no need and are repugnant to an ever larger segment of our society. Often, our only reason for continuing these classes results from a fear that what we perceive as a dominant male majority culture will oppose any change to nonintegrated classes.
   (d) *Community Participation*
       Our rhetoric and public statements now support the idea of community participation, but how long it took us to reach this point and how little relationship there is between the generalization of philosophical support and the actuality of real support and leadership in the specific situation. How often the comment is heard in our meetings, "We believe in community participation and we're working on it, but we have a long way to go yet." It is the author's fear that a kind of "absolution" technique has emerged as a substitute for actual commitment; as long as we say we're

working at achieving a desirable goal, it relieves us of any responsibility to do a damned thing.

(e) *Understanding and Support for the Disadvantaged*

It is a relatively simple task to create a sense of "busyness" at most parks or recreation centers. There are a certain percentage of kids and adults who would show up and play basketball and picnic, etc., regardless of whether we had any staff present or not. But while we revel in this semblance of success, we often are guilty of overlooking the disadvantaged—whether they be so because of reasons which are physical, spiritual, economic, or other, the people who need us the most we often ignore, or worse, make them feel unwelcome. We didn't, on our own, redesign our facilities so that they could be comfortably used with dignity by a cripple or a blind person. We were *forced* into design changes by the special interest groups who must look out for the welfare of the blind, the lame, the old, the retarded. We still have not developed programs which provide positive answers to the problems generated from the drug culture, even when we know that a considerable percentage of our young people are comforted by this culture.

4. Lastly, we are not identified with the major problems and their solutions which confront our total American society. In 1900, 60.3 percent of our population lived in rural areas, 39.7 percent were resident in urban society. By 1970, the situation was reversed—rural 26.5 percent and urban 73.5 percent. And yet we still persist in debating whether urban needs shall be our primary concern. In today's world, we face the reality of a mounting anger often typified by a rising violence and terrorism and antisocial behavior. And instead of coming forth with new substantive *predelinquency* type solutions (one reason for our existence), we are "copping out" and joining in the push for more police and police protection *(postdelinquency)* as the answer. And today when you speak privately to the creative leaders in our Movement, the real "shakers" and "movers," they inevitably describe to you their sense of isolation because they dare to be innovative and because they defy the party line. How unfortunately similar to Ibsen's "Enemy of the People" who became concerned with the polluting of the town's water supply by the major industry—and who was kicked out of polite society for his attempt at reform.

This is one view of our America and our Recreation and Park Movement today. It is a pessimistic summary, one filled with deep concern and disappointment. It doesn't mean to overlook the accomplishments, but in all candor, it is our view that the next thirty years must be one of solid achievement and leadership if our Movement is to fulfill our hopes and dreams, and if we are to assume a major role in building an America which is rich in human and spiritual blessing.

PART II ● The Future of American Society

Today change is occurring in response to visions dimly grasped but widely and powerfully felt that deal with who we are, what we might do, and what we can be in the light of the limits and potentials we see in the human dimension. There is a broad and growing humanistic ethic permeating America. It sees the great need of our nation in human terms. It would not rank improved technology or an improved economy as central needs in our national life. It would see the primary social needs as human development, improved processes of human interaction, and protection and restoration of our environment as central. It is precisely in these fields that the Recreation and Park Movement must operate. It is in these fields the Movement finds its mission and identity.

In our country there is a rapidly changing vision of what we want our lives to be. At the root of the great change in self-perception that is now evolving is the way we feel about ourselves and the way we conceive of ourselves as human beings. Our sensation of being alive, our sense of individual existence, and our vision of identity are all being revised. In short, our whole concept of what it means to be human is undergoing profound change. America is turning inward. We are reexamining our thoughts, our ideals, our motives. Our method is introspection and our goal is self-discovery. The new frontier is the exploration of inner space. The motive is a deeper participation in life. The really significant problems in our country lie in the area of human interaction. It is in these relationships that human destruction or human development take place. It is precisely here that a new society will be created, if there is to be a new society. Something very, very important is happening and it is possible that those of us who devote our lives to the Recreation and Park Movement may have a part in it. If we recognize what we are about, it may be a significant part.

The American Institute of Planners in their "Fiftieth Year Consultation" expressed the national purpose as: "To assure the primary importance of the individual, his freedom, his widest possible choice, his access to joy and opportunity, his impetus to self-development, his responsible relation to his society, the growth of his inner life, and his capacity to love." This glowing vision of our potential future we have not yet attained. One of the things swift social and technological change is demonstrating is that our cultural heritage mutates faster than our physical and biological heritage.

Prepared by David E. Gray, Vice-President for Administration, California State University, Long Beach, California.

Abraham Maslow has suggested that human motives are arranged in a pyramid that ranges from "physiological" needs at the bottom, through "safety," "belongingness and love" or social needs, "esteem" including self-respect and feelings of success, to "self-actualization" which has been attained when the individual has become all he is capable of becoming. A rising number of Americans are no longer content at the physiological and security of that structure. They have set out to climb the pyramid. They seek experience at the center of existence—not the experience of escapism but a deeper participation in life.

As a nation, we are beginning to perceive that health is more than the absence of disease. There is a great national debate going on over the goals of health care. The growing concept is the idea of health as well-being and the debate centers on the issue of keeping people well versus curing them after they are sick. The Recreation Movement has a stake in that debate. As therapists, recreation personnel have a role in curing the sick but as members of the Recreation and Park Movement, we all have a role in developing a society that will help keep people well.

The World Health Organization has defined health as "a state of complete physical, mental, and social well-being, and not merely the absence of disease and infirmity." To be free of illness, discomfort, and disability is of itself highly desirable, but the absence of these conditions is not the highest expression of human potential. When the individual lives constructively and creatively beyond a level of ordinary effectiveness, he is beginning to fulfill his potential. Then he is approaching the full state of health. Then he will be making the most of life. Health is not an end in itself, it is a state of being that permits people to make the most of themselves. Health improves the vitality of mankind and releases people for the creative life. Recreation is one aspect of that life. It is a cliché to talk of poor adaptation to the freedom granted by increasing free time but cliché or not, it is true and the results of maladaptation have significant human consequences. Poor adjustment shows itself in various kinds of sociopsychological disturbances. Sando Ferenczi, in a classic study published in 1926, identified a pattern of "Sunday neurosis," that is now being reconfirmed by England in a study that shows an increase in psychosomatic phenomenon, including depression and suicides, during holidays and vacations. Other reactions to free time are excessive guilt, compulsive work, and self-alienation.

"Mobility" has been widely discussed as a significant social phenomenon for several years, but we have recently come to realize that "mobility" which suggests movement from place to place, is inadequate to indicate the pervasiveness and social consequences of the conditions we are experiencing. The word recently adopted for that is "transience" which may be defined as the rapid turnover of relationships with people, places, and things. The current high rate of mobility in the United States produces relationships of short duration and low intensity with other people, with places, and with things. Motion which was originally a means, has become an end. For many, transience is the essence of life. We see it in the mobility of habitation, in the "Dixie Cup" approach to possessions, in the "serial monogamy" of marriage. Transience is evident all around us. Cars are rented, dolls are traded in, dresses are discarded after a single wearing, friendships come and go, marriages last for a few months or years. In a transient society where there are no long-term commitments, there must be a feeling for the temporary that makes something as good as it can be, while it lasts.

The small group is the essential vehicle and unit of learning, and of life support. The forces at work in our culture are tearing apart the old small groups that have been central in our society. Groups based on family, work, and friendship decline. New forms like collectives, communes, liberation groups, "growth centers," ecology and consumer action organizations, and liberation units have evolved to replace them. These groups are not random; they are attempts to bring people together in an organization capable of coping with the world in flux. If we are to help mitigate the human toll of transience, it is our task to develop nuclei around which small groups can form, and to speed up group process so that the benefits of group membership can be experienced before transience tears it apart again.

Learning is a lifetime enterprise. It begins with the first breath and ends with the last. It is the central activity of life; in a very real way, it is life. It varies in pace and intensity but it goes on day and night, year after year. Learning expands awareness, stores information, develops conditioned responses, establishes identity; it governs perceptions, regulates human interaction, influences health. Learning determines who we are and how we behave. The most significant kinds of learning do not take place in school. Education as we are coming to know it, goes beyond developing skills. The new emphasis is on development of individual human capabilities, to enhance the quality of life in all its aspects, and to enhance individual and social well-being. Developmental psychologists have established beyond any doubt the intimate relationship between playing and learning. A child's learning is best centered on his own experience. For most children, play experience is the thing life is made of. If people are not learning, they are probably not enjoying recreation. We must be deeply involved in learning. We have learned to sustain life; now we want to enhance it.

Our cities do not work as they should. In the typical suburban neighborhood today there is no commons, no public meeting place—where the people of the neighborhood can interact. The predilection of the city planner for sorting land use by functions and putting all like uses together, has segregated residential areas into compounds which include only houses. These sterile areas often do not provide even a corner store where one might pass the time of day with a neighbor.

Recreation activities operate *within* the social environment and *form a part* of the total social environment of the community and the nation. In many communities they are a conspicuous part of the pattern of social interaction. In areas where the neighborhood has lost its social significance as an organizing device for human association, recreation activities are the primary arena beyond work and kinship. In communities with high rates of mobility, recreation may be more effective as a social nucleus than kinship. Open space is social space. In the great urban parks of the nation a daily open house takes place that brings together people of the neighborhood in a no-host social event. An essential task is to provide the commons where the people of the city can interact.

It is tempting but unsatisfactory when one considers the impact of change on the Recreation and Park Movement to concentrate on technological change which is a physical embodiment and is, therefore, easier to perceive. It is unsatisfactory because, in spite of the widespread influence of technological change, it is not the most significant force impacting the Movement. That force is social change. That illusive combination of changes in technology, economics, politics, philosophy, environmental perceptions, and religion is remaking man's view of the universe and what it means to be human. We only dimly perceive how pervasive social change is and what it may portend for us. Even that dimly lit vision, confirms that things cannot remain as they are.

The Recreation and Park Movement, and the agencies that administer programs, exist in a political and social environment that is increasingly complex. The state and most communities are politicized to a degree we have not experienced before. Concurrent and interwoven into this increase in the tempo and intensity of political activity are technological and social developments that are changing the social environment dramatically. It is in this rapidly changing social environment that the Recreation and Park Movement must operate. The magnitude of social change is so great it defies description; it may defy comprehension until it is seen in the framework of history, but some trends can already be seen as highly influential.

Among them the changing pattern of family relationships, deterioration of the sense of neighborhood, the development of an urban man, altered conditions of work, the changing role of women in society, race relations, sorting of society on the basis of age, and revolutionary changes in our system of values appear to be highly significant.

Failure of the Recreation and Park Movement to deal with change continually will inevitably lead to crisis. An adaptive mechanism that denies change or denies the significance of change can only lead to major crisis in place of a whole series of more or less manageable problems that will permit incremental adaptation. Adjustment to change requires flexibility and a short response time. Managing change requires a preferred vision of the future. We need images of potential tomorrows, conceptions of possible tomorrows, identification of our probable tomorrows.

The central concepts of the Recreation and Park Movement are ideas whose time has come. The concern for people that has been and is the primary theme in the philosophical foundations of the Recreation Movement has become the major thrust of contemporary life in this country. It is apparent in the humanistic movement that is sweeping the nation and the world. We see it in humanistic psychology, attacks on the abuses of technology, the peace movement, empathy for the poor, the drive for improved medical care, the move to reject possessions as the symbol of identity, the effort to improve education, women's lib, race relations, and in a thousand other ways. These ideas are being acted out in programs and demonstrations and individual efforts all around us.

The fundamental themes of the Park Movement are also a major national obsession. Conservation and ecology are the watchwords of the age. The realization that human beings are not independent of nature but a part of it, has seeped into the national consciousness. The few that have been concerned about survival of the endangered species are now joined by the thousands who are deeply concerned about the survival of man in the cities of man. We now see mankind as an endangered species. It is a frightening prospect.

THE FUTURE OF THE RECREATION AND PARK MOVEMENT

Alvin Toffler has suggested, "No serious futurist deals in prediction." It is not our purpose to predict the future, rather it is our intent to examine some of the alternatives and to suggest what some elements of the preferred future for the Recreation and Park Movement are.

It is time for us to devote increasing thought to the role recreation services should play in the community and what recreation should mean to the individual. We can begin to rethink the content of recreation programs by noting the nature of the promise of the human species. Contribution to fulfillment of that promise is the reason for recreation and park programs. A central purpose of community recreation programs is to help improve the quality of living. A great many park and recreation people have not made the connection between parks and the environment or recreation and the quality of life.

We must give more attention to the recreation concept and improve our definition of it. Current definitions ignore or give little attention to the psychological implications of recreation. They are activity centered. Definition in terms of activities is unsatisfactory because a given activity may provide recreation for one individual and not for another; worse yet, it may provide recreation for a person at one time but not at another. Current definitions work within a time frame—leisure—but recreation may occur at any time. They hold out for inherent reward, but many recreation responses are dependent on feedback from others, and it is not clear why acceptance of material reward invalidates the experience. Some mandate social acceptability. A little introspection will reveal the absurdity of that criterion.

We should have discovered long ago the nature of the business we are in, but we have not. Only now are we beginning to rethink what recreation is. In the emerging view it is not activities, or facilities, or programs that are central, it is what happens to people. Recreation is not a specific event, a point in time, or a place in space, it is a dimension in life; it is a state of being. The proposed definition is:

> Recreation is an emotional condition within an individual human being that flows from a feeling of well-being and self-satisfaction. It is characterized by feelings of mastery, achievement, exhilaration, acceptance, success, personal worth, and pleasure. It reinforces a positive self-image. Recreation is a response to aesthetic experience, achievement of personal goals, or positive feedback from others. It is independent of activity, leisure, or social acceptance.

Following that definition, recreation is feeling good about yourself. It is a peak experience in self-satisfaction. It stems from aesthetic experience—the sense of being a significant part of a vast and mysterious whole; it comes from establishing a personal goal and achieving it—the higher the standard, the more intense the recreational experience; it comes from favorable reactions of others—the kind of support that builds a self-image of personal affection and competence. Recreation has nothing to do with leisure, it can occur at any time. It has nothing to do with activity; it can occur in tennis or accounting, but it may not happen in either tennis or accounting. It has nothing to do with social acceptance. In short, our traditional definitions of recreation do not advance our understanding of it. For thirty or forty years or more the Park and Recreation Movement has been deluded by a false perception of recreation. This has warped our services, given us false priorities, prevented effective evaluation of results, and inhibited our ability to interpret what we do. Worst of all, it has prevented us from developing an understanding of our goals and methods. The popular understanding of recreation in our field cannot sustain further development. The concept is bankrupt.

Recognition of recreation as an internalized emotional response is comparatively easy. Acting on that knowledge in recreation and park agencies will be far more difficult, but it is necessary if we are to substantially improve our services. Adopting the suggested definition, or something like it, is the first step toward improving our contribution to the quality of life. Developing the methods of implementing the definition is the second.

Some implications of this proposed new definition are already clear:

- We must alter our programs and the way they are conducted to emphasize human development, well-being, and development of a positive self-image.
- We must enhance the possibility that people can experience the peak experience described in the definition—in short, the opportunity for aesthetic response, achievement of personal goals, and positive feedback from others.
- We must rethink competition and the way it is used in recreation programs.
- We must accept responsibility for the human consequences of what we do.
- We must evaluate everything we do in human terms. The critical questions are not, "How many were there?" or "Who won?" The critical question is, "What happened to Jose, Mary, Sam, and Joan in this experience?"

We must reorient our approach to services, to think not only in terms of activities and programs, but also in terms of human experience. The recreation program should help each individual extend his intellectual and emotional reach. The three-dimensional man is the man who is a participant in the creative process. He is one who has something to say, a way to say it, and someone to listen. Recreation improves awareness, deepens understanding, stimulates appreciation, develops one's powers, and enlarges the sources of enjoyment. It promotes individual fulfillment. It encourages self-discovery. It helps give meaning to life.

People who grew up on the frontier a century or two ago were isolated because of physical separation; today people in the cities are isolated because of emotional separation. Factors which inhibit self-expression through recreation may be physical, social, or economic. They may be inherent in the social or political system, but the most severe limitations are often self-generated. Lack of skill, insecurity, little knowledge of opportunity, fear of failure and a variety of other internalized factors can limit or destroy motivation. Overcoming these inhibitions often requires competent leadership. Learning to serve in this way is a very personal process. It is a matter of extending one's experience by sharing the experience with others, assimilating it, and eventually drawing on it. It is a search for attitudes rather than methods. It is more a matter of being than a matter of doing. The highly personal patterns of human interaction that are at the root of successful service in this field are not established procedures. They are expressions of experience and attitudes. What one thinks and feels about oneself and other people comes through. The recruitment and training of personnel who can give adequate leadership will require methods we have not yet invented.

We must have better planning processes. Critics argue that much planning is antihuman and in many cases they are right. It is easy to lose social, cultural, and psychological values in the overwhelming desire to maximize economic efficiency. The answer to the criticism is not to act without plan; that approach generates its own tyranny. Rather it is to devise a planning method that embraces these values. We desperately need a method of planning that permits *social cost-benefit* analysis. Lacking such a system, we are turning control of our social enterprises over to the accounting mind. The accounting mind reaches decisions by a method in which short-range fiscal consequences are the only criterion of value. Recreation and park services will not survive in that kind of an environment. Most of the great social problems that disfigure our national life cannot be addressed in a climate dominated by that kind of value system.

We do not need irrationality, rigid traditionality, passive acceptance of change, despair, or witless revolution. We need a powerful, rational strategy for the management of change. We need planning based on an accurate assessment of the world and our place in it. We need an understanding of purpose. We need a consensus broad enough to sustain united action. We need programs that provide essential human services, and we need informed, articulate spokesmen who can help create a climate in which our agencies can prosper.

Human needs are met through experiences; the method of providing experience is program; participation in program is based on interest. The interests to be met, the programs to be conducted, the experiences to be provided are determined by organizational goals. Organizational goals must be immediately responsive to the needs and wishes of those the organization was created to serve. Since different people experience physical and social conditions in different ways, it is imperative that facilities and programs be designed with particular clientele and particular reference groups in mind. The idea that there exist "universals" of human behavior and human response is the idea that produces stereotyped programs and stereotyped facilities. There may be a few near universals like the physical and aesthetic response to water, but there are not many and even here the response to water is expressed in different ways by different people. The imperative is that persons planning programs and parks must know intimately the culture, wishes, social patterns, and life-style of the people who are to use them; the park or program must fit those conditions. There is no such thing as a universal man and there is no such thing as a universal park, and there is no such thing as universal recreation. There is an individual, emotional response, by an individual person, in an individual park.

We must recognize the potential role of recreation in the development of people. The goals of organized recreation programs are to provide people opportunities for the exercise of their powers, opportunity for recreational experience, opportunity for the development of a positive self-image. Any program that receives a participant whole and sends him back damaged in self-respect, self-esteem, or relationships with others is not a recreation program. The fact that it may be a basketball program with games played during leisure is irrelevant. Such a program is not a recreational program unless the emotional response of the participant is positive.

We have need for challenge and risk-taking in recreation programs. Such elements must be regulated to assure the penalties for failure are not too high. They can be graduated to all levels of skill and risk but they are an essential element that has great relevance to self-discovery, self-development, and self-enhancement. Risk and challenge are not only present in physical activities, they can be an ingredient in social activities also. Challenge is present in a broad range of pursuits from skydiving to sailing, and from acting to angling.

Recreation programs can offer a chance for experiencing the joys of mastery. In modern life it is a rare experience for one to prove himself or to exhibit mastery. To run a risk, meet a challenge, to see the results of one's own effort are all important means of developing a positive self-image. To be competent, confident, and recognized is a powerful feeling. Recreation pursuits are often the only arena where such a feeling can be experienced.

How we *feel* about things is enormously important. Open space, for example, is usually justified because it provides recreational opportunity, conserves scenic and natural resources, and gives form to metropolitan communities. None of these reasons says much about how open space serves people. It implies much but says little, because it does not communicate the human needs served by open space and how we feel about it. The study of "Open Space for Human Needs" provides some insights on the contributions open space can make to the people of the city. In the view of those who completed the study, open space in a metropolitan area provides psychic relief from the urban landscape. It provides choices not otherwise available. It gives perspective, changing vistas, orientation. It permits other perceptions of the relationship between the world and self. It aids exploration of other facets of one's identity. Open space generates a different psychological response than a strictly urban landscape. We feel differently about it. The benefits of an open space system identified in the study are to manipulate material directly, to exhibit mastery, to meet a challenge or run a risk, opportunity for low level stimuli as a release from the density of personal encounter in the urban world, relaxation, contrast, social contact free of the usual restraints of city living, opportunity to try new social roles, achievement of a sense of being part of the natural order of things, extension of one's intellectual and emotional reach. This is not the typical list of the landscape designer or the activity specialist. What is being explored here is the meaning open space has for the user. The list helps define psychological need and intellectual and emotional response.

The recreation movement must draw on its own independent research and on the social sciences, particularly sociology, psychology, and social anthropology. We need the concepts and theories these disciplines can offer, to rationalize, extend, and improve the services of recreation agencies. We must evaluate and select what we use in terms of human need. We must interpret what we take in terms of human values, and the development of human effectiveness. To operate effectively in this kind of a mission, we will need to be able to measure not only participation in recreational events, but also perceptions and emotional reactions to these events.

Every social agency in our nation is under test. Either they will adapt to the new time now developing or they will die. Drawing all the wagons in a circle and defending the status quo, will not keep out the night. Educational institutions, churches, youth organizations, recreational agencies, fraternities, women's clubs, and many other institutions are substantially out of phase with the wishes and perceived needs of their intended clientele. Organizational obsolescence is widespread and growing. Social and technological change is overwhelming most institutions, because the processes of change are more rapid than the processes of adaptation. What is needed is a continuous process of organizational renewal that updates the agency values, programs, and procedures at a pace equal to the process of social and technological change. None of us knows how to do that precisely, but we must learn to do it.

A very live question in our society today is whether the institutions of our nation can change. The nation retains the hope that our institutions are capable of generating the will to change internally. Park and recreation agencies have not yet been the object of intense criticism as the educational system, the police, the church, and lately the prison system have been because we have not been important enough in national priorities. As a result, we have not had the enormous external pressure for change some other institutions have had. Therefore, the question of whether we can change of our own volition is a significant one.

We are moving toward greater citizen involvement in community affairs and in local government. Many programs supported by the federal government require it and the times demand it. We ought to foster that principle. One way to involve more citizens in a useful way is to form an advisory council for each center. Some administrators are reluctant to do that. There is a fear of citizen participation that centers around loss of control, but when such councils are formed properly and utilized skillfully, the benefits far outweigh any liabilities. We must learn to work successfully with large numbers of citizen groups.

Our vision of appropriate government demands participation of *all* the people because it is right and because it is more effective. An adequate set of goals for a recreation agency cannot be set by a few people sitting alone. As the number of social components grows and change makes the whole system less stable, it becomes less and less possible to ignore the demands of political minorities. Goals set without consultation of those who are affected will be increasingly difficult to execute. We must find a way to involve hundreds of people in each community in the question that is so rarely asked, "What kind of a community do you want in ten, twenty, or thirty years?" It is time we addressed the all-important question of what our goals are. What kinds of services do we wish to render and to whom? What are the social benefits of those services? How will we know whether these goals are being reached? If we are short of resources, as we probably will be, what are our priorities?

The Recreation and Park Movement cannot be an effective political force until it is unified, aware, willing to pursue its ideals in legislation, and skilled in the political arena. We must gain legislative support for the Park and Recreaton Movement and for our individual agencies.

The vehicle that holds us together nationally is the Recreation and Park Movement. The Movement requires nurture, too. It needs mass, a sense of mission, renewal, leadership, ideas, identity, goals, political sophistication, and a social conscience. Collectively we must give it what it needs. Without the Movement, we are a collection of disconnected parts.

There is the fear, and it may not be an unfounded fear, that the forces in American society are centrifugal. Our aspirations for a more humanistic society rise faster than our progress in developing such a society. This aspiration gap is a source of much frustration. The world is far from perfect but it is not unalterable. There is progress. The fact that our perceptions of a quality life exceed our ability to make it a reality should not be a cause for despair. It produces frustration, of course, particularly in the "new generation," but the dream always precedes the reality. It is significant that we can now dream of a better society. There is a chance the dream may become the reality and that is the promise that makes the social turmoil we are now going through worthwhile.

We, in the Recreation and Park Movement, are now caught with a vast conceptual attic, filled with ideas that are no longer useful but that are too good to throw away. To adjust to our future, it will be necessary to discard some facets of the past. We often perceive our institutions as change agents but evidence suggests otherwise. Many social institutions are created to control and inhibit change and they are often effective. Even among those not specifically organized to preserve tradition and manage the status quo, a generally conservative approach is common. Whether we can generate the will to change and the sense of direction necessary to adapt to our changing environment is a question we must now face.

Many people feel powerless in the swift flowing stream of change. They feel swept along by currents, and they feel they cannot steer. In reality it is not the future that is beyond our grasp and beyond our ability to influence. It is the present that cannot be mastered. A common reaction to "future shock" is to seize the present and try to hold it. More common still is an attempt to turn back to a time that looks in retrospect, more orderly, more pleasant, less threatening. These are the responses that are beyond control. One cannot hold today; one cannot regain yesterday, it is only tomorrow that is subject to planning and control.

We are all engaged in the struggle to make an imperfect society work. There is the distinct possibility that American society and the Recreation and Park Movement are on divergent courses. If we fail to deal effectively with the future, it may be because we have none. It is time we devoted ourselves to the complex question of what our purposes are, and it is time we devoted ourselves to the achievement of those purposes. Here is an action program to begin these tasks.

PART III ● An Action Program for the Recreation and Park Movement

A. To reorient the primary thrust of the Movement and to accelerate the processes of change, we recommend the National Recreation and Park Association, the agencies and the individuals active in the park and recreation field, undertake accomplishment of these goals:

1. Using this statement as a working paper, rethink the future of the Movement in terms of its meaning for the people of the local community, nation, and of the world.

2. Adopt a humanistic ethic as the central value system of the Movement.

3. Develop and act on a social conscience that focuses park and recreation services on the great social problems of our time, and develop programs designed to contribute to the amelioration of those problems.

4. Develop a set of guidelines for programs that emphasizes human welfare, human development, and social action.

5. Foster integration, coherence, and growth in the Recreation and Park Movement because our movement represents a major potential in the world-wide thrust for positive life experience.

6. Reorganize and reorient our agencies in a way that will renew their energies, improve their sense of mission, and make them more responsive to human need and social change.

7. Establish common cause with the environmentalists and other social movements that embrace a value system similar to our own.

8. Establish a substantial research effort designed to investigate the nature of recreational experience, to improve our understanding and definition of it, and to strengthen our ability to stimulate it.

9. Develop evaluation methods capable of measuring the contribution of park and recreation experience to human welfare which can make us accountable for the human consequences of what we do.

10. Develop an effective interpretation program capable of articulating to a national and world-wide audience the meaning of park and recreation experience in human terms.

11. Revise recreation and park curricula to emphasize development of a social mission, a humanistic ethic, the processes of human

Prepared by Sy Greben and David E. Gray.

development throughout life, the psychology of park and recreation experience, group processes, and human ecology.

12. Take the data, values, and concepts thus assembled and promote them as central themes in a comprehensive in-service training effort in recreation and park agencies throughout the nation, an in-service training effort which is clear about where we are and where we wish to proceed.

13. Organize the members of the Recreation and Park Movement as an effective political force capable of affecting local and national political processes.

B. In support of the goals, we recommend *The National Recreation and Park Association:*

1. Accept responsibility for stewardship and leadership of the Recreation and Park Movement.

2. Create an organizational structure and a program which can attract to the Association and successfully involve thousands of lay and professional members. Lay membership must be encouraged and the Association must frontally attack a situation in which the large majority of our "professionals" do not see any reason for joining their own Association. This is a commentary on the commitment of the personnel and a judgment of the effectiveness of NRPA. As historically constituted, the Association has failed to prove to its prospective members that there is a viable purpose for membership. The hopeful signs of change already visible must be pursued vigorously. The Association must draw the bulk of its support from its own members.

3. Promote recognition of intelligent use of our leisure as a national issue which has enormous implications for American society; move quickly to define the issue, suggest appropriate responses, and to elicit the national attention the issue deserves.

4. Take the lead in developing broad understanding and acceptance of these concepts:

   a. participation, not winning, is the legitimate goal of leisure utilization, and participation, not merely watching, is basic to health and development;

   b. working together rather than working alone to provide fulfillment and recognition is a legitimate goal of leisure activities;

   c. the function of leisure is unrealized when the participant receives no real sense of gratification from an experience or when gratification is achieved as an antisocial, destructive phenomena associated with another person's discomfort or disgrace.

There is urgent need to accept these concepts and act upon them beginning with the park and recreation profession.

5. Take the lead in integrating recreation and parks into a single entity with an appropriate name that encompasses both recreation and parks and which reflects concern for productive living in a healthy, creative, leisure life.

6. Provide national leadership to the environmental movement which enlists the forces of park and recreation personnel in the cause of restoring and preserving our natural environment; begin to formulate immediately a national strategy that will make the move for a better environment local and urban, as well as rural.

7. Develop and advocate an open space policy for America that articulates the meaning of open space in human terms.

8. Become a leading participant in the major social movements of our day with specific emphasis on the need for equal opportunity for all Americans including racial minorities, minorities based on age, and minorities based on sex; begin this task by increasing its sensitivity and responsiveness to its own minority membership.

9. Extend and improve the excellent work already begun in providing the national government information required to help our leaders formulate effective legislation; formulate annually an NRPA legislative program.

10. Take action to reduce and hopefully eliminate the pattern of internal and persistent bickering which has been so much a part of the relationships among the branches, the state organizations, the National Council, and other units of the Association.

C. To further these goals, we recommend *local governmental units including counties, cities, and special districts:*

1. Closely identify with the total planning process commitment to planning, not only to the obvious factors of open space requirements and total park acreage based on population density, but also to matters of set-back ordinances, requirement for underground utilities, sign and billboard regulation, control over automobiles and truck traffic through green belts, noise abatement, and street tree planting. As an immediate goal, recreation

and park agencies should be regularly represented and assume leadership roles on the local planning body and should develop, publicize, and support a comprehensive master plan for the community.

2. Carry out a regular legislative function, symbolized specifically by development annually of a legislative program which it actively pursues, and which becomes the primary basis for program implementation.

3. Develop a statement of goals and objectives, which is known and understood by the total staff of the organization, the community, the citizens, and government leaders; the statement must be ever-changing, dynamic, and a reflection of our highest ideals. It must also include reference to:

    a. Our belief in, and identity with, community leadership and citizen participation; not "lip service" to community participation, but true joint planning and operating involving the energy and resources of the people in the communities and the park and recreation staff.

    b. The responsibility of our total staff to know and understand what we mean when we refer to "positive leisure experience." There must be recognition that this can be accomplished only if we are completely committed to this ideal, and that we are willing to continuously communicate these ideals.

    c. Support of the aspirations of the many subcultures in the community and our conviction that we must assume a leadership role in assuring equal opportunity and participation for all our citizens.

    d. Our deep commitment to the preservation of a healthy environment and our definition of the specific responsibilities which must be assumed by the staff in making this goal possible.

    e. Problems that must be confronted, priorities, and commitment to seeking workable solutions.

4. Recruit, develop, and support individuals to lead recreation and park agencies who are capable of occupying positions of community leadership, who are seen as leaders by the members of the community, who represent the ideals of the Movement, who are strong enough to fight for an unpopular cause without losing the ability to lead, and who are skillful enough to accomplish the agency's goals.

5. In individual departments, there are specific goals that we can and should start achieving now. A partial list would include the following:

   a. The total staff, and particularly those responsible for individual centers or activities, must understand the concept of recreation as a positive and pleasurable experience for the participant, and as a means of emphasizing human development.

   b. The total staff must be committed to the importance of its mission. It is when we settle for minimum commitment that we achieve minimum response from our communities —and it is when we lack commitment that we assume a low priority of importance in our communities.

   c. Employees must stop being parks *or* recreation staff members and recognize a oneness that is defined by the recipients of our services, not by the emptiness of our internal conflicts. We should aim to eliminate organizational definitions such as Parks Division, or Recreation Branch for the nomenclature is no longer relevant and by its continued existence it tends to perpetuate an expensive, outdated fiction of the past.

   d. Begin now to eliminate all artificial restraint from program participation based upon sexual and ethnic distinctions. These bars are useless and arbitrary and they help to perpetuate a condition in our society that is repugnant.

   e. Develop an affirmative action program intended to off-set the limitations on employment that have historically hampered minorities and women; eliminate job requirements which discriminate in any way against individual or group because of race, sex, or any other irrelevant factor.

   f. Define a set of responsibilities for community participation, for each facility or activity director, and a time table for achieving the increments of this participation; community participation should be viewed as including evidence of an active, viable, *representative* community support group which participates in major decision-making including land acquisition, development, program planning, *budgeting*, and program scheduling.

   g. Assign environmental and planning responsibilities for its *entire* field staff, particularly those staff members who minimize their environmental role by thinking only in terms of recreation programs. These assignments should include at least some of the following:

    (1) Development of an active environmental organization at each center, well supported by the total staff.

    (2) Organization of programs which improve the environment of the center, and the environment of the community. These should include tree planting (and maintenance) programs, painting, and clean-up campaigns, improvements of drainage, mural painting, organized community action in combatting vandalism, and participation in community action to protect the environment against undesirable intrusion.

    (3) Presentation of lectures and other programs in conjunction with local schools and environmental matters.

    (4) Maintaining facilities with concern for maximum use and aesthetics.

  h. Ascertain that individual centers and activities function at times most convenient for the public, not the staff. This may mean expanded evening and weekend schedules, and it may demand innovative experimentation with various types of flexible work schedules.

D. In pursuit of these goals, we recommend the *colleges and universities:*

  1. Reexamine the scope of their commitment to the Park and Recreation Movement, to think through the nature and goals of the Movement, its potential contribution to American life, the kind of education candidates for careers in the field should have, articulation and improvement of research efforts, and organization and extension of the literature.

  2. Undertake a systematic investigation of the outcomes of park and recreation experience and develop a taxonomy of human benefits.

  3. Establish contacts with park and recreation agencies that will strengthen in-service and reentry education services.

  4. In concert with other segments of the Movement, develop an interpretation program for recreation and park services that focuses on the contribution these services make to human development and welfare.

E. To achieve these goals, we recommend *individuals* in the Recreation
   and Park Movement:

    1. Develop a commitment not only to the agencies of local service,
       but also to the Movement and to the organizations that sustain it.
    2. Provide ideas, financial and political support, and leadership to
       the National Recreation and Park Association.
    3. Develop a national perspective, an understanding of the forces
       of social change, and appreciation of the potential of the Move-
       ment, and avenues of professional service through study of the
       field, participation in professional meetings, interaction with
       others active in park, recreation, conservation, and public affairs.
    4. Aid in local and national arenas the processes of change and the
       improvement and expansion of park, recreation, city planning,
       public administration, and conservation services.

selected bibliography

Anderson, Charles, and Gordon, Milton. "The Blue-Collar Worker at Leisure."
In *Blue Collar World: Studies of the American Worker,* edited by Arthur
B. Shostak and William Gomberg, pp. 407-416. Englewood Cliffs, New
Jersey: Prentice-Hall, Inc., 1964.

Bannon, Joseph J., ed. *Outreach—Extending Community Service in Urban Areas.*
Springfield, Illinois: Charles C Thomas Publishing Co., 1973.

Bennis, Warren, and Slater, Philip E. *The Temporary Society.* New York: Harper and Row, Publishers, 1968.

Berger, Bennett, "Hippie Morality—More Old Than New," *Transaction* 5:19-23,
26-27.

———. *Looking for America.* Englewood Cliffs, New Jersey: Prentice-Hall, Inc.,
1971.

———. "The Sociology of Leisure: Some Suggestions." *Industrial Relations* 1:31-
45.

Best, Fred. *The Future of Work.* Englewood Cliffs, New Jersey: Prentice-Hall,
Inc., 1973.

Brickman, William W., and Lehrer, Stanley. *Automation, Education and Human Values.* New York: Thomas Y. Crowell Co., 1966.

Brightbill, Charles K. *Educating for Leisure—Centered Living.* Harrisburg,
Pennsylvania: Stackpole Books, 1966.

———. *The Challenge of Leisure.* Englewood Cliffs, New Jersey: Prentice-Hall,
Inc., 1963.

Burch, William R., Jr.; Cheek, Neil H., Jr.; and Taylor, Lee. *Social Behavior,
Natural Resources and the Environment.* New York: Harper and Row,
Publishers, 1972.

Burdge, Rabel J. "Levels of Occupational Prestige and Leisure Activity," *Journal of Leisure Research* 1:262-274.

Butler, George O. *Introduction to Community Recreation,* 4th ed. New York:
McGraw-Hill Book Co., 1967.

Carlson, Reynold; Deppe, Theodore; and MacLean, Janet. *Recreation in American Life,* 2nd ed., Belmont, California: Wadsworth Publishing Co. Inc.,
1972.

Charlesworth, James C., ed. *Leisure in America: Blessing or Curse?* Monograph
#4, American Academy of Political and Social Science, April, 1964.

229

Cunningham, David A.; Montoye, Henry J.; Metzner, Helen L.; and Keller, Jacob B. "Active Leisure Activities as Related to Occupation." *Journal of Leisure Research* 2:104-111.

deGrazia, Sebastian. *Of Time, Work and Leisure.* New York: The Twentieth Century Fund, 1962.

Dubin, Robert. "Industrial Worker's World: A Study of 'Central Life Interests' of Industrial Workers." *Social Problems* 3:131-142.

Dunston, Maryjane, and Garlan, Patricia. *Worlds in the Making: Probes for Students of the Future.* Englewood Cliffs, New Jersey: Prentice-Hall, Inc., 1970.

Eason, Jean. "Life-Style Counseling for a Reluctant Leisure Class." *Personnel and Guidance Journal* 51:127-132.

Ellis, M. J. *Why People Play.* Englewood Cliffs, New Jersey: Prentice-Hall, Inc., 1972.

Fabun, Don. *The Dynamics of Change.* Englewood Cliffs, New Jersey: Prentice-Hall, Inc., 1967.

Farina, John. "Towards A Philosophy of Leisure." *Convergence* 2:14-16.

Feldman, Saul D., and Thielbar, Gerald W., eds. *Life Styles: Diversity in American Society.* Boston: Little, Brown and Co., 1972.

Faught, Millard C. *More Timewealth For You.* New York: Pyramid Books, Inc., 1969.

Gerstl, Joel. "Leisure, Taste and Occupational Milieu." *Social Problems* 9:56-58.

Gold, Seymour M. *Urban Recreation Planning.* Philadelphia: Lea & Febiger, 1973.

Gray, David E. "Exploring Inner Space." *Parks and Recreation* 7:18-19, 46.

———. "The Case for Compensatory Recreation." *Parks and Recreation* 4:23-24, 48-49.

———. "The Tyranny of the Chain-Link Fence." *California Parks and Recreation* 10:10.

———. "This Alien Thing Called Leisure." Paper presented at Oregon State University, Corvallis, Oregon, July 8, 1971.

Gray, David E., and Pelegrino, Don, eds. *Reflection on the Recreation and Park Movement.* Dubuque, Iowa: Wm. C. Brown Co. Publishers, 1973.

Green, Thomas F. *Work, Leisure and the American Schools.* New York: Random House, 1968.

Guggenheimer, Elinor C. *Planning for Parks and Recreation Needs in Urban Areas.* New York: Twayne Publishers, Inc., 1969.

Hatry, Harry, and Dunn, Diana. *Measuring the Effectiveness of Local Services: Recreation.* Washington, D.C.: The Urban Institute, 1971.

Haun, Paul. *Recreation: A Medical Viewpoint.* New York: Bureau of Publications, Columbia Univ., 1965.

Havighurst, Robert J., and Feigenbaum, Kenneth. "Leisure and Life-Style." *American Journal of Sociology* 64:396-405.

Howe, Louise Kapp. *The White Majority: Between Poverty and Affluence.* New York: Vintage Books, 1970.

Jenkins, Shirley. *Comparative Recreation Needs and Services in New York Neighborhoods.* New York: Community Council of Greater New York, 1963.

Jensen, Clayne R. *Outdoor Recreation in America.* Minneapolis: Burgess Publishing Co., 1970.

Johnston, Denis F. "The Future of Work: Three Possible Alternatives." *Monthly Labor Review* 95:3-11.

Kaplan, Max. "Leisure and Design." Paper presented at the American Iron and Steel Institute, Chicago, Illinois, March 23, 1972.

———. *Leisure in America.* New York: John Wiley and Sons, Inc., 1960.

Kaplan, Max, and Bosserman, Phillip, eds. *Technology, Human Values and Leisure.* Nashville: Abingdon Press, 1971.

Kerr, Walter. *The Decline of Pleasure.* New York: Simon and Schuster, Inc., 1962.

Klapp, Orrin E. *Collective Search for Identity.* New York: Holt, Rinehart and Winston, 1969.

Knopp, Timothy B. "Environmental Determinants of Recreation Behavior." *Journal of Leisure Research* 4:129-138.

Kraus, Richard. *Public Recreation and the Negro.* New York: Center for Urban Education, 1968.

———. *Recreation and Leisure in Modern Society.* New York: Appleton-Century-Crofts, Inc., 1971.

———. *Recreation and the Schools: Guides to Effective Practices in Leisure Education and Community Recreation Sponsorship.* New York: The Macmillan Co., 1964.

———. *Urban Parks and Recreation: Challenge of the 1970s,* New York: Community Council of Greater New York, 1972.

Lejeune, Robert. *Class and Conflict in American Society.* Chicago: Markham Publishing Co., 1972.

Leonard, George B. *Education and Ecstasy.* New York: Dell Publishing Co., Inc., 1968.

Linder, Staffan B. *The Harried Leisure Class.* New York: Columbia University Press, 1969.

Lystad, Mary. *As They See It: Changing Values of College Youth.* Cambridge, Massachusetts: Schenkman Publishing Co., Inc., 1973.

McLuhan, Marshall. *The Medium Is the Massage.* New York: Bantam Books, Inc., 1967.

Malcolm, Henry, *Generation of Narcissus.* Boston: Little, Brown and Co., 1971.

232   selected bibliography

Martin, Alexander Reid. *Leisure Time—A Creative Force.* New York: The Council on the Aging, 1963.

Maslow, Abraham H., ed. *New Knowledge in Human Values.* Chicago, Illinois: Henry Regnery Co., 1959.

May, Rollo. *Man's Search for Himself.* New York: New American Library, Inc., 1967.

Michael, Donald N. *The Future Society.* New Brunswick, New Jersey: Transaction, Inc., 1970.

Miller, Norman, and Robinson, Duane. *The Leisure Age.* Belmont, California: Wadsworth Publishing Co., Inc., 1963.

Murphy, James F. "Community Recreation: A Dynamic Process." *California Parks and Recreation* 23:14.

———. ed. *Concepts of Leisure: Philosophical Implications.* Englewood Cliffs, New Jersey: Prentice-Hall, Inc., 1974.

———. "The Counter Culture of Leisure." *Parks and Recreation* 7:34, 41-42.

Nash, Jay B. *Philosophy of Recreation and Leisure.* Dubuque, Iowa: Wm. C. Brown Co. Publishers, 1953.

Niepoth, E. William. "A Conceptualization of Leisure Service." In *Leisure Service Delivery System: A Modern Perspective,* James F. Murphy, John G. Williams, E. William Niepoth and Paul D. Brown, Philadelphia: Lee & Febiger, 1973.

———. "Users and Non-users of Recreation and Park Services." In *Reflections on the Recreation and Park Movement,* edited by David E. Gray and Donald A. Pelegrino, Dubuque, Iowa: Wm. C. Brown Co. Publishers, 1973, pp. 131-142.

Nesbitt, John A.; Brown, Paul D.; and Murphy, James F. *Recreation and Leisure Service for the Disadvantaged.* Philadelphia: Lea & Febiger, 1970.

Parker, Stanley. *The Future of Work and Leisure.* New York: Praeger Publishers, Inc., 1971.

Pieper, Josef. *Leisure: The Basis of Culture.* New York: Pantheon Books, Inc., 1952.

Poor, Riva, ed. *4 Days, 40 Hours: Reporting a Revolution in Work and Leisure.* Cambridge, Massachusetts: Bursk and Poor Publishing Co., 1970.

Recreation in the Nation's Cities: Problems and Approaches. Washington, D.C.: Department of Urban Studies, National League of Cities, 1968.

Reich, Charles. *The Greening of America.* New York: Random House, 1970.

Reissman, Leonard. "Class, Leisure and Social Participation." *American Sociological Review* 10:75-84.

Report of the National Advisory Commission on Civil Disorders. New York: Bantam Books, Inc., 1968.

Roberts, Kenneth. *Leisure.* London: Longmans, Green and Co., Ltd., 1971.

Roszak, Theodore. *The Making of a Counter Culture*. New York: Doubleday and Co., 1969.

Sexton, Patricia Cayo, and Sexton, Brendon. *Blue Collar and Hard Hats*. New York: Vintage Books, 1971.

Slater, Philip. *The Pursuit of Loneliness*. Boston: Beacon Press, 1970.

Spergel, Irving A. *Community Problem Solving: The Delinquency Example*. Chicago: The University of Chicago Press, 1969.

Staley, Edwin J., and Miller, Norman P. *Leisure and the Quality of Life*. Washington, D.C.: American Association for Health, Physical Education and Recreation, 1972.

Stein, Thomas A., and Sessoms, H. Douglas, eds. *Recreation and Special Populations*. Boston: Holbrook Press, Inc., 1973.

Teich, Albert H. *Technology and Man's Future*. New York: St. Martin's Press, 1972.

"The Leisure Enigma." *Quest*, Monograph #5, The National Association for Physical Education of College Women and the National College of Physical Education for Men, December, 1965.

Theobald, Robert. *An Alternative Future for America II*. Chicago: Swallow Press, 1970.

Toffler, Alvin. *Future Shock*. New York: Random House, 1970.

———. *The Futurists*. New York: Random House, 1972.

Weiner, Myron E. *Systems Approach to Municipal Recreation*. Storrs: Institute of Public Service, University of Connecticut, 1970.

Wilensky, Harold L. "The Uneven Distribution of Leisure: The Impact of Economic Growth on Free Time." *Social Problems* 9:32-56.

Wurman, Richard Saul; Levy, Alan; and Katz, Joel. *The Nature of Recreation*. Cambridge, Massachusetts: MIT Press, 1972.

Index

Adventure playgrounds, 69-72
  supervisor, role of, 70, 72
Aging
  characteristics of, 147
  dynamics of, 146-50
  ill aged, 147
  leisure services for, 148-50
  retirement communities, 149-50

Berger, Bennett, 110, 112, 124
Bishop, Doyle, 3, 33
Blacks
  initial recreation provision of, 44
  racial discrimination of, 47
Bureau of Colored Work, 44
Bureau of Outdoor Recreation, 35, 47-
    48

Community
  characteristics of, 56
  concept of, 56
  temporary, 57
Community Action Project, 58-59
Community catalyst, 3, 61-63, 68-69,
    96-98
  advantages of, 98
  humanistic consideration of, 164
  preparation of, 166
  program examples of, 97-98
  qualities of, 63
  role of, 68-69
Community education
  objectives for, 159-60
Community life, 56-57
  developmental process of, 57
Community recreation
  new strategy for, 67-68
Consciousness
  individual, self-concept of, 31
  leisure-based, definition of, 31

Counseling
  behavioral approach, 87
  humanistic approach, 89-92
  humanistic life-style, 87-91
  participant-centered approach, 87
Cyberculture, 193-94
  definition of, 193
Cybernation
  definition of, 11

DeGrazia, Sebastian, 5
Drug subculture, 85-86
Dulles, Foster Rhea, 28

Education
  humanistic, goals of, 161-62
  society's task in, 154
Electric technology
  process of, 188-89
Ellis, Michael, 14
Environment
  ecological concerns for, 135
  energy problem, 137
  future scenarios, 137
  leisure service guidelines, 135-36

Farina, John, 8
Frye, Virginia, 7
Future shock
  definition of, 188, 200

Gold, Seymour, 65-66, 67, 74, 76, 131
Gray, David, 7, 13-14, 40, 63, 64, 136,
    140-41, 143, 169

Howard, Dennis, 3, 33, 34, 35
Human development, 71
Humanism, 2, 212

Humanistic ethic
  definition of, 3
  implications of, 63-65
  increase in, 182
  values of, 41, 42t
Humanistic psychology, 2, 40, 212

Identity
  collective search for, 83-84

Johnston, Denis, 10

Kaplan, Max, 7, 127, 142
Kraus, Richard, 7, 23, 25, 27-28, 29,
      49, 119, 120, 135, 148, 158

Leisure
  activity preferences, 34
  behavioral view, 31-32
  concepts of, 5-9
    antiutilitarian perspective, 8
    classical perspective, 5-6
    discretionary perspective, 6-7
    holistic perspective, 8-9
    social instrument perspective, 7-
      8, 58
  ecology of, 194-96
  education for, 154-70
  historical social orders of,
    feudal order, 20-21, 26
      Greek and Roman cultures, 24-
        26
      medieval communities, 26
      Renaissance, 27
    industrial order, 21, 27-30
      Puritan folk festivals, 28
      Civil War era, 28-29
    postindustrial order, 23
    primitive order, 20, 23-24
    transitional order, 21, 23
  life-style perspectives, 35-36, 85
  measuring value of, 195-96
  mental health, 144-46
  personality indicators, 34
  problem of, 190-91
  quality of life, 192
  redefinition of, 200-227
  school's responsibility for, 156-58
  self-actualization, 143-44

  student views on, 110-11
  working class, 114-17
Leisure education
  goals of, 158-59
  thrust of, 160
Leisure ethic, 50-51, 145, 183-85
Leisure service
  chain-link fence philosophy, 61
  comparative need for, 130-31
  deprived groups, provision for, 130
  dissatisfaction in, 96
  dynamics of, 86-87
  filters of change, 142-43
  institution of, 57
  measurement of, 65-67
  minority group approach, 119
    special responsibility for, 128-32
  objective of, 85
  philosophical commitment of, 92-
    98
    cafeteria service approach, 93
    direct service approach, 93
    enabling service approach, 93
    expressive goals, 93-94
    instrumental goals, 93-94
    interactionist service approach,
      93-94, 96
    prescriptive service approach, 93
  postbureaucratic leadership in, 68-
    69
  satisfaction in, 96
  threshold in, 49, 129
Leisure service personnel
  change agents, 58-59
  community workers, role of, 59-61
    advocate, 59-61
    developer, 60
    enabler, 59-61
    organizer, 60
  future role of, 193-94
  identifying competencies of, 72-73
Leisure studies, 161-70
  curriculum design, 163
  learning, levels of, 168-69
  Resource Awareness Center, 162-63
  two track curriculum, 169-70
Life-style
  alternative forms of, 107-20
    blue-collar, 114-18
    counterculture, 111-12

minority expressions, 118-20
  youth subculture, 108-12
definition of, 102
examples of, 103-4
guidelines for, 127-28
range of, 103
subcultures, 105, 131
types of, 104-5

Maslow, Abraham, 64, 209

National Advisory Commission on
      Civil Disorders, 118
Niepoth, E. William, 32, 84

Office of Economic Opportunity, 48-
      49, 128
Organizational Renewal, 68-69
Organizational strategy, new, 76-77

Parker, Stanley, 184-85, 189-90
Peters, Martha, 7
Pieper, Josef, 5
Place, sense of, 139-42
Play
  arousal-seeking view, 13-14
  perspectives on, 33-36
Playground Association of America, 43
Protestant work ethic
  background of, 8, 27
  erosion of, 182
  values of, 41, 42t

Recreation
  humanistic expression of, 2-5
  outcomes of, 74
  psychological definition of, 213-14
    implications of, 214-15
  reorientation of, 160-61
Recreation and leisure service
  agency commitment to, 32
  developmental concern, 13
  effective approach of, 33
  humanistic approach of, 2, 4
  outreach approach of, 49, 164-65
  pluralistic approach of, 36
  primary objective of, 14-15
Recreation and Park Movement
  action program for, 221-27

colleges and universities, 226-27
local government units, 223-26
National Recreation and Park
      Association, 222-23
Recreation and Park Movement,
      221-22
challenge of, 4
development of, 4, 40
history of, 41-51
problems of, 204-7
"Recreation for all," concept of, 45
Recreation experience
  activity view, 32
  behavioral view, 32-33, 84
  individual need, 33, 84
  nature of, 13-15
  psychological response of, 13
Rhythm of life, 105-7
  outsiders, 105-6
Roberts, Kenneth, 106-7, 158, 190-91
Rogers, Carl, 2-3, 125
Roszak, Theodore, 109

Sessoms, Doug, 126
Social change, 188-89, 211
Sport
  Esalen Sports Center, 133
  new dimensions in, 132-34
  new philosophy of, 132

Time
  cyclical perspective, 12
  eclectic perspective, 12
  mechanical perspective, 12
  psychological perspective, 12
Toffler, Alvin, 56, 188, 200, 212
Transience, 210

Urban recreation planning
  innovative approach to, 75-76
  self-renewal, 138, 142-43
  societal renewal, 138
  traditional approach to, 65-66

Values
  crisis in, 126-28
  definition of, 127
  formulation of, 124
  technological changes, 127

Witt, Peter, 3, 33
Work
  concepts of, 9-12
    blue perspective, 10
    green perspective, 10
    turquoise perspective, 10-12
  four-day week, 181-83
  historical meanings of, 175-77

  holistic pattern of, 180-81, 183-85
  human goals of, 178-81
  integration of, 177-78
  monotony in, 175
  moral integration, sources of, 174
World War I, 44-45
World War II, 45-46